Mometrix
TEST PREPARATION

OSAT®

I0880290

Agricultural Education (042) Secrets Study Guide

Dear Future Exam Success Story

First of all, **THANK YOU** for purchasing Mometrix study materials!

Second, congratulations! You are one of the few determined test-takers who are committed to doing whatever it takes to excel on your exam. **You have come to the right place.** We developed these study materials with one goal in mind: to deliver you the information you need in a format that's concise and easy to use.

In addition to optimizing your guide for the content of the test, we've outlined our recommended steps for breaking down the preparation process into small, attainable goals so you can make sure you stay on track.

We've also analyzed the entire test-taking process, identifying the most common pitfalls and showing how you can overcome them and be ready for any curveball the test throws you.

Standardized testing is one of the biggest obstacles on your road to success, which only increases the importance of doing well in the high-pressure, high-stakes environment of test day. Your results on this test could have a significant impact on your future, and this guide provides the information and practical advice to help you achieve your full potential on test day.

Your success is our success

We would love to hear from you! If you would like to share the story of your exam success or if you have any questions or comments in regard to our products, please contact us at **800-673-8175** or **support@mometrix.com**.

Thanks again for your business and we wish you continued success!

Sincerely,
The Mometrix Test Preparation Team

Need more help? Check out our flashcards at:
http://MometrixFlashcards.com/CEOE

Written and edited by the Mometrix Exam Secrets Test Prep Team
Printed in the United States of America

TABLE OF CONTENTS

Introduction

Thank you for purchasing this resource! You have made the choice to prepare yourself for a test that could have a huge impact on your future, and this guide is designed to help you be fully ready for test day. Obviously, it's important to have a solid understanding of the test material, but you also need to be prepared for the unique environment and stressors of the test, so that you can perform to the best of your abilities.

For this purpose, the first section that appears in this guide is the **Secret Keys**. We've devoted countless hours to meticulously researching what works and what doesn't, and we've boiled down our findings to the five most impactful steps you can take to improve your performance on the test. We start at the beginning with study planning and move through the preparation process, all the way to the testing strategies that will help you get the most out of what you know when you're finally sitting in front of the test.

We recommend that you start preparing for your test as far in advance as possible. However, if you've bought this guide as a last-minute study resource and only have a few days before your test, we recommend that you skip over the first two Secret Keys since they address a long-term study plan.

If you struggle with **test anxiety**, we strongly encourage you to check out our recommendations for how you can overcome it. Test anxiety is a formidable foe, but it can be beaten, and we want to make sure you have the tools you need to defeat it.

Secret Key #1 – Plan Big, Study Small

There's a lot riding on your performance. If you want to ace this test, you're going to need to keep your skills sharp and the material fresh in your mind. You need a plan that lets you review everything you need to know while still fitting in your schedule. We'll break this strategy down into three categories.

Information Organization

Start with the information you already have: the official test outline. From this, you can make a complete list of all the concepts you need to cover before the test. Organize these concepts into groups that can be studied together, and create a list of any related vocabulary you need to learn so you can brush up on any difficult terms. You'll want to keep this vocabulary list handy once you actually start studying since you may need to add to it along the way.

Time Management

Once you have your set of study concepts, decide how to spread them out over the time you have left before the test. Break your study plan into small, clear goals so you have a manageable task for each day and know exactly what you're doing. Then just focus on one small step at a time. When you manage your time this way, you don't need to spend hours at a time studying. Studying a small block of content for a short period each day helps you retain information better and avoid stressing over how much you have left to do. You can relax knowing that you have a plan to cover everything in time. In order for this strategy to be effective though, you have to start studying early and stick to your schedule. Avoid the exhaustion and futility that comes from last-minute cramming!

Study Environment

The environment you study in has a big impact on your learning. Studying in a coffee shop, while probably more enjoyable, is not likely to be as fruitful as studying in a quiet room. It's important to keep distractions to a minimum. You're only planning to study for a short block of time, so make the most of it. Don't pause to check your phone or get up to find a snack. It's also important to **avoid multitasking**. Research has consistently shown that multitasking will make your studying dramatically less effective. Your study area should also be comfortable and well-lit so you don't have the distraction of straining your eyes or sitting on an uncomfortable chair.

The time of day you study is also important. You want to be rested and alert. Don't wait until just before bedtime. Study when you'll be most likely to comprehend and remember. Even better, if you know what time of day your test will be, set that time aside for study. That way your brain will be used to working on that subject at that specific time and you'll have a better chance of recalling information.

Finally, it can be helpful to team up with others who are studying for the same test. Your actual studying should be done in as isolated an environment as possible, but the work of organizing the information and setting up the study plan can be divided up. In between study sessions, you can discuss with your teammates the concepts that you're all studying and quiz each other on the details. Just be sure that your teammates are as serious about the test as you are. If you find that your study time is being replaced with social time, you might need to find a new team.

Secret Key #2 – Make Your Studying Count

You're devoting a lot of time and effort to preparing for this test, so you want to be absolutely certain it will pay off. This means doing more than just reading the content and hoping you can remember it on test day. It's important to make every minute of study count. There are two main areas you can focus on to make your studying count.

Retention

It doesn't matter how much time you study if you can't remember the material. You need to make sure you are retaining the concepts. To check your retention of the information you're learning, try recalling it at later times with minimal prompting. Try carrying around flashcards and glance at one or two from time to time or ask a friend who's also studying for the test to quiz you.

To enhance your retention, look for ways to put the information into practice so that you can apply it rather than simply recalling it. If you're using the information in practical ways, it will be much easier to remember. Similarly, it helps to solidify a concept in your mind if you're not only reading it to yourself but also explaining it to someone else. Ask a friend to let you teach them about a concept you're a little shaky on (or speak aloud to an imaginary audience if necessary). As you try to summarize, define, give examples, and answer your friend's questions, you'll understand the concepts better and they will stay with you longer. Finally, step back for a big picture view and ask yourself how each piece of information fits with the whole subject. When you link the different concepts together and see them working together as a whole, it's easier to remember the individual components.

Finally, practice showing your work on any multi-step problems, even if you're just studying. Writing out each step you take to solve a problem will help solidify the process in your mind, and you'll be more likely to remember it during the test.

Modality

Modality simply refers to the means or method by which you study. Choosing a study modality that fits your own individual learning style is crucial. No two people learn best in exactly the same way, so it's important to know your strengths and use them to your advantage.

For example, if you learn best by visualization, focus on visualizing a concept in your mind and draw an image or a diagram. Try color-coding your notes, illustrating them, or creating symbols that will trigger your mind to recall a learned concept. If you learn best by hearing or discussing information, find a study partner who learns the same way or read aloud to yourself. Think about how to put the information in your own words. Imagine that you are giving a lecture on the topic and record yourself so you can listen to it later.

For any learning style, flashcards can be helpful. Organize the information so you can take advantage of spare moments to review. Underline key words or phrases. Use different colors for different categories. Mnemonic devices (such as creating a short list in which every item starts with the same letter) can also help with retention. Find what works best for you and use it to store the information in your mind most effectively and easily.

Secret Key #3 – Practice the Right Way

Your success on test day depends not only on how many hours you put into preparing, but also on whether you prepared the right way. It's good to check along the way to see if your studying is paying off. One of the most effective ways to do this is by taking practice tests to evaluate your progress. Practice tests are useful because they show exactly where you need to improve. Every time you take a practice test, pay special attention to these three groups of questions:

- The questions you got wrong
- The questions you had to guess on, even if you guessed right
- The questions you found difficult or slow to work through

This will show you exactly what your weak areas are, and where you need to devote more study time. Ask yourself why each of these questions gave you trouble. Was it because you didn't understand the material? Was it because you didn't remember the vocabulary? Do you need more repetitions on this type of question to build speed and confidence? Dig into those questions and figure out how you can strengthen your weak areas as you go back to review the material.

Additionally, many practice tests have a section explaining the answer choices. It can be tempting to read the explanation and think that you now have a good understanding of the concept. However, an explanation likely only covers part of the question's broader context. Even if the explanation makes perfect sense, **go back and investigate** every concept related to the question until you're positive you have a thorough understanding.

As you go along, keep in mind that the practice test is just that: practice. Memorizing these questions and answers will not be very helpful on the actual test because it is unlikely to have any of the same exact questions. If you only know the right answers to the sample questions, you won't be prepared for the real thing. **Study the concepts** until you understand them fully, and then you'll be able to answer any question that shows up on the test.

It's important to wait on the practice tests until you're ready. If you take a test on your first day of study, you may be overwhelmed by the amount of material covered and how much you need to learn. Work up to it gradually.

On test day, you'll need to be prepared for answering questions, managing your time, and using the test-taking strategies you've learned. It's a lot to balance, like a mental marathon that will have a big impact on your future. Like training for a marathon, you'll need to start slowly and work your way up. When test day arrives, you'll be ready.

Start with the strategies you've read in the first two Secret Keys—plan your course and study in the way that works best for you. If you have time, consider using multiple study resources to get different approaches to the same concepts. It can be helpful to see difficult concepts from more than one angle. Then find a good source for practice tests. Many times, the test website will suggest potential study resources or provide sample tests.

Practice Test Strategy

If you're able to find at least three practice tests, we recommend this strategy:

Untimed and Open-Book Practice

Take the first test with no time constraints and with your notes and study guide handy. Take your time and focus on applying the strategies you've learned.

Timed and Open-Book Practice

Take the second practice test open-book as well, but set a timer and practice pacing yourself to finish in time.

Timed and Closed-Book Practice

Take any other practice tests as if it were test day. Set a timer and put away your study materials. Sit at a table or desk in a quiet room, imagine yourself at the testing center, and answer questions as quickly and accurately as possible.

Keep repeating timed and closed-book tests on a regular basis until you run out of practice tests or it's time for the actual test. Your mind will be ready for the schedule and stress of test day, and you'll be able to focus on recalling the material you've learned.

Secret Key #4 – Pace Yourself

Once you're fully prepared for the material on the test, your biggest challenge on test day will be managing your time. Just knowing that the clock is ticking can make you panic even if you have plenty of time left. Work on pacing yourself so you can build confidence against the time constraints of the exam. Pacing is a difficult skill to master, especially in a high-pressure environment, so **practice is vital**.

Set time expectations for your pace based on how much time is available. For example, if a section has 60 questions and the time limit is 30 minutes, you know you have to average 30 seconds or less per question in order to answer them all. Although 30 seconds is the hard limit, set 25 seconds per question as your goal, so you reserve extra time to spend on harder questions. When you budget extra time for the harder questions, you no longer have any reason to stress when those questions take longer to answer.

Don't let this time expectation distract you from working through the test at a calm, steady pace, but keep it in mind so you don't spend too much time on any one question. Recognize that taking extra time on one question you don't understand may keep you from answering two that you do understand later in the test. If your time limit for a question is up and you're still not sure of the answer, mark it and move on, and come back to it later if the time and the test format allow. If the testing format doesn't allow you to return to earlier questions, just make an educated guess; then put it out of your mind and move on.

On the easier questions, be careful not to rush. It may seem wise to hurry through them so you have more time for the challenging ones, but it's not worth missing one if you know the concept and just didn't take the time to read the question fully. Work efficiently but make sure you understand the question and have looked at all of the answer choices, since more than one may seem right at first.

Even if you're paying attention to the time, you may find yourself a little behind at some point. You should speed up to get back on track, but do so wisely. Don't panic; just take a few seconds less on each question until you're caught up. Don't guess without thinking, but do look through the answer choices and eliminate any you know are wrong. If you can get down to two choices, it is often worthwhile to guess from those. Once you've chosen an answer, move on and don't dwell on any that you skipped or had to hurry through. If a question was taking too long, chances are it was one of the harder ones, so you weren't as likely to get it right anyway.

On the other hand, if you find yourself getting ahead of schedule, it may be beneficial to slow down a little. The more quickly you work, the more likely you are to make a careless mistake that will affect your score. You've budgeted time for each question, so don't be afraid to spend that time. Practice an efficient but careful pace to get the most out of the time you have.

Secret Key #5 – Have a Plan for Guessing

When you're taking the test, you may find yourself stuck on a question. Some of the answer choices seem better than others, but you don't see the one answer choice that is obviously correct. What do you do?

The scenario described above is very common, yet most test takers have not effectively prepared for it. Developing and practicing a plan for guessing may be one of the single most effective uses of your time as you get ready for the exam.

In developing your plan for guessing, there are three questions to address:

- When should you start the guessing process?
- How should you narrow down the choices?
- Which answer should you choose?

When to Start the Guessing Process

Unless your plan for guessing is to select C every time (which, despite its merits, is not what we recommend), you need to leave yourself enough time to apply your answer elimination strategies. Since you have a limited amount of time for each question, that means that if you're going to give yourself the best shot at guessing correctly, you have to decide quickly whether or not you will guess.

Of course, the best-case scenario is that you don't have to guess at all, so first, see if you can answer the question based on your knowledge of the subject and basic reasoning skills. Focus on the key words in the question and try to jog your memory of related topics. Give yourself a chance to bring the knowledge to mind, but once you realize that you don't have (or you can't access) the knowledge you need to answer the question, it's time to start the guessing process.

It's almost always better to start the guessing process too early than too late. It only takes a few seconds to remember something and answer the question from knowledge. Carefully eliminating wrong answer choices takes longer. Plus, going through the process of eliminating answer choices can actually help jog your memory.

Summary: Start the guessing process as soon as you decide that you can't answer the question based on your knowledge.

How to Narrow Down the Choices

The next chapter in this book (**Test-Taking Strategies**) includes a wide range of strategies for how to approach questions and how to look for answer choices to eliminate. You will definitely want to read those carefully, practice them, and figure out which ones work best for you. Here though, we're going to address a mindset rather than a particular strategy.

Your odds of guessing an answer correctly depend on how many options you are choosing from.

Number of options left	5	4	3	2	1
Odds of guessing correctly	20%	25%	33%	50%	100%

You can see from this chart just how valuable it is to be able to eliminate incorrect answers and make an educated guess, but there are two things that many test takers do that cause them to miss out on the benefits of guessing:

- Accidentally eliminating the correct answer
- Selecting an answer based on an impression

We'll look at the first one here, and the second one in the next section.

To avoid accidentally eliminating the correct answer, we recommend a thought exercise called **the $5 challenge**. In this challenge, you only eliminate an answer choice from contention if you are willing to bet $5 on it being wrong. Why $5? Five dollars is a small but not insignificant amount of money. It's an amount you could afford to lose but wouldn't want to throw away. And while losing $5 once might not hurt too much, doing it twenty times will set you back $100. In the same way, each small decision you make—eliminating a choice here, guessing on a question there—won't by itself impact your score very much, but when you put them all together, they can make a big difference. By holding each answer choice elimination decision to a higher standard, you can reduce the risk of accidentally eliminating the correct answer.

The $5 challenge can also be applied in a positive sense: If you are willing to bet $5 that an answer choice *is* correct, go ahead and mark it as correct.

Summary: Only eliminate an answer choice if you are willing to bet $5 that it is wrong.

Which Answer to Choose

You're taking the test. You've run into a hard question and decided you'll have to guess. You've eliminated all the answer choices you're willing to bet $5 on. Now you have to pick an answer. Why do we even need to talk about this? Why can't you just pick whichever one you feel like when the time comes?

The answer to these questions is that if you don't come into the test with a plan, you'll rely on your impression to select an answer choice, and if you do that, you risk falling into a trap. The test writers know that everyone who takes their test will be guessing on some of the questions, so they intentionally write wrong answer choices to seem plausible. You still have to pick an answer though, and if the wrong answer choices are designed to look right, how can you ever be sure that you're not falling for their trap? The best solution we've found to this dilemma is to take the decision out of your hands entirely. Here is the process we recommend:

Once you've eliminated any choices that you are confident (willing to bet $5) are wrong, select the first remaining choice as your answer.

Whether you choose to select the first remaining choice, the second, or the last, the important thing is that you use some preselected standard. Using this approach guarantees that you will not be enticed into selecting an answer choice that looks right, because you are not basing your decision on how the answer choices look.

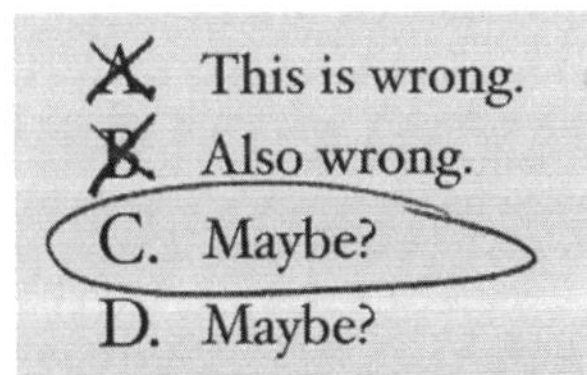

This is not meant to make you question your knowledge. Instead, it is to help you recognize the difference between your knowledge and your impressions. There's a huge difference between thinking an answer is right because of what you know, and thinking an answer is right because it looks or sounds like it should be right.

Summary: To ensure that your selection is appropriately random, make a predetermined selection from among all answer choices you have not eliminated.

Test-Taking Strategies

This section contains a list of test-taking strategies that you may find helpful as you work through the test. By taking what you know and applying logical thought, you can maximize your chances of answering any question correctly!

It is very important to realize that every question is different and every person is different: no single strategy will work on every question, and no single strategy will work for every person. That's why we've included all of them here, so you can try them out and determine which ones work best for different types of questions and which ones work best for you.

Question Strategies

☑ Read Carefully

Read the question and the answer choices carefully. Don't miss the question because you misread the terms. You have plenty of time to read each question thoroughly and make sure you understand what is being asked. Yet a happy medium must be attained, so don't waste too much time. You must read carefully and efficiently.

☑ Contextual Clues

Look for contextual clues. If the question includes a word you are not familiar with, look at the immediate context for some indication of what the word might mean. Contextual clues can often give you all the information you need to decipher the meaning of an unfamiliar word. Even if you can't determine the meaning, you may be able to narrow down the possibilities enough to make a solid guess at the answer to the question.

☑ Prefixes

If you're having trouble with a word in the question or answer choices, try dissecting it. Take advantage of every clue that the word might include. Prefixes can be a huge help. Usually, they allow you to determine a basic meaning. *Pre-* means before, *post-* means after, *pro-* is positive, *de-* is negative. From prefixes, you can get an idea of the general meaning of the word and try to put it into context.

☑ Hedge Words

Watch out for critical hedge words, such as *likely, may, can, often, almost, mostly, usually, generally, rarely,* and *sometimes.* Question writers insert these hedge phrases to cover every possibility. Often an answer choice will be wrong simply because it leaves no room for exception. Be on guard for answer choices that have definitive words such as *exactly* and *always.*

☑ Switchback Words

Stay alert for *switchbacks.* These are the words and phrases frequently used to alert you to shifts in thought. The most common switchback words are *but, although,* and *however.* Others include *nevertheless, on the other hand, even though, while, in spite of, despite,* and *regardless of.* Switchback words are important to catch because they can change the direction of the question or an answer choice.

✓ Face Value

When in doubt, use common sense. Accept the situation in the problem at face value. Don't read too much into it. These problems will not require you to make wild assumptions. If you have to go beyond creativity and warp time or space in order to have an answer choice fit the question, then you should move on and consider the other answer choices. These are normal problems rooted in reality. The applicable relationship or explanation may not be readily apparent, but it is there for you to figure out. Use your common sense to interpret anything that isn't clear.

Answer Choice Strategies

✓ Answer Selection

The most thorough way to pick an answer choice is to identify and eliminate wrong answers until only one is left, then confirm it is the correct answer. Sometimes an answer choice may immediately seem right, but be careful. The test writers will usually put more than one reasonable answer choice on each question, so take a second to read all of them and make sure that the other choices are not equally obvious. As long as you have time left, it is better to read every answer choice than to pick the first one that looks right without checking the others.

✓ Answer Choice Families

An answer choice family consists of two (in rare cases, three) answer choices that are very similar in construction and cannot all be true at the same time. If you see two answer choices that are direct opposites or parallels, one of them is usually the correct answer. For instance, if one answer choice says that quantity *x* increases and another either says that quantity *x* decreases (opposite) or says that quantity *y* increases (parallel), then those answer choices would fall into the same family. An answer choice that doesn't match the construction of the answer choice family is more likely to be incorrect. Most questions will not have answer choice families, but when they do appear, you should be prepared to recognize them.

✓ Eliminate Answers

Eliminate answer choices as soon as you realize they are wrong, but make sure you consider all possibilities. If you are eliminating answer choices and realize that the last one you are left with is also wrong, don't panic. Start over and consider each choice again. There may be something you missed the first time that you will realize on the second pass.

✓ Avoid Fact Traps

Don't be distracted by an answer choice that is factually true but doesn't answer the question. You are looking for the choice that answers the question. Stay focused on what the question is asking for so you don't accidentally pick an answer that is true but incorrect. Always go back to the question and make sure the answer choice you've selected actually answers the question and is not merely a true statement.

✓ Extreme Statements

In general, you should avoid answers that put forth extreme actions as standard practice or proclaim controversial ideas as established fact. An answer choice that states the "process should be used in certain situations, if..." is much more likely to be correct than one that states the "process should be discontinued completely." The first is a calm rational statement and doesn't even make a definitive, uncompromising stance, using a hedge word *if* to provide wiggle room, whereas the second choice is far more extreme.

✓ Benchmark

As you read through the answer choices and you come across one that seems to answer the question well, mentally select that answer choice. This is not your final answer, but it's the one that will help you evaluate the other answer choices. The one that you selected is your benchmark or standard for judging each of the other answer choices. Every other answer choice must be compared to your benchmark. That choice is correct until proven otherwise by another answer choice beating it. If you find a better answer, then that one becomes your new benchmark. Once you've decided that no other choice answers the question as well as your benchmark, you have your final answer.

✓ Predict the Answer

Before you even start looking at the answer choices, it is often best to try to predict the answer. When you come up with the answer on your own, it is easier to avoid distractions and traps because you will know exactly what to look for. The right answer choice is unlikely to be word-for-word what you came up with, but it should be a close match. Even if you are confident that you have the right answer, you should still take the time to read each option before moving on.

General Strategies

✓ Tough Questions

If you are stumped on a problem or it appears too hard or too difficult, don't waste time. Move on! Remember though, if you can quickly check for obviously incorrect answer choices, your chances of guessing correctly are greatly improved. Before you completely give up, at least try to knock out a couple of possible answers. Eliminate what you can and then guess at the remaining answer choices before moving on.

✓ Check Your Work

Since you will probably not know every term listed and the answer to every question, it is important that you get credit for the ones that you do know. Don't miss any questions through careless mistakes. If at all possible, try to take a second to look back over your answer selection and make sure you've selected the correct answer choice and haven't made a costly careless mistake (such as marking an answer choice that you didn't mean to mark). This quick double check should more than pay for itself in caught mistakes for the time it costs.

✓ Pace Yourself

It's easy to be overwhelmed when you're looking at a page full of questions; your mind is confused and full of random thoughts, and the clock is ticking down faster than you would like. Calm down and maintain the pace that you have set for yourself. Especially as you get down to the last few minutes of the test, don't let the small numbers on the clock make you panic. As long as you are on track by monitoring your pace, you are guaranteed to have time for each question.

✓ Don't Rush

It is very easy to make errors when you are in a hurry. Maintaining a fast pace in answering questions is pointless if it makes you miss questions that you would have gotten right otherwise. Test writers like to include distracting information and wrong answers that seem right. Taking a little extra time to avoid careless mistakes can make all the difference in your test score. Find a pace that allows you to be confident in the answers that you select.

⊘ KEEP MOVING

Panicking will not help you pass the test, so do your best to stay calm and keep moving. Taking deep breaths and going through the answer elimination steps you practiced can help to break through a stress barrier and keep your pace.

Final Notes

The combination of a solid foundation of content knowledge and the confidence that comes from practicing your plan for applying that knowledge is the key to maximizing your performance on test day. As your foundation of content knowledge is built up and strengthened, you'll find that the strategies included in this chapter become more and more effective in helping you quickly sift through the distractions and traps of the test to isolate the correct answer.

Now that you're preparing to move forward into the test content chapters of this book, be sure to keep your goal in mind. As you read, think about how you will be able to apply this information on the test. If you've already seen sample questions for the test and you have an idea of the question format and style, try to come up with questions of your own that you can answer based on what you're reading. This will give you valuable practice applying your knowledge in the same ways you can expect to on test day.

Good luck and good studying!

Agricultural Business, Economics, and Marketing

Economic and Marketing Principles in Agribusiness

Using Supply and Demand to Determine Price of Agricultural Commodities

Supply refers to how much of a **commodity** (good) is available at a given time for purchasing. **Demand** refers to the consumer's wanting to purchase a given commodity. Usually a lower price for any given commodity increases the demand for the commodity. Agricultural commodity prices, like many other commodities, are determined by the producer. This is due to several factors: the perishable nature of unprocessed foods, relationships between peak quality and prices of fruits and vegetables, and producer's inability to completely control production of eggs, meat, crops, and dairy products once production has started. Demand can also be affected by unforeseen factors (i.e., Romaine lettuce recall due to salmonella), and producers have to take a cut in profits due to consumer demand being lowered. Agricultural cooperatives have allowed producers to negotiate prices for large volumes of agricultural commodities.

Law of Diminishing Returns

The **law of diminishing returns** states that if one aspect of production and all other inputs are held constant, then eventually a point will be reached where the returns will begin to decrease. An example of this can be seen in a car manufacturing facility. If the number of workers is continually increased, eventually the workers will get in the way of one another, and productivity will decrease. A phrase commonly used to describe the law of diminishing returns is "the gain is not worth the pain." An example of this can be seen in crop production. A farmer may plant 100 acres of corn each year. This year, he or she may increase his nitrogen fertilizer spraying rates by 5%. The corn crop will likely increase due to the extra fertilizer. However, if he or she increases the fertilizer rate by 50%, the farmer won't get any more corn than he or she would have gotten if he or she increased the rate by only 5%. Therefore, the farmer has lost profit due to the increase in fertilizer cost.

Fixed and Variable Costs

Fixed costs are costs that generally don't change over time. If they do change, it occurs slowly over time. Fixed costs would include costs such as land rent, machinery, building rent, and so on. Noncash costs that are also fixed costs would include some tractor depreciation, implement depreciation, and land charges. **Variable costs** are costs that are subject to change more rapidly. Variable costs may be costs such as wages or salaries, utilities, or material costs. Agricultural variable costs would be costs such as seed, feed, fertilizers, chemicals, and so on. Some noncash costs that are associated with agribusiness that are also variable costs would include tractor depreciation or interest. Typically, variable costs are going to increase at a constant rate with labor and capital.

Marginal Cost and Marginal Return

Marginal cost is the change in opportunity cost that arises when the quantity produced is incremented by one unit, or the extra cost of producing one additional unit. Marginal cost includes the cost of inputs to create the next unit. For example, in the automobile industry, manufacturers will pay the hourly wages that often include manufacturing of parts for the next automobile. **Marginal return**, or the marginal revenue, is the addition to total revenue that results from the sale of one more unit of the product. The marginal return equals the change in total revenue divided by change in output. When capital is fixed, a diminishing return can occur in the short term.

Depreciation

Depreciation is the measure of the value lost in an asset. Typically, depreciation is taken for assets that are continuously updated. Depreciation commonly occurs with vehicles and technology such as computers, copiers, printers, fax machines, and so on. Depreciation is calculated yearly and is considered an annual expense. Depreciation would be listed under expenses on an income statement. Depreciation, although considered an expense, can lead to a decrease in other expenses. An example of this would be seen with a farm truck. A farmer uses the truck daily, and over time the truck loses value. Eventually the truck will not run anymore and holds no value to the farmer. However, as the truck gets older, the cost of insuring that truck will decrease. To calculate depreciation use the formula: (purchase price – salvage price)/life expectancy.

Inputs and Outputs

Outputs are the end product, or goal, of production. **Inputs** are resources that are used to create the output. For a cotton farmer, the output would be bales of cotton, and the inputs would be fuel, seed, fertilizers, labor, and so on. The average product is the total output per number of input. The equation used to calculate this is: average product equals the total product divided by units of labor. To produce an output, a company or producer uses resources (inputs) to create outputs. The cost and availability of the inputs will generate costs. The cost of production is the sum of the costs of all inputs used during production. An input with a lower availability typically equates to a higher cost, whereas an input with a higher availability equates to a lower cost.

Current and Noncurrent Assets and Liabilities

Current assets are assets that will provide a benefit within the next year. Examples of current assets include cash, merchandise on hand, and supplies. **Noncurrent assets**, also called long-term assets, are assets that will still provide a benefit, just not within the next year or for more than one year. Examples of noncurrent assets include land, buildings, equipment, and furnishings. Total assets equal current assets plus noncurrent assets. **Current liabilities** are debts that require immediate payment. Examples of current liabilities include accounts payable, salaries, utilities, equipment rentals, and interest payable. Examples of noncurrent liabilities include notes payable long term, installment contracts payable, and mortgages. **Noncurrent liabilities** are debts that can be paid long term.

Opportunity Costs Within an Agribusiness

Opportunity cost is the cost of not using an asset with the intention of making a profit elsewhere. Opportunity costs are useful when considering an alternative plan for agricultural resources and assets. For example, if a farmer owns 100 acres of row crop field, he or she could rent that land out to another farmer for $150 per acre. He or she could potentially profit $15,000 from renting that land out to a neighbor, so the opportunity cost would be $15,000. He or she would need to make more than $15,000 from those 100 acres to make a profit. If the farmer cannot make more than $15,000 from the 100 acres, then it would make more sense for him or her to rent the land out to a neighbor. Opportunity cost can also be looked at from the perspective of satisfaction given up by not making a consumption decision. A farmer may forgo purchasing a new enclosed cab tractor to install a new swine barn. In agricultural businesses, there is often a fine line between investment decisions and consumption decisions.

Diversification and Specialization

Diversification involves reallocating a farm's productive resources to other farmers. Resources are moved from a low-value commodity to a high-value commodity. Producers can add shops and restaurants to incorporate value-added products. Diversification also moves producers away from one major crop production. Diversification can be used by producers to reduce risk, meet changing consumer demands, meet changing government policy, and mitigate external shocks and the newer need to reduce climate change. **Specialization** is the opposite of diversification. Specialization involves a producer focusing on one commodity or market. Producers can specialize in a commodity to offer a high-quality product. Specialization is common when contracts are used to sell commodities.

Commodity Futures and Options Trading

A **commodity futures contract** is an agreement to buy or sell a particular commodity at a predetermined place and date. A price and amount are agreed upon at the time of the contractual agreement. A **commodity futures option** gives the buyer the ability to buy or sell a futures contract at a future date for a particular price. Traded futures contracts allow for the transfer of risk and provide a price discovery mechanism for the commodities in the contract. The Commodity Futures Trading Commission (CFTC) regulates futures trading in the United States. Livestock futures prices are determined through bids and offers between buyers and sellers.

Hedging and Speculation

Speculation tries to make a profit from a price change. Speculation seeks to profit from betting on the direction an asset will be moving. **Hedging** seeks to reduce the amount of risk that is associated with a price change. Hedging prevents risk of any losses but also restricts the potential gains. Speculators assume the market price risk while seeking profit. Speculators add to market liquidity, aid in price determination, and facilitate hedging. Hedging involves taking a futures position that is opposite to one's current cash market position. For a hedge to be successful, there must be correlation between the cash and futures markets.

Key Factors Involved in Marketing

Successful marketing designs a place, promotion, product, and price that attracts the target market and creates sales. The **target market** is a group of people identified as potential customers who have similar wants and needs. To successfully market a product, a business must have abundant **product knowledge**. Product knowledge is understanding a product's features and benefits. To market a service requires **service knowledge**. A business should be able to use the value, problem-solving ability, and specialization of a service to persuade customers to use it. **Customer knowledge** is understanding potential customers. Businesses should identify who they are, what they want and need, and understand their buying patterns and consumer needs.

Promotional Campaign

A **promotional campaign** is a series of advertisements used by a business to promote a product, service, or event. Various media outlets can be used in a promotional campaign. Promotional campaigns are more than just advertising to potential customers. Promotional campaigns are used to communicate with a target audience. The first step involves identifying the target audience. Then, the appropriate communication channel can be chosen (social media, billboard, etc.). Specific, measurable, attainable, realistic/relevant and time bound (SMART) goals should be set for the campaign. Then the promotional mix can be determined. Clear and unambiguous messages to the target audience are created. The budget is allocated for the campaign. Each promotional campaign should be evaluated for effectiveness.

Effects of Market Prices and Cycles on Agricultural Commodities

Agricultural commodities are affected by **seasonality**. Seasonality is a phenomenon that causes commodity prices to behave in a somewhat predictable manner each year. Crop seasonality generally has two major components: the harvest lows and the post-harvest rally. Most major crops grown in the United States have a single harvest season. This means the total supply of the crop becomes available in a short period of time, flooding the market and therefore lowering the commodity prices. The supply of crop commodities is reduced due to domestic use and exporting to foreign markets. The prices therefore increase during the post-harvest rally. When conducting commodity analysis, crops can be split into two categories: **short crop years** and **normal years**. Short crop years are years during which yields were significantly lower than normal due to uncontrollable environmental conditions. Short crop years have higher commodity pricing than normal years due to the lowered supply. Normal years are the years that are not short crop years.

Agribusiness Management and Entrepreneurship

Basic Management Skills

Management is the coordination and organization of a business's activities to achieve certain goals. Effective scheduling is a key component of management. **Scheduling** is the process of developing, maintaining, and communicating schedules for time and resources. Whether scheduling timetables for projects or scheduling employee work hours, managers should ensure all gaps are covered and be prepared for unexpected setbacks. Another key role managers play is **hiring** new employees. When hiring new employees, managers will take potential candidates through an application and interview process. The best-qualified candidate should be hired. Managers are also often tasked with making **purchasing** decisions for a business. When purchasing, managers should conduct research to find the best products and suppliers in terms of the best value, delivery schedule, and quality. Purchasing should be done with long-term business goals in mind.

Management Decision-Making Process

There are five steps in the **management decision making process**. The first step involves **defining the problem** and understanding it. Next, the potential causes for the problem should be **identified**. This is done by asking employees and pinpointing the issue. After potential causes are identified, **alternative approaches** to solve the problem can be identified. Input of employees can also be taken at this step. The appropriate approach can be chosen that will best solve the problem for the long term. Next, an action plan can be created to **implement** the best alternative. The implementation should be monitored closely to ensure the implementation remains on schedule and actually solves the problem successfully. Last, management should closely **monitor** the situation to ensure the problem remains resolved.

Agribusiness Plan

The main purpose of an **agribusiness plan** is to communicate where a potential business is headed and how it intends to get there. A business plan is created to communicate this information to potential lenders and investors. There are five key components to a business plan. The first section should be the **executive summary**. The executive summary describes the products and services that will be offered, the type of ownership, strengths of the business, expertise and skills of the owners, and a market analysis. The second portion of a business plan is the **business description and analysis**, which includes the business type, the mission and vision statements, the location, any analysis, and product descriptions. The third portion is the **proposed organization,** which details managers, education, or experience requirements of employees and details about ownership type, proposed product supplies, manufacturing plans, and the marketing plans. The fourth portion is the

financial plan, which details the sources of capital as well as expected expenses and income sources. The last portion is for additional documents and leaves room for letterheads, business cards, employee rules, and any other supporting documents.

Individual Proprietorships, Partnerships, Cooperatives, and Corporations

An **individual proprietorship** is a business that is owned and operated by one individual. A **partnership** is a business that is owned and run by two or more people. Partnerships combine the skills, capital, and labor of multiple people for profit. A **corporation** is a business that has legally undergone the process of being authorized to act as an individual entity. Corporations can make decisions and take action that cannot affect the members of the corporation or its owners. A **cooperative** is a business organization that is owned and operated by a group of individuals for their mutual benefit. Agricultural cooperatives, often referred to as co-ops, can minimize risk for producers, reduce farm production costs, and assist producers in marketing and selling their commodities.

Sectors of Agribusiness

A **producer** is an individual who creates a good or commodity that can be marketed and sold. This could be a grower, farmer, rancher, fisher, and do on. A **consumer** is someone who purchases a good or service. Changes in consumer taste and preference have an impact on what producers are growing, raising or providing. In agriculture, the consumers have a large impact on the price of the goods or commodities that producers sell. A **service** is an action or activity that one person performs for another. Services are typically purchased similar to goods, but they are intangible. **Processing** is the steps of taking a good and creating a value-added product or preparing the product for sale. **Marketing** is advertising a commodity, service, or business to increase public awareness to increase sales and profit.

Reducing Risk in an Agribusiness

Financial risk is the risk of losing capital during periods of adverse conditions. To avoid financial risk, agribusinesses can maintain credit reserves and savings, spread out sales during production, diversify commodities, and participate in forwarding contracting, hedging, and futures contracts. Futures contracts are sales contracts created with agreed-upon prices and commodity quantities. Producers can reduce risk in an agribusiness by keeping the amount of cash available to the business strong. Many agribusiness expenses can be prepaid, so if there is a bumper-crop year, producers can prepay expenses. Thoroughly analyzing spending that is farm related ensures that the best decision is reached.

Contract Components

A **contract** is a legally binding agreement between two parties. For a contract to be valid, it must serve a legal purpose. There has to be mutual voluntary agreement over the contract by both parties. Both parties must agree upon the transaction and terms fully. A typical contractual agreement will follow a series of steps beginning with the offer. One party offers the other party terms as the basis for the agreement. The offered party can then choose to accept the transaction. After acceptance, both parties recognize that there is value to the agreement and go into a period of consideration. Once both parties are content with the stipulations of the contract, they will mutually accept the agreement. This usually ends in the creation of a legally binding written document that gives details of the agreement.

Lease Components

A popular contract is that of a **lease**. A lease document should include several key components. The first major item to be included is the property description. The description should list the address, building number, and a detailed building description. A lease should clearly list the tenants and landlords. The rental amount should clearly be listed in a lease. The forms of acceptable payment should also be included (cash, check, etc.). The landlord must clearly indicate how the payment can be received. There should also be clear statements regarding the consequences of late payments. Eviction clauses must also be included in the lease document. There should be a clear start and end date to the lease.

Enterprise Records

Enterprise records allow producers to assign income and expense information to farm enterprises that generated the cost or profit. The term *enterprise* refers to types of farm production. A farm may have a cotton enterprise and a wheat enterprise. Enterprises may be split up within one commodity. A beef cow farm could be divided into a grass-fed enterprise and a feed lot enterprise. When a producer grows feed for the livestock, these must be included on enterprise records. The grain grown on the farm would be credited as income to the grain enterprise while being an expense to the livestock enterprise. Enterprise records are useful when producers are creating multiple commodities. These records show producers where income and expenses are being generated on the farm. Enterprise records can be used to show proof of profitability in certain commodities that are produced.

Enterprise Budget

An **enterprise budget** allows producers to evaluate expected costs and returns for a production year. There are five sections included in an enterprise budget. The first section shows the total receipts on a sales unit and land unit. The second section records costs of producing the commodity. The third section shows the harvest component where pre-harvest and harvest expenses are combined to show total variable costs. The fourth section illustrates ownership costs for fixed resources. The last section summarizes the returns. The total costs equal variable costs plus ownership costs. The return over variable equals total receipts minus the total variable costs. The return over all costs equals the total receipts minus combined variable and ownership costs.

Balance Sheet

A **balance sheet** is a key component in a set of financial statements for an agribusiness. A balance sheet lists assets, liabilities, and net worth at a given time. It shows producers the current state of financial conditions at a given time. A balance sheet should be completed at the beginning of the agribusiness's fiscal year. Assets are usually grouped as current, intermediate, and long-term assets. Liabilities are usually grouped as current, intermediate, and long-term liabilities. The total assets must be balanced out by the total liabilities and net worth. Net worth equals total assets minus total liabilities. A balance sheet can be used to analyze the liquidity and solvency of an agribusiness. Liquidity measures the ability to meet short-term obligations without disrupting operations. Solvency measures the overall capital structure.

Cash-Flow Statement

A **cash-flow statement** is used to show changes in balance sheet accounts and how income affects profits. It also breaks the analysis down into operating, investing, and financing activities. To calculate a cash flow statement, start with net income. Start deducting changes made in cash, accounts receivable, inventory, depreciation, and accounts payable. A business should show a positive cash flow from operations to be profitable. These cash flow statements are used to map out where money comes into and leaves a business. They are used by analysist groups to determine the validity of a group. Cash flow statements should be prepared on a regular basis and can be a powerful tool in keeping a business profitable.

Completed Inventory

An **inventory** includes the finished and unfinished goods that have not been sold by a business. There are four components of a complete inventory: raw materials, work in progress, completed goods, and goods for resale. **Raw materials** are materials used to make a product. **Work in progress** goods are raw materials that have begun transformation to finished goods. **Finished goods** are ready for sale, and **goods for resale** are previously sold and returned goods that can be sold. Inventories count as assets on a business's balance sheet. There are two ways that inventories can be recorded: perpetually and periodically. A periodic system requires physically counting goods on hand. A perpetual system is a continuous system that records receipt and disbursement of every item.

Income/Expense Statement

An **income** or **expense statement** can also be called a profit or loss statement. It serves as a summary of a business's profit or loss for a given period of time (monthly, quarterly, and annually). It serves as a place to record all revenues and operating expenses. Income/expense statements can be used to determine the financial success of a business. They can also be used to calculate a business's tax liability. Income and expense statements are usually required by potential lenders and investors to determine credit limits for a business. The bottom line of an income and expense statement shows the net profit or loss for a business.

Single- and Double-Entry Methods of Accounting

Double-entry accounting is the most common method of accounting used by businesses. In the double-entry method, for every financial transaction, it will affect at least two accounts. Therefore, if there is an increase in one account, there is an opposite and equal decrease in another. Double-entry accounting increases accountability and is the best method to use when investors are involved. Most accounting software uses the double-entry method. The **single-entry** method of accounting is commonly used for small businesses or entrepreneurships. The single-entry method works similar to balancing a checkbook. Income is recorded once, and expenses are also recorded once.

Break-Even Analysis for an Enterprise

A **break-even analysis** can help determine how soon a business will be profitable and can cover its expenses. It allows businesses owners to determine how much product or profit to make or sell in a given time period to "break even." The formula for calculating the break-even point is: break-even point = fixed costs/(unit selling price – variable costs). Farmers can benefit from using a break-even calculator to analyze their financial situation. A break-even calculator can help farmers decide when to sell a crop. For example, if the break-even point comes to $3.80 a bushel and market prices hit $3.90 a bushel, then the farmer should sell some of the crop. A break-even analysis can also help farmers decide what to plant and what they can afford to pay for seed, chemicals, and fertilizer. This will allow them to see if they can afford to prepay or if they need to negotiate prices. A break-even analysis will also allow producers to calculate if they can afford to purchase a new piece of equipment or land.

Important Financial Ratios and Calculations

The basic accounting equation is: assets = liabilities + owner's equity. This takes many financial ratios and calculations into account. Assets are anything that a company has that is of value (commodities, savings, cash on hand, etc.). Assets can be split up into short-term and long-term assets. Liabilities are the opposite and represent money that is owed (salaries, loans, etc.). Liabilities can also be split up into short-term and long-term liabilities. **Net worth** is found with the equation (net worth = assets – liabilities). **Debt to equity** is a ratio that shows the shareholders' equity and any debts that are used to finance a company. **Solvency** refers to the amount of assets a company has over its liabilities. Solvency occurs when there is a positive net worth.

Savings and Investment Plans

Savings provides funds for emergencies and for making purchases in the near future (usually purchases that will be made within the next three years). Savings generally yield a low rate of return and are kept in a way that is easily turned into cash. A savings plan is used to reach short-term goals. **Investing** is used for long-term goals and involves financial risk. Investing is used to increase net worth and has higher return values. Generally, savings come first, then investing. A strong savings and investment plan can create financial stabilities for an agribusiness. Producers may have short crops or be forced to accept lower prices for commodities. Extra funds can help support producers through short years.

Sources of Credit

Agricultural credit is different from other business credit as it is adapted to meet the unique needs of farmers. Agricultural businesses are often subject to the planting, harvesting, and breeding seasons as well as marketing cycles. Loans, notes, bills of exchange, and banker's acceptances can all serve as forms of credit. The **Federal Farm Credit System** (FFCS) is a major component in providing agricultural credit. The FFCS is a network of institutions that provide credit. The **Farm Credit System** (FCS) is a nationwide system of financial institutions that provide credit to agricultural businesses. The **Commodity Credit Corporation** (CCC) is an agency of the US Department of Agriculture that supports and protects farm goods and agricultural prices.

Building and Maintaining Credit

There are five components that are viewed by potential lenders and creditors when determining a credit score: payment history, level of debt, credit age, mix of credit, and recent credit. Paying bills on time can positively impact credit. Late payments, especially ones left unpaid or ones in collections, will negatively impact credit scores. Credit card balances should remain less than 30% of the credit limit. High credit card balances negatively impact credit scores. Credit card accounts should remain open, especially older accounts. The lower the amount of debt, the easier it is to have a higher credit score. New credit inquiries can negatively impact credit score if there are too many recent inquiries, so it's best to inquire only about credit lines that are necessary.

Business Proposal

A **business proposal** is a written, formal offer to a prospective buyer or lender. An informally solicited proposal is usually the result of a verbal conversation. An unsolicited proposal is used to advertise and open the potential of a sale. A business proposal is based on research and follows a specific format. All business proposals have a clear title or title page. An abstract is used to state the situation, goal, method, and expected outcome in less than 200 words. The business proposal should detail the statement and method. A budget with clear costs and expected returns should be thoroughly researched and included. Any pertinent biographical and market information that was researched should also be included. Business proposals can be used to secure additional markets or credit.

Chapter Quiz

Ready to see how well you retained what you just read? Scan the QR code to go directly to the chapter quiz interface for this study guide. If you're using a computer, simply visit the online resources page at **mometrix.com/resources719/osatagred** and click the Chapter Quizzes link.

Animal Science

Animal Anatomy and Physiology

INTEGUMENTARY SYSTEM

The **integumentary system** is the system that encloses the body. This includes structures such as skin, feathers, hair, scales, nails, and so on. The integumentary system prevents pathogens from entering the body. The integumentary system encloses the outside of the body as well as covers and lines many internal structures as well. The internal integumentary structures help keep organs separated and tissues enclosed. The integumentary system also prevents the body from losing water and prevents dehydration. The integumentary system in livestock serves as an adaptation to prevent heat loss and maintain homeostasis. In birds, it has allowed for flight. Many species also use specialized hair or feathers to attract mates. The integumentary system can provide protection from not only pathogens but larger organisms as well.

MUSCULAR SYSTEM

The **muscular system** is responsible for providing movement in the body. There are three muscle groups, each serving its own function. Skeletal muscle allows for the movement of an animal. Skeletal muscle is unique because it requires voluntary movement. Skeletal muscle is composed of long muscle fibers that are bundled together. The skeletal muscles are attached to bones with tendons. Smooth muscle makes up much of the digestive tract and aids in digestion. Smooth muscle movement is involuntary and cannot be controlled by thought. Cardiac muscle is the muscle tissue that makes up the heart. Cardiac muscle movement is involuntary and cannot be controlled by thought. Cardiac muscle tissue is striated in appearance.

SKELETAL AND REPRODUCTIVE SYSTEMS

The **skeletal system** is responsible for providing structure to the body and includes bones, tendons, cartilage, and ligaments. The amount of bones varies in each species of livestock. Bones provide structure and support to the body. The skeletal system is the adaptation that has allowed animals to grow upright against the force of gravity. The inner portion of bones is spongy and soft. The spongy bone is responsible for making blood cells. The hard outer portion of bone also serves as a mineral storage.

The **reproductive system** is the system that allows for the production of offspring. The reproductive structures are unique to male and female animals. Males produce sperm cells, and females produce egg cells. In the livestock species, females are responsible for growing the offspring in the uterus and giving birth.

RESPIRATORY AND DIGESTIVE SYSTEMS

The **respiratory system** is the system that is responsible for the exchange of gases. The respiratory system includes the lungs, nasal cavity, diaphragm, bronchi, and trachea. Air is pulled into the lungs through the nasal cavity. Once in the lungs, oxygen is pulled into the body, and carbon dioxide is released. Carbon dioxide is exhaled.

The **digestive system** is responsible for the breakdown and absorption of nutrients as well as the excretion of wastes. The digestive system begins in the mouth and esophagus, continues into the stomach, large intestine, and small intestine, and ends with the anus. There are several types of digestive systems in livestock species and can include structures such as the crop and gizzard in chickens, a four-compartment stomach in ruminants, and the cecum in horses. The overall goal of the digestive tract is the same; it breaks down food and absorbs nutrients while excreting unwanted material and wastes.

Excretory System

The **excretory system** is responsible for removing waste materials from the body. The excretory system includes portions of the urinary system as well as portions of the digestive system. The kidneys filter waste and toxins from the blood. These wastes are excreted into the urine and pass out of the body with urine. The digestive system, responsible for absorbing nutrients and water, does not absorb all materials that are ingested. The materials ingested that are not nutrients are passed out of the body in the form of solid waste. These materials exit the body as feces via the colon and anus.

Nervous System

The **nervous system** is responsible for the senses, pain reception, and cognitive function. The nervous system is comprised of two major systems. The peripheral nervous system is the portion of the nervous system that extends through the body and limbs. The **peripheral nervous system** relays messages about the extremities of the body and the environment back to the brain. The **central nervous system** includes the brain, brain stem, and spinal cord. The brain is responsible for all thought and memory function and is composed of dense nervous tissue. The spinal cord acts as the connection between the brain and the peripheral nervous system. The spinal cord is housed within the vertebra of the spine.

Immune and Lymphatic Systems

The **immune system** is responsible for fighting off any potential threats to the body. The immune system recognizes pathogens that can cause illness and works to destroy them. The immune system uses white blood cells to attack and engulf pathogens. Most pathogens are bacterial or viral. The white blood cells have a unique ability to "remember" pathogens that it has encountered before and can quickly attack these pathogens. (This is why vaccines are effective.) The **lymphatic system** is composed of lymph nodes that are located all over the body. Lymph nodes are filled with lymphatic fluid. Lymphatic fluid carries white blood cells to the site of infection. Lymphatic fluid also carries waste materials and toxins to the bloodstream so that it can be filtered out by the kidneys.

Endocrine and Cardiovascular Systems

The **endocrine system** is the system that is responsible for the excretion and movement of hormones in the body. Hormones act as chemical messengers and are responsible for regulating many processes in the body. Growth, reproduction, and development are directly affected by the endocrine system. Organs included in the endocrine system include the pancreas (secretes insulin), the pituitary gland (secretes many hormones including growth hormone), the ovaries (secretes estrogen), the adrenal glands (secrete adrenaline), hypothalamus (secretes oxytocin), as well as the thyroid gland (secretes thyroxin).

The **cardiovascular system** is responsible for the transportation of gases, nutrients, and wastes in the body. The cardiovascular system includes the heart, arteries, veins, capillaries, and blood. The heart is responsible for pumping the blood and circulating the blood throughout the body. Arteries carry oxygenated blood and appear red in color. Veins carry deoxygenated blood and appear blue in color. Capillaries act as the meeting point where oxygen and nutrients can be dropped off to tissues. The blood, composed mostly of water, red blood cells, and antibodies, serves multiple functions. Red blood cells carry oxygen and act as iron storage. Antibodies fight off pathogens to prevent illness.

Animal Taxonomy and Classification

Taxonomical Classification System of Animals

The classification system that is used to classify all organisms was created by Carl Linnaeus. This classification system is called **taxonomy**. Taxonomy organizes living things into groups based on their similarities. Each group is given a scientific name that is universal among different languages. This allows scientists to communicate across language barriers about the same organism. The classification system begins with the largest group and continues to create smaller and smaller groups until the end, which is the individual species. The classification system is broken into these categories (beginning with largest): domain, kingdom, phylum, class, order, family, genus, and species. It is important to note that the genus and species are always written in italics with the genus name capitalized and the species name written in lowercase (e.g., *Homo sapiens*). All animals, including livestock species will fall under the domain Animalia. All livestock species are vertebrates and therefore will be classified under the phylum Chordata.

Major Species of Livestock

There are several species of livestock that play a key role in the agriculture industry. **Cattle, goats, sheep, pigs, chickens** and **horses** are the main livestock species. Cattle (*Bos taurus* or *Bos indicus*) are livestock species that typically weigh around 1,000 lbs. Cattle breeds are broken into either beef breeds or dairy breeds. Beef breeds of cattle are used for meat production. Dairy breeds of cattle are used for milk and dairy production. Goats are rising rapidly in popularity in the United States. Goats (*Capra hircus*) can be split into meat and dairy goats. Sheep (*Ovis aries*) are raised for either wool fibers or meat. Sheep raised for meat are processed into either lamb or mutton and are more commonly raised in Australia than in the United States. Pigs (*Sus scrofas*) are raised as meat animals throughout the United States. Chickens (*Gallus gallus domesticus*) are raised for either egg or meat production. Horses (*Equus caballus*), although not used for meat production in the United States, are a popular species of livestock that are used for recreational purposes.

Terms Used to Distinguish Animals by Sex and Age

Cattle, Horses, and Sheep

Cattle refer to a group of cows that are either male or female. A **cow** is a female that has given birth. A **heifer** is a female that has not given birth yet. A **bull** refers to a mature male cow. A **steer** is a castrated male cow, usually raised to send to market. A **calf** is a young cow and can be used to describe a male or a female. The term bull-calf can be used to describe a male calf. More than one horse is referred to as a **herd.** The term **stallion** is used to describe an uncastrated male that is sexually mature. A castrated male horse is called a **gelding**. A female horse is called a **mare.** A young horse that is less than one year old is called a **foal.** A female foal is called a **filly,** and the term **colt** is used for male foals. A group of sheep is called a **flock.** A mature female sheep is called a **ewe.** A mature uncastrated male is called a **ram.** A castrated male sheep is called a **wether.** A young sheep is referred to as a **lamb.**

Goats, Chickens, and Pigs

A female goat is called a **doe,** and a male goat is referred to as a **buck** or a **billy.** Castrated male goats are called **wethers.** A baby goat of either sex is called a **kid.** Male kids can also be called bucklings. A chicken that is a mature female is called a **hen.** A mature male chicken is called a **rooster.** The term **pullet** is used to describe a female chicken that is not sexually mature. A **cockerel** is the term used to describe a male chicken that is not sexually mature. A baby chicken of either sex is called a **chick. Capons** are castrated male chickens. A female pig that has not given birth is called a **gilt.** A female pig that has given birth is called a **sow.** A male pig that has been castrated is called a **barrow.** A male pig that has not been castrated is called a **boar.** Baby pigs of either sex are called **piglets.**

Terms Used to Distinguish Animals by Physical Traits in Livestock

When viewing livestock, it is possible to describe colors, hair length, or type and other physical characteristics. Many livestock breeds can be solid colors such as red, black, grey, or white. Livestock can also be spotted or "belted." Many breed associations have strict color requirements that the animals must meet. Sheep have different hair types and can be "hair" sheep or wool sheep. There are mohair breeds of goats. Animals can also be described by the structures of their bodies. Terms like knock-kneed, cow-hocked, and pigeon-toed can be used to describe the leg structure of animals. The topline of an animal describes the back of the animal, where the underline refers to the stomach of the animal. Market terms referring to cuts of meat can also be used to describe animals.

Animal Facilities and Environmental Conditions

Common Styles of Facilities for Common Livestock Production

Dairy cattle are kept in open barns with access to pastures. The dairy barn is usually connected to the milking parlor. The milking parlor is the building where cows are milked. The dairy barn is open to allow for adequate ventilation as dairy cattle stay hot. The barns are equipped with long feeding troughs so that cattle can be fed high-energy feed. Beef cattle are raised on pasture or in feedlots. Many beef cattle that are raised on pasture are finished on feedlots. Feedlots are areas where large amounts of beef cattle are contained in smaller pens and are fed high concentrations of feed. Beef cattle should have access to shelter. Producers will also have barns or pens with squeeze chutes to work the cattle in. Sheep are raised on pasture with access to shelter. Pigs are raised in hog barns. Pig barns are well ventilated and temperature controlled. The barns are created with concrete, slatted floors. The slatted floors allow waste to be washed down into a holding tank underneath the barn. The waste is flushed out into lagoons or holding tanks. Goats are raised on pasture with access to shelter.

Safe and Effective Facility Designs

Producers should always have a safe way to work animals. Ideally, animals should be worked in a way that allows workers to handle the animals with a barrier between them. With cattle, this usually means working them through a chute system. Smaller livestock species can be handled more physically. When producers are loading animals into a trailer, facilities that have chute systems that can be funneled to the trailer work best. Animals will not willingly move into areas that are dark, so the barns, trailer, and chute system should have adequate sunlight. Producers also need to ensure that surfaces are not slick, especially when working around frightened animals. Livestock that need to be loaded into a trailer need to be given an access to a ramp that has a gradual slope.

USDA Inspection Process for Livestock Processing and Handling Facilities

The USDA's Food Safety and Inspection Service (FSIS) is responsible for ensuring safe production of meat, poultry, and processed egg products. The FSIS also ensures products are accurately labeled. The FSIS ensures these by following and enforcing the Federal Meat Inspection Act, the Poultry Products Inspection Act, and the Egg Products Inspection Act. FSIS also ensures compliance with the Humane Methods of Slaughter Act for livestock. Slaughter facilities can conduct slaughter operations only if an FSIS slaughter inspector is present. To sell commercial products, a slaughter establishment must be federally inspected. An FSIS inspector conducts carcass inspections and ensures slaughterhouses maintain proper sanitation procedures. FSIS inspectors inspect animals before slaughter for signs of disease. If an animal is down or appears ill, an FSIS veterinarian must inspect the condition of the animal and determine the cause of illness.

Equipment for Safe and Effective Handling of Common Livestock Animals

Squeeze chutes are most commonly used with cattle, but smaller varieties do exist to work with smaller livestock species. Squeeze chutes prevent the animal from moving forward or backward and can put pressure on the animal's sides to prevent side-to-side movement. Squeeze chutes are used when vaccinating, worming, or branding animals. A **twitch** is a tool that can be used when handling horses. The twitch has a loop that can be put around the horse's upper lip as a restraining method. **Grooming stands** differ for large livestock and small livestock. For small livestock, they may be elevated to avoid putting pressure on the handler or groomer's back. For large livestock such as cattle, it usually includes a nonslip floor with a head restraint so that the body can be worked on. Goats and lambs can be dehorned. To do this safely, they should be placed in a **disbudding box**. A disbudding box is an enclosed box that the animal's entire body goes into. The top of the box has a hole in it that the animal's head and neck come out of. This allows the producer to disbud the animal safely without them moving, thrashing, or kicking.

Effects of Environmental Conditions on Animal Agriculture

The environment plays a big role in animal production, especially for animals that are raised outdoors. Livestock need to have access to barns or shelter to escape the elements. Dairy cattle cannot cool themselves off easily and need access to misting fans during the warmer months. For this reason, many dairy cattle farms are located in northern states. Beef cattle can cool themselves off, but they still need access to shade and adequate water. Pigs cannot sweat and therefore need access to misting fans in the warmer months. Many pig barns are fully equipped to be temperature controlled to ensure the best environmental conditions. Humid air conditions make it harder for animals to cool themselves off because the sweat cannot evaporate as easily. All animals need unlimited access to clean, fresh drinking water. Many animals will opt to cool themselves off in ponds or streams if they have access to them.

Effects of Detrimental Environmental Conditions on Livestock

If an animal is in a poor environment, it will affect them physically. Animals that are cold will shiver to generate heat. If the animal cannot warm itself, it will continue to shiver and expend energy to warm itself. This will lower the amount of energy available to be used for growth and development and will decrease the animal's production. Animals that cannot cool themselves off will go into heat stress. Pigs are highly susceptible to heat stress because they cannot sweat. Animals that live in tropical conditions often have reproductive issues due to the almost constant heat stress that they are under. If animals cannot access water, they will quickly become dehydrated and start to show health issues. Animals that are exposed to the elements can die due to heat stress, freezing, or lightning strikes.

Environmental Conditions Affected by Animal Production

Livestock can have a large impact on the environment. Pasture-raised animals require large amounts of grass. Producers have to clear large fields and prevent trees from growing in the fields so that grasses can grow. This can disrupt the environment and ecosystems around the farm if the area falls within an area that is naturally wooded. Producers have to take care to not allow chemicals or medications that are used with animal agriculture to seep into the ground. The chemicals can affect the soil biome and seep into the ground water supply. Producers also have to take precautions to ensure that other wastes such as feed bags, hay strings, and other materials do not become litter. Animal waste is a by-product of animal agriculture that should be disposed of properly so that it doesn't leach into the ground.

Animal Production and Management

Domestication of Animals

Animals were thought to be domesticated around 10,000 to 12,000 years ago. Dogs were one of the first animals that were domesticated. It is thought that dogs could have been domesticated as early as 14,000 years ago. Today's dogs are descendants of wolves and wild dogs. The first livestock species domesticated was the goat. There are dated paintings that show domesticated goats that date back to 10,000 to 12,000 years ago. Goats were used as a source of both meat and milk. The skins of goats were often used as well. Cattle, sheep, and horses were later domesticated. Horses and oxen were used as draft animals. Only recently have horses been used as recreational animals rather than draft animals. Cattle were domesticated as a source of meat and milk. Sheep were domesticated and raised for their meat and wool.

Past, Current, and Emerging Trends Related to Animal Agricultural Industry

In the past, most animals were raised on a family farm. Animals were fatty, and the focus was on fatty tissue rather than lean muscling. Currently, the majority of livestock are raised on commercial farms, where thousands of animals are raised together. Producers aim to raise animals that produce large amounts of muscle on minimal amounts of feed. Producers don't raise fatty animals but focus on lean meat. Producers can use reproductive technologies to breed their animals for certain traits. Selective breeding, artificial insemination, and embryo transfer are a few ways that producers today can breed their animals to more consistently produce a trait or characteristic. As these processes are researched more, producers will see lowered cost with using these processes. Genetic editing and engineering is opening up as an option to create higher quality genetic variations and potentially prevent the breeding of animals with disorders or disease.

Selecting Market and Breeding Livestock Based on Visual Assessment

Animals that will be used for market should have clear muscle definition. There should be adequate shape to the muscle and correct muscling in the areas that are of most value in the species. For example, lambs should be long and muscular through the rack and hindquarters. All species should have large amounts of muscling. Breeding animals should be selected based on muscling qualities as well as other qualities. Correct conformation and frame are important for breeding animals. Breeding animals should have correct leg structure. In breeding females, the female should have a feminine appearance. Females should also have enough body capacity to carry a fetus to term comfortably. Animals with poor conformation, framework, or muscling qualities should not be used as breeding animals as these traits will be passed on to offspring.

Selecting Animals to Cull Based on Performance Data

Animals that are not performing at a high level should be culled. Performance data tells the producer how well the animal is performing in terms of producing offspring, meat and muscle tissue, or dairy production. Producers need to keep records of how much feed the animal is consuming and how productive the animal is being. Some common types of performance data in meat animals include average daily gain, weight per day of age, loin eye area, or weight at X days. Breeding animals will have performance data such as weaning weight, litter weight, productivity index, or number born alive. Dairy animals will have data that show pounds of milk, pounds of butterfat, somatic cell counts, and number of dry days. All of this data can be compared by producers to choose the animals that are the lowest performing. Low-performing animals should be culled first (e.g., a beef cow that consistently weans smaller calves should be culled from the herd). Performance data gives the producer a better idea of how an animal is producing when compared to the other animals in the herd.

Grading Systems of Livestock

Grading systems allow prediction of feedlot performance and carcass characteristics of finished cattle. Cattle **feeder grades** are determined by frame size, muscling, and thriftiness. There are three frame sizes: small, medium and large. There are four muscle grades: #1, #2, #3, and #4. Grade #1 are heavily muscled animals and #4 are extremely lightly muscled animals. Carcass **quality grading** is based on factors that affect meat palatability. These grades are based on degree of marbling and degree of maturity. Marbling grades include prime, choice, select, and standard. Carcass maturity grades are given based on cartilage ossification of thoracic buttons. **Yield grades** estimate the amount of boneless, closely trimmed retail cuts from high-value parts of the carcass. Yield grades range from 1 to 5 and are determined by external fat, visceral fat, hot carcass weight, and loin eye area.

Management Procedures for Effective Livestock Production

There are many procedures that need to take place when effectively managing livestock. Feeding, providing water, and vaccinating animals provides the bare minimum. Male animals that will not be used for breeding and that are being raised for meat production will need to be castrated. **Castration** involves removing the testicles. Castration prevents the animal's body from producing testosterone, which can affect meat quality. Sheep and pigs routinely have their tails **docked**. Pigs will chew on other pigs' tails and cause injury, so the tails are removed at a young age. Sheep tails are docked to prevent fecal matter from getting caught in the wool on the tail. Piglets also have their needle teeth clipped at a young age. Calves, sheep, and goats that are horned can be dehorned. **Dehorning** animals prevents the animal from growing horns and involves removing the buds that will grow into horns. Horned animals are more likely to injure people, injure each other, or get their heads caught in fencing. Chickens that are used for egg production will have their top beak trimmed to prevent the chickens from pecking one another and causing injury.

Importance of Proper Nutrition for Animal Production

Proper nutrition is imperative in animal production. In animals that are raised for meat, producers aim to spend as little money on feed while still quickly raising animals. The less money that is spent on feed, the more profit the producer gains. Meat animals are harvested primarily for muscle tissue. Feed for meat animals should provide adequate amounts of protein to build muscle mass while also providing enough fats and carbohydrates to provide the animal with energy. A proper balance of vitamins and minerals is also necessary for proper growth. Animals that are raised for dairy purposes should be given a diet high in calories. Dairy animals are usually in a nutrient deficiency, so caloric intake is important in dairy animals. The limiting nutrient in all animals is water. This means that normal body processes cannot occur without water; therefore, water is the most important nutrient.

Ruminant and Nonruminant Digestion

Ruminants are animals that have a complex stomach. A ruminant stomach has four compartments. The four compartments are the rumen, reticulum, omasum, and abomasum in that order. The rumen is the largest compartment and is the holding compartment. Fermentation by bacteria takes place in the rumen. The rumen also sends feed and roughages back up to the mouth to be chewed. The reticulum, often called the honeycomb, absorbs nutrients and water. The omasum is lined with many folds that absorb water and prevent larger particles from moving forward. The omasum is often called the "leaves of the Bible" due to the folds of tissue. The last compartment is the abomasum and is considered the true stomach. Ruminant animals take in food without chewing it, it goes into the rumen where it starts to ferment, then it is moved back into the mouth so that it can be chewed and swallowed again. Cattle, sheep, goats, and deer are ruminants. **Nonruminants** are called monogastrics. The term *monogastric* means "simple stomach." Humans, pigs, dogs, and cats are monogastrics.

Major Groups of Nutrients

Proteins are macromolecules that are composed of amino acids. Proteins are used as a source of amino acids but generally not for energy. **Carbohydrates** are used as a quick source of energy and comprise simple sugars such as starch and glucose. Carbohydrates are the primary source of energy in an animal's diet. **Fats** are used as a long-term energy storage and are densely packed with energy. **Minerals** are nutrients that are required for bodily processes, but they cannot be created by the body. These must be ingested and are found abundantly in nature. Minerals can be sorted into trace and macrominerals. Trace minerals are required in the diet in small amounts; macrominerals are required in the diet in larger amounts. Salts are examples of minerals. **Vitamins** are nutrients that are required for proper bodily processes to take place. Vitamins can be categorized into water-soluble and fat-soluble vitamins. Vitamins A, D, E, and K are examples of vitamins required in the diet. Water is the most limiting nutrient and therefore is the most important.

Balancing a Ration

A **ration** is the combination of feed given to an animal in a 24-hour period. The purpose of a **balanced ration** is to nourish an animal, that is, provide the animal's body with essential nutrients in forms that the body can use all while reducing waste. Reducing waste both lowers feed costs and reduces wasted materials entering the environment. A properly balanced ration includes both forages and grain. To create a balanced ration, the nutritional needs of the animal need to be determined based on age, weight, workload, status, and any other individual variations, such as pregnancy, lactation, disease, and so on. The energy and protein needs are the greatest and should be met first. Energy forms should be digestible energy. Calcium, phosphorus, vitamin A, and other vitamin and mineral needs should be met.

Pearson's Square Method of Calculating a Balanced Ration

The Pearson square ration formulation is a process designed for creating simple rations. The nutrient contents of ingredients and the nutrient requirements must be expressed in the same way (i.e., as-fed or dry-matter). The value in the middle of the square represents the nutritional requirement of an animal for a specific nutrient. This value must fall between the two numbers on the left of the square, or the calculation would not be possible. Subtract the nutrient value from the nutritional requirement on the diagonals to get a number in parts. The parts can then be added and divided by the total parts to calculate the ration in percentages.

Example:

You are making a feed mix from soybean meal (SBM) and corn. SBM is 45% CP (crude protein) and corn is 10% CP. How much of each do you need to make a 200 lb. mix that is 17% CP?

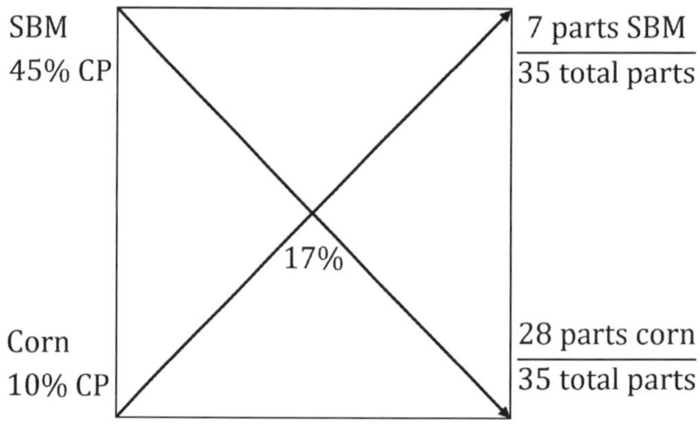

$$45\% - 17\% = 28 \text{ parts Corn}$$
$$17\% - 10\% = 7 \text{ parts SBM}$$
$$28 + 7 = 35 \text{ Total Parts}$$

$$\frac{28}{35} = \frac{4}{5} = 80\% \text{ corn; } 200\ lb. \times 80\% = 160\ lb.$$
$$\frac{7}{35} = \frac{1}{5} = 20\% \text{ SBM; } 200\ lb. \times 20\% = 40\ lb.$$

Therefore, a 200 lb mixture at 17% CP would require 160 *lb.* of corn and 40 *lb.* of soybean meal.

Symptoms of Common Nutrient Deficiencies

Goiter, or iodine deficiency, in pigs is common. Iodine deficiency can cause birth of weak or dead pigs that are hairless with a mucinous edema on the body. Iron deficiency is also common in pigs and is characterized by loss of body condition, lesions, and death. Rickets is a disease that affects growing bone tissue caused by a deficiency of calcium, phosphorus, or vitamin D. Rickets can affect all livestock and causes poor growth, short stature, and deformed weight-bearing long bones. Grass tetany is caused by a magnesium deficiency and is most common in cattle and sheep. Grass tetany causes abnormal gait, tremors, and convulsions. Polio encephalomalacia is a disease caused by a thiamin deficiency and is characterized by circling, muscular incoordination, and head pressing. Many nutritional deficiencies cause poor weight gain or weight loss, lethargy, infertility, and poor production.

Normal and Abnormal Behavior in Common Livestock Animals

Normal animal behavior includes animals eating normally, excreting waste normally, and being calm. **Abnormal** animal behavior occurs when an animal's eating habits change, their personalities change, or their waste excretion changes. Animals can go off of their feed, eat too much feed, or eat different foods. Sometimes animals will consume nonfeed items. Animals that have digestive changes may have diarrhea, may be constipated, or may have trouble urinating. It's important for producers to monitor the animal's fecal and urinary patterns so they can recognize when there is a change. Animals that are in pain may become aggressive or lethargic. Animals that are lame may have a noticeable limp or have problems moving around. Animals that aren't normally aggressive may become aggressive, and animals that aren't usually calm may become too calm. Uncomfortable animals will pace, have a rapid breathing rate, or become vocal.

Causes of Abnormal Behavior in Common Livestock Animals

Abnormal behavior in animals usually has a cause related to a health or comfort issue. Animals that have trouble with waste excretion or urination may have digestive or urinary issues. Diarrhea can indicate an infection or that the animal ingested something that it shouldn't have. An animal that constantly looks at its stomach is probably experiencing abdominal pain. Dogs and cats will commonly eat grass to try to settle their stomachs. Animals that paw at their face or shake their heads frequently may have ear issues. An animal that seems unusually lethargic may have an illness that causes it to lack energy.

Safe Animal-Handling Procedures

Always work with livestock in a calm manner. Speak quietly to the animals, and don't make sudden movements or loud noises. It is best in the long term to work slowly with animals until they are comfortable. Don't approach an animal from its blind spot. Most animals cannot see directly behind them, leaving a blind spot in their field of vision. Animals that have a strong flight response will move according to how they are approached. If you approach the animal from the head, it will typically back up. If you approach the animal from the hip or at an angle from behind, it tends to move forward. Approach an animal from the shoulder to prevent it from moving. Animals can also be worked with a squeeze chute. This prevents the animal from moving when it is receiving a vaccination, being branded, or receiving any uncomfortable treatment. Always be aware of the animal and the surroundings. Monitor the animal's behavior, and look for signs of nervousness or stress (ear pinned, stomping, etc.). Always have an escape route when working with animals.

Animal Welfare and Animal Rights

Animal welfare refers to the humane treatment of animals. Animals can be used to produce meat, milk, or fiber but must be cared for properly. The idea of animal welfare was put into legislation in the form of the Animal Welfare Act, which was put into law in 1966. Under the AWA, animals that are being used for meat, milk, fiber production, or research should live comfortably and be well cared for. These animals should not experience suffering and should have their basic needs of food, water, and shelter met. **Animal rights** is a belief that animals should not be used for human purposes and therefore should not be used for meat, milk, fiber, or research purposes. Animal rights activists believe there is no difference in the value of life of people or animals.

Waste-Management and Animal-Disposal Plan for Livestock Operations

Animal waste is a by-product of animal agriculture that should be disposed of properly so that it doesn't leach into the ground. Animal waste is composed of large amounts of nitrogen, phosphorus, and potassium. These chemicals can leach into the ground soil and make their way into nearby waterways. These chemicals can feed algae and cause algal blooms, which is undesirable. Neighbors of large farms often complain about the overwhelming smell of animal production, especially swine production. Producers should have a waste-management program in place that can include holding tanks, decomposing systems, or lagoons. These systems break the waste down into nutrients and can be used by farmers to fertilize crop fields. When animals are raised in large concentrations, there will be animal fatalities, and producers should prepare for that. Carcasses can be disposed of by rendering, burial, composting, or incineration.

Safety and Biosecurity Plan for a Specific Class of Animals

Biosecurity is a system of management practices that prevent or significantly reduce the risk of introducing or spreading disease on a farm. Pathogens can be spread from animal to animal, or in the case of zoonotic diseases, from animal to human. Pathogens can be transmitted through aerosols, direct contact, vectors, fomites, and orally, so precautions should be taken to prevent all transmission forms. When adding a new animal to a herd, make sure the animal has up-to-date health records, a veterinarian inspects the animal prior to purchase, and the animal is isolated for a minimum of 30 days (60 for swine), and do not cross use shovels, buckets, or other equipment between isolated animals and others. Workers should clean hands, boots, and clothes if necessary between barns. Limit contact with neighboring livestock, wildlife, and stray animals.

Animal Reproduction and Management

Selective Breeding, Artificial Insemination, and Embryo Transfer

Selective breeding is a breeding tactic that has been used for thousands of years with livestock. In selective breeding, producers choose two animals for certain desirable traits and breed them to create offspring with those desirable traits. **Artificial insemination** is the process of taking viable sperm from a male and inserting it into the female reproductive tract. Sperm is collected from the male and then separated into smaller doses. Females that are fertile and in estrus will be bred and will receive a dose of semen with an artificial insemination rod. Artificial insemination allows producers to use semen from superior males at a small price. **Embryo transfer** is done when producers have an exceptional female and want to get more offspring from her than they would be able to if they just bred her each year. The female is given hormones that cause her to superovulate, and then the eggs are flushed out of her and collected. The eggs are fertilized in a lab and then placed in a surrogate mother's body.

Crossbreeding, Grading Up, Inbreeding, Linebreeding, and Purebred Breeding

Crossbreeding refers to the process of crossing purebred animals from two different breeds to create a hybrid animal. Crossbreeding is commonly used in market breeding systems as it creates the highest level of hybrid vigor, or heterosis. **Grading up** is a breeding system used to improve a producer's herd. The producer will cull the low-performing animals each year and will only continue to breed the highest-performing animals. Females are bred to a high quality male to improve the genetics of the herd each year. **Inbreeding** is a breeding system that involves breeding related animals to one another. **Linebreeding** is a form of inbreeding. Linebreeding is done by breeding an animal and its offspring back to the same animal repeatedly. Linebreeding can be harmful in the long term as it can uncover harmful genes. **Purebred breeding** is a breeding system that is used most commonly with show or replacement animals. Purebred animals are animals that are qualified to be registered with a breed association. A purebred breeding system breeds purebred animals to purebred animals.

Castration, Estrous, Gestation, Lactation, and Parturition

Castration is the removal of the testicles in male animals. Males that are raised for meat and will not be used for breeding are castrated. Castrated animals cannot be used for breeding. **Estrous** is the term used to describe the heat cycle that females go through. Estrous is the time when females are receptive to a male and are fertile. Gestation is the term used to describe pregnancy. **Gestation** spans from the time of fertilization to the time of parturition. **Parturition** is the term used to describe the act of giving birth. Parturition in swine is called farrowing. Parturition in cattle is called calving. Parturition in horses is called foaling, and parturition in sheep is called lambing.

Parturition in goats is called kidding. **Lactation** is the term used to describe the time period when mothers are actively nursing their young.

EPDs

Expected progeny differences (EPDs) provide estimates of the genetic value of an animal as a parent. Differences of EPDs between two individuals within the same breed predict differences in performance of future offspring. EPDs are calculated for birth, growth, carcass, and maternal traits for the major species of livestock. EPD values are reported by breed associations, and two different breed EPDs may not directly correlate. EPD data is created by using performance data on the animal itself and data from ancestors, collateral relatives, and progeny. Accuracy of EPDs is improved with additional progeny data. EPDs allow producers to make more educated decisions about breeding animals. Some examples of EPD data include birth weight, weaning weight, birth type (single, twin, or triplet), number born alive, loin eye area, milking ability, sow productivity index (SPI), and so on.

Processes Involved in Cell Division

Somatic cells constantly divide through the process of **mitosis**. Mitosis results in two genetically identical daughter cells. Sex cells, or gametes, divide through the process of meiosis. **Meiosis** results in haploid cells, which contain only half the number of chromosomes as the adult organism should have. During meiosis, a process called **crossing over** occurs. During crossing over, genes are swapped between homologous chromosomes. This swapping of genes results in genetic variation between the gametes. The creation of sperm cells through meiosis is called **spermatogenesis**. The creation of egg cells, or ova, is through the meiosis process of **oogenesis**. Chromosomes carry the genes for an organism, and these serve as the blueprint for the organism's characteristics such as hair color, polled or horned, and so on.

Punnett Squares

Punnett squares are used to show all of the possible gene combinations for specific traits between two animals. To complete a Punnett square, you must be able to identify the trait and the alleles that the animal has for that trait. This is best illustrated with an example.

		Heterozygous Mother with Black Hair	
		B	**b**
Homozygous Father with Red Hair	**b**	Bb	bb
	b	Bb	bb

In this example, a female cow that is heterozygous for black hair is crossed with a male cow that is homozygous for red hair. Half of the offspring could be expected to have black hair; half could be expected to have red hair from this cross.

For two-factor crosses, use the genotypes to create the possible gene combinations for each parent, and plug them into a two-factor square.

		Heterozygous Black Polled Cow (Bbpp)			
		Bp	**bp**	**Bp**	**bp**
Homozygous Red Bull with Horns (bbPp)	**bP**	BbPp	bbPp	BbPp	bbPp
	bp	Bbpp	bbpp	Bbpp	Bbpp
	bP	BbPp	bbPp	BbPp	bbPp
	bp	Bbpp	bbpp	Bbpp	bbpp

In this example, we have crossed a heterozygous black, polled cow with a homozygous red, horned bull. The Punnett square shows you an expected ratio of animals based on the hair color and the presence of horns from this cross.

Phenotype and Genotype of Animals

The **phenotype** refers to the appearance of an animal. Phenotypes are traits that can be seen or measured. Examples of phenotypes would be hair color, height, weaning weight, or the possession of horns or being polled. **Genotype** tells the genes that the animal has. Phenotypes can give you clues about the genotypes that the animal has. The genotype will tell the actual alleles that the animal has for a certain trait. It will show whether the animal is homozygous or heterozygous for a trait. It will also show whether the alleles are dominant or recessive. An example of this can be seen with polled animals. Being polled is recessive, so an animal that is polled would have a genotype of hh. A horned animal would have a genotype of either HH or Hh because being horned is a dominant trait. Genotypes are used to complete Punnett squares and predict the traits of potential offspring.

Role of the Estrous Cycle, Ovulation, Heat Detection, and Fertilization

There are four stages of the **estrous cycle**: proestrus, estrus, metestrus, and diestrus. Proestrus is the time when a female will start to show signs of heat but may not be receptive to a male yet. Estrus is the time when a female is receptive to a male and is fertile. Metestrus is the time period right after ovulation and until the corpus luteum develops. Diestrus is the time period after metestrus until the corpus luteum regresses. **Ovulation** is the term used to describe the releasing of an ovum (egg) or multiple ova from the ovaries. **Heat detection** is usually done by the male in natural mating. In artificial insemination, heat detection methods are used to ensure that the female is receptive and ready for breeding. **Fertilization** occurs when a sperm and egg cell merge and attach to the wall of the uterus to begin the development process.

Animal Disease Control and Prevention

Vaccination and Immunization in the Animal Science Industry

Vaccines are used by producers to prevent animals from catching a disease. Many diseases are expensive to treat; therefore, it is cheaper in the long run for producers to prevent the disease than it is to treat the disease. Vaccines will vary for livestock species as well as the location of the animal. Animals that don't leave the farm will require minimum vaccinations. Animals that frequently leave the farm, such as breeding and show animals, will require more vaccinations because they will potentially come into contact with more diseases. **Immunization** refers to giving vaccines to boost the animal's immune system. When a vaccine is given, the injection includes either a weakened or dead pathogen that causes a disease. The animal's immune system learns how to fight off the pathogen, so if it comes into contact with the live pathogen, it can destroy it before it makes the animal sick.

Routes of Administration of Medications and Vaccines on Animal Species

There are two main ways of providing **medications** to animals. Some medications must be injected into the tissue of the animal; some can be given orally. Oral medications can be poured or mixed into the feed of the animal. Some oral medications are given as a paste or gel and are squirted into the animal's mouth using a syringe. Medications are used to treat some illness or infection. **Vaccines** are used to prevent an illness and boost the animal's immune system. Vaccines are given as shots. They are administered either intramuscularly (IM) or subcutaneously (SQ). Intramuscular vaccines are given into the muscle tissues and injected into areas of large muscle mass such as the neck or hindquarters. Subcutaneous injections are given into the tissues of the skin. Subcutaneous injections are commonly given into the neck tissue.

Procedures for Handling Animal Materials

When handling animal medications, one should use caution. Animal medications are often a much higher dosage than what humans would be exposed to. **Vaccinations** are given with a needle and syringe. The animal receiving the vaccination should be calm and restrained. The needle should be uncapped, the vaccination given, and then the needle should be immediately recapped and discarded into a sharps container. Needles should not be shared from one animal to another, even if the animal appears healthy. When giving an animal an oral **supplement** in the form of a paste or gel, it is typically squirted into the mouth with a plastic syringe. The animal should be calm and restrained before the supplement or medication is given. Once the medication is given, the syringe should be thrown away. Pour-on medications or supplements should be dressed onto the animal's feed, and exposure to the skin should be limited. All animal medication and supplement containers should be discarded properly.

Methods of Controlling Parasites of Livestock

There are two types of parasites that can affect livestock. **External parasites** attach to the animal from the outside. Examples of external parasites would be fleas, ticks, and mites. **Internal parasites** are ingested by the animal and affect the animal internally, living within the tissues of the animal. Internal parasites that can affect livestock are parasitic worms such as tapeworms, hookworms, roundworms, and coccidia. There are sprays and topicals available to producers that can repel external parasites. There are feed additives that can be fed to help expel external parasites. Internal parasites can be treated with antiparasitic drugs. Many of these are administered orally and work by killing the internal parasites that are then passed out with digestive wastes. Parasites can develop a resistance to antiparasitic drugs, so it's important to use these only when the animal has too many parasites. Producers can use rotational grazing to help prevent the spread of internal parasites. Cograzing different species of livestock can also be used to lower parasite loads in livestock. Goats are exceptionally prone to anemia due to parasites and should be checked frequently using FAMACHA scoring.

Noninfectious and Infectious Diseases and Disorders

An **infectious disease** is a disease that can be spread from animal to animal. Infectious diseases are caused by pathogens such as bacteria and viruses. Animals with infectious diseases should be quarantined and treated to prevent spreading of the disease to other animals in the herd or group. All newly purchased animals should be checked for infectious diseases before being allowed into the group of the other animals. A noninfectious disease is a disease that is not spread to other animals. Noninfectious diseases can be caused by nutritional deficiencies or toxicities, genetic diseases or disorders, or other disease or disorders such as cancer. A noninfectious disease requires treatment of some kind, but the animal does not need to be separated from the herd during treatment as the illness will not spread to the rest of the group.

Chapter Quiz

Ready to see how well you retained what you just read? Scan the QR code to go directly to the chapter quiz interface for this study guide. If you're using a computer, simply visit the online resources page at **mometrix.com/resources719/osatagred** and click the Chapter Quizzes link.

Plant and Soil Science

Principles of Soil Science

Horizons Within a Soil Profile

A **soil profile** is the cross section of soil that shows all of the different layers, or **horizons**, of soil. Horizons are labeled, and each horizon has different characteristics. Starting from the surface, Horizon O is the first horizon. It is named **Horizon O** as this is the layer of organic material found at the surface of the soil. Horizon O is sometimes called the humus layer. The next horizon is Horizon A. **Horizon A** is made up of a mixture of organic and inorganic material. The substantial proportion of organic material causes it to be darker in color than the lower horizons. The next horizon is **Horizon B**. This layer is often called the subsoil. It is slightly more compact and lighter in color than Horizon A. It is rich in minerals that drained from the A horizon. The next horizon is **Horizon C**. This horizon is composed of weathered parent material and bedrock and is extremely hard. Some soils will have an E horizon. Horizon E is eluviated material that has leached through the A horizon and sits in between the A and B horizons.

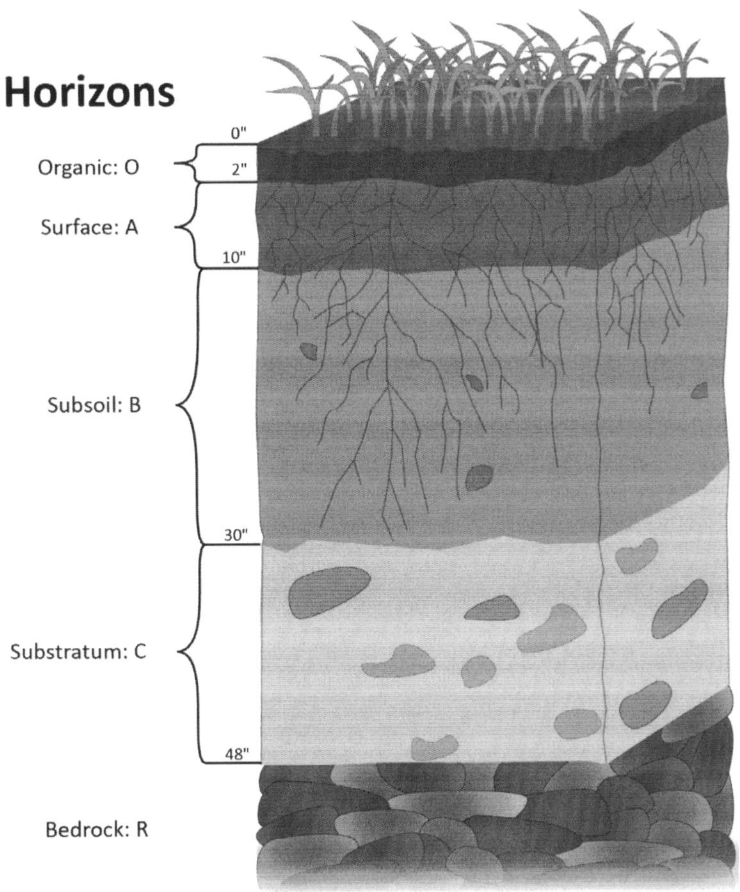

Soil Structure and Texture

Soil is made up of sand, silt, clay, organic materials, living organisms, and the pores where water and air are located. **Sand** particles are the largest, followed by **silt**, leaving **clay** particles as the smallest. Sandy soils are well drained and often lack enough water and nutrients for plants to grow.

Clay soils are usually poorly drained and hold excessive water, preventing proper plant growth. The ideal soil is almost equal amounts of sand, silt, and clay. This is referred to as **loamy** soil. Soil should be roughly half solid matter (sand, silt, clay, minerals, and organic materials) and roughly half air and water (equal parts air and water). An ideal soil allows plant roots to grow deep into the soil as there is adequate water, air, and nutrients for growth.

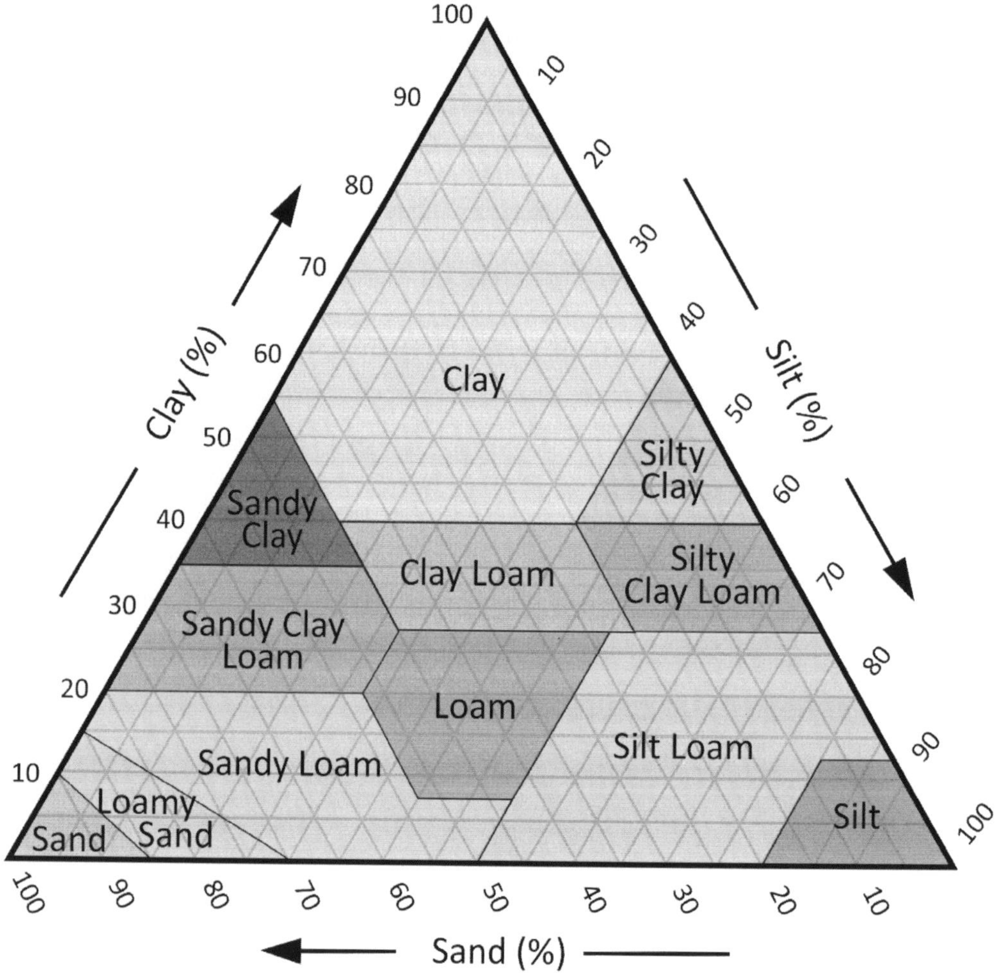

TYPES OF WATER IN SOIL

There are multiple types of water in the soil. Soil has pores where water can be found.

- **Gravitational water** is unavailable to plants. It is pulled down through the soil and either becomes groundwater or drains into streams.
- **Capillary water** is the water held within the pores of the soil in between the soil particles. There are three types of capillary water: free moving capillary water, available capillary water, and unavailable capillary water.
- **Free moving capillary water** moves constantly in all directions through the soil.
- **Available capillary water** is what remains in the soil once the capillary movement stops. This water is available and can be use by plants.
- **Unavailable capillary water** is held tightly around soil particles and cannot be used by plants.

- **Hygroscopic water** refers to the thin layer of water that binds tightly to soil particles due to adhesion forces, rendering it inaccessible to plants.
- **Interstitial water** refers to water located in the small spaces between soil particles, and it can be available to plants if it is not too tightly bound to the soil particles.

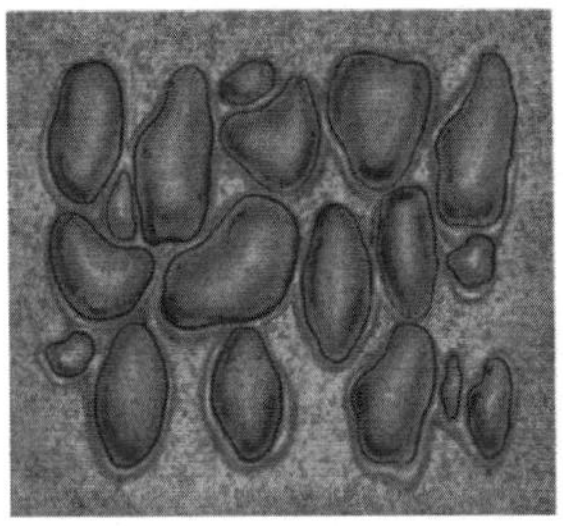

Hydroscopic water

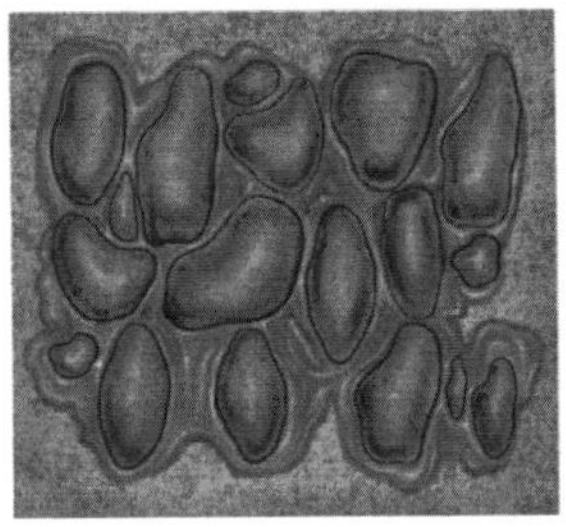

Capillary water

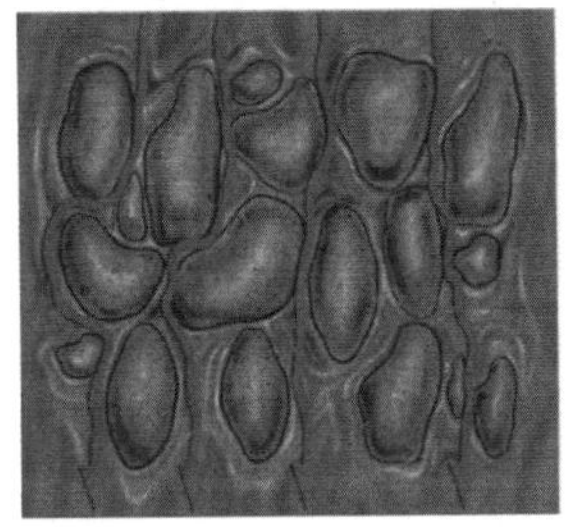

Gravitational water

Role of Soil pH in Plant Production

Most plants prefer to grow in soil with a pH between 5.6 and 7.0. The pH scale indicates the amount of hydrogen and hydroxide ions or whether a substance is **acidic** or **alkaline**. A pH of 7.0 is neutral. The pH scale ranges from 0 to 14. A pH lower than 7.0 is considered acidic, whereas a pH above a 7.0 is considered alkaline, or basic. Soil tends to be acidic in areas where there is acidic parent material and more precipitation than is able to evaporate from the soil. In areas where there is more soil evaporation than precipitation reaching the soil, salts build up in the soil. This causes the soil to become alkaline and can even become so basic that plant growth is limited or prevented. When the soil it too alkaline and the pH needs to be lowered, sulfur or acids such as vinegar can be added to the soil to lower the pH, allowing plants to grow. If the soil is too acidic and needs to be raised, lime can be added to the soil. An incorrect pH can cause the soil to hold essential nutrients in place, preventing the plant from gaining and using those nutrients.

Materials Used in Soilless Media

Soilless media is used in many commercial growing operations in place of soil. Soilless media are used to provide support to the plant in the absence of soil. They are commonly used in hydroponics systems. Soilless media have the benefit of being both cleaner and cheaper for growers. **Vermiculite** is a growing media made from hydrated silicate minerals. When heated, vermiculite expands. Vermiculite retains water and nutrients. **Perlite** is a growing medium made from volcanic glass. Similar to vermiculite, when perlite is heated, it expands. It also holds both water and nutrients. **Sphagnum moss**, or peat moss, is a growing media. Sphagnum moss comes from more than 300 types of moss that grow in bogs and are harvested. **Horticultural sand** is a medium commonly used for cuttings. Horticultural sand promotes aeration when added to media mixtures.

Soil Conservation Practices

Soil conservation uses methods of agriculture to prevent or reduce soil lost each year. Most soil loss results from water erosion. **Water erosion** occurs in three steps: detachment, transport, and deposition. The amount of soil removed by water erosion is affected by soil texture and structure, slope, surface roughness, and soil cover. Erosion due to water can be lessened by reducing raindrop impact, reducing or slowing runoff, and safely removing water from fields. Conservation tillage methods, soil cover, crop rotation practices, grass waterways, terraces, contour tilling, and strip-cropping can reduce water erosion. Dry areas with high winds are more likely to experience wind erosion. **Wind erosion** can occur as saltation, suspension, or surface creep. Soil texture, structure, roughness, climate conditions, field length, and vegetative cover affect the amount of soil lost to wind erosion.

Plant Classification, Morphology, and Physiology

Taxonomical Classification of Plants and the Binomial Nomenclature

Most plants have more than one common name, which would make it confusing for scientists discussing these plants as two completely different plants may have the same common name. The **binomial nomenclature system** of naming and classifying organisms was developed by Carolus Linnaeus. The taxonomical classification includes (broadest to most specific) domain, kingdom, phylum, class, order, family, genus, and species of every organism. The genus and species for an organism are considered the scientific name for that organism and are written as Latin words. Latin is used because it is a dead language. Species of plants are often further classified into **varieties**. Varieties are plants that resemble another plant but have slight differences that are inherited. Plants also have another subdivision of classification called the cultivar. The term **cultivar** means cultivated variety.

Classification of Plants According to Use and Growth Habits

Agronomic plants include crops that are grown on a large scale for food. Forages, such as hay crops, are also considered agronomic plants because they are grown on a large scale for livestock feed. Agronomic crops provide the basis of our food supply and include rice, corn, and wheat. **Horticultural** crops include vegetables, fruits, and flowering and ornamental plants. Horticultural plants can both enhance our diets as well as our living environment. Horticultural crops are grown on a smaller scale than agronomic crops. **Annuals** are plants that perform their entire life cycle within one growing season, leaving the entire plant to die. **Perennials** are plants that live year after year. The top portion of perennials may die back, but the root system survives, and the plant regrows.

USDA Plant Hardiness Zone Maps

The **USDA Plant Hardiness Zone Map** breaks North America into 11 zones. The zones are based on the average annual minimum winter temperatures for a 30-year period. Each zone represents a 10-degree difference and is divided again into two 5-degree a and b zones. Zone 1 on the map is the coldest zone. Zone 11 is the warmest zone. These zones are frequently used by plant catalogs, landscapers, and commercial growers to indicate suitable planting climates. The USDA Plant Hardiness Zone Map is color-coded with colder temperatures represented as blues and purples, temperate climates as greens and yellows, and warmer climates as oranges and reds.

Monocots and Dicots

Flowering plants can be divided into two categories: **monocots** and **dicots**. The differences between the two start when the plants are embryos. Monocots are named so because they have only one cotyledon. Dicots have two cotyledons. Monocots have parallel leaf veins, whereas dicots have branched leaf veins. Monocots have stomata on the top side and underside of the leaf. Dicots have stomata only on one side. Monocots have flowers with petals in multiples of threes and do not bear fruit. Dicots have flowers with petals in multiples of four or five and can bear fruit. Monocots have fibrous root systems, and dicots have taproot systems. Monocots have bundles of vascular tissue throughout the stem and lack a cortex. Dicots have bundles of vascular tissue that is arranged in a ring. Monocots are herbaceous plants such as wheat or corn. Dicots can be woody or herbaceous plants such as oak or tomatoes.

Vegetative Plant Parts

The **vegetative** parts of a plant include the leaves, stems, and roots. **Leaves** are where food is produced. They are green in color due to the large amount of chlorophyll that they contain. The chlorophyll captures sunlight, which is used in the process of photosynthesis. Photosynthesis takes place within the leaves. **Stems** have two main functions: movement of materials and support. Stems move water and minerals up from the roots into the leaves. They transport food produced by the leaves down into the plant and roots for storage. **Roots** have several functions for plants. They anchor the plant down into the soil, which helps hold the plant upright. Roots absorb water and minerals from the soil and bring it into the plant. Roots also store large amounts of food. In some plants, roots can even be used to propagate and reproduce.

Reproductive Plant Parts

The **reproductive** structures of a plant include flowers, fruits, and seeds. **Flowers** have four main parts: sepals, petals, stamens, and the pistil. The **sepals** are the green, leaflike structures that cover and protect the flower before the flower opens. **Petals** are technically leaves and are a brightly colored portion of the flower. They are brightly colored to attract pollinators. The **stamen** is the male part of the plant and includes the filament and anther. The anther is where pollen is held. The **pistil** is the female part of the flower and produces eggs called ovules. The pistil includes the stigma, which is sticky to grab pollen. The pistil also includes the style, ovary, and the ovule. Fertilized eggs become **seeds,** and the ovary becomes a fruit or seed coat. The **fruit** protects the seed and acts as a means of dispersal.

Herbaceous and Woody Plants

One of the key differences between herbaceous and woody plants is found in the stem. **Herbaceous** plants have soft, flexible stems. Herbaceous plants can be annuals or perennials. The top portion of herbaceous plants can die back each year with new growth appearing the following year. **Woody** plants produce wood tissue to provide structure. Woody plants are perennials. New wood tissue is added each year and can be seen in a cross section of the trunk or stem as rings. Woody plants have stems and a trunk that is covered in bark. The wood tissue creates sturdy structure, allowing the plant to survive and grow even during harsh conditions. Because of this, woody plants are the largest terrestrial plants.

Major Plant Processes

There are three key processes that plants need to survive: photosynthesis, respiration, and transpiration. **Photosynthesis** is the process that plants use to create food. Photosynthesis requires water, carbon dioxide, and sunlight. Photosynthesis creates glucose molecules that can be broken down and used as energy for the plant. The cellular **respiration** process breaks glucose molecules into usable energy for the cell. Respiration requires oxygen to take place, so the plants take in oxygen. **Transpiration** is the process of plants losing water through their leaves. Plants can control the amount of water lost through their leaves. Water is lost through stomata on the underside of the leaves. Stomata can be opened and closed by guard cells.

Effects of Temperature, Light, Moisture, and Air on Plant Growth

Environmental factors including temperature, light, moisture, and air can all impact plant growth. **Temperature** is the most important environmental factor determining plant growth. The temperature needs vary for different plants. Tender plants will not grow in cold conditions. Plants use photosynthesis to create food. For photosynthesis to take place, plants need **light**. Without light, plants cannot produce food and will die. Water is essential for all life, including plants. **Water** is the main component of plant cells and helps keep the plant turgid. A plant without water will wilt and die. Water is required in photosynthesis and is used to transport nutrients in the plant. **Air** is required for both the production of food (photosynthesis) and the breakdown of food into energy (respiration).

Macronutrients and Micronutrients Needed for Plant Growth

The **macronutrients** needed for plant growth include nitrogen, phosphorus, potassium, calcium, magnesium, and sulfur. The **micronutrients** needed for plant growth include boron, copper, chlorine, iron, manganese, molybdenum, zinc, and nickel. Plants require large amounts of the macronutrients, therefore giving them the name macronutrients (macro = large). The micronutrients are required by the plant in smaller amounts, leading to their name (micro = small). The macronutrients can be divided into two groups: the major nutrients and the secondary nutrients. The **major nutrients** include nitrogen, phosphorus, and potassium. The **secondary nutrients** include calcium, magnesium, and sulfur. Plants require a balance of nutrients to stay healthy. Deficiencies of any of the nutrients will present symptoms and health issues.

Role of Nitrogen, Phosphorus, and Potassium in Plant Growth

Nitrogen has a profound effect on plants. Nitrogen encourages vegetative growth and creates dark green leaves. Nitrogen helps regulate the use of the other major elements. It also creates tender vegetative growth, which is desired in leafy vegetables. Too much nitrogen can lower resistance to disease, weaken the stem, lower fruit quality, and delay maturity. Too little nitrogen stunts root and top growth and causes leaves to yellow. **Phosphorus** encourages plant cell division, prevents flowers and seeds from forming, hastens maturity, encourages the growth of strong root systems, increases disease resistance, and improves fruit crop quality. Deficiencies of phosphorus lead to reduced flowering and fruiting, poor-quality fruit, and susceptibility to cold and disease. **Potassium** increases disease resistance, encourages healthy roots, encourages efficient carbon dioxide use, and is essential for starch, chlorophyll, and tuber development.

Sexual Reproduction in Plants

Sexual reproduction in plants involves flowers. The processes of fertilization, pollination, and germination must occur for sexual reproduction to be successful. The sex cells of plants include **pollen grains** (male sex cells) and the **ovules** (female sex cells). Pollination occurs when pollen grains from the anther land on the stigma. **Pollination** can be through self-pollination or cross-pollination. The pollen tube grows down through the style into the ovary and merges with an ovule. A single sperm cell travels down the pollen tube to fertilize the egg. **Fertilization** occurs when the male and female cells join. Only fertilized ovules can become seeds. **Germination** occurs with the growth of a root through the seed coat of a new plant. Sufficient warmth, water and air are required for germination to take place.

Crop Production and Management

Development of Human Use of Plants

Thousands of years ago, humans were nomadic and traveled in search of food. As nomads, humans used plants they foraged for food, shelter, and medicinal purposes. The domestication of crops allowed human civilization to begin to develop. Crops allowed humans to settle in a location and create permanent homes and settlements. Plants were grown for food, feed for animals, and medicine. Fiber plants would eventually be grown and used for clothing to replace skins of animals. Wood and timber were used to create log shelters or the framework for homes. Today, plants still provide many things for humans. They provide food, fiber, shelter, medicines, recreation, and aesthetic value.

Major Milestones and Advances of Plant Science

There are many major milestones and advances of plant and soil science that have occurred. Plant breeding has occurred for thousands of years as farmers selectively bred crop plants for desired traits. Gregor Mendel studied genetic traits in pea plants in the 1800s. Often called the father of genetics, his pea plant studies allowed him to discover the Law of Segregation, the Law of Independent Assortment, and the Law of Dominance. Many scientists would follow and further explore his findings, leading to the mapping of plant genomes. In the early 1990s, tobacco plants were being experimentally genetically modified. In 1994, the first genetically modified crop was available for sale in the United States, the FlavrSavr tomato. Primitive farmers understood the value of adding nutrients to the soil around crops and would often use fish or other waste materials to fertilize their crops. In the 1800s, Justus von Liebig studied the role of nutrients in soil and created the framework for modern soil science. The US Soil Conservation Service studied soils extensively to improve soil fertility, reduce soil erosion, and maintain US soils after the Dust Bowl.

Importance of Plants in the Global Food Supply

Human ancestors' diets consisted of mainly plant matter. As humans hunted more efficiently and began to domesticate livestock, meat became a larger portion of human diets. Plants still make up a large percentage of human diets and therefore the global food supply. Estimates show that between 50% and 75% of the global diet comprises plant-based foods. Corn, wheat, and rice are dominating crops in the global food supply. Many scientists agree that plants will be the answer to feeding the growing population. Plants can be grown virtually anywhere with today's agricultural practices. Plants also require little space to grow. Livestock, however, is more limited and requires large amounts of space. The amount of arable land is limited, and agricultural production will need to be significantly increased to feed the global population; therefore, plants will play an even larger role in the global food supply in the future.

Types of Cultivation for Agronomic Crops

Cultivation involves preparing the soil, planting crops, and maintaining the soil as a farming system. Conventional row cropping is a type of cultivation called **intensive cultivation**. Intensive cultivation requires increased maintenance, capital, fertilizers, and pesticides. It also results in higher crop yields per land unit. This cultivation over long periods is damaging to the soil and can lead to poor soil quality and erosion. **Extensive cultivation** uses reduced maintenance, fertilizers and capital. The soil is tilled much less, if at all, allowing the soil health and productivity to increase naturally. **Monoculture** is the cultivation of a single crop in a field at a time. **Crop rotation** is the practice of rotating plants to improve soil structure and fertility.

Equipment Used in Cultivating and Harvesting Agronomic Crops

The most commonly used piece of equipment on an agronomic crop farm is the **tractor**. Tractors are versatile and can be used to pull implements to work the soil, spread seed, water or fertilizer, harvest crops, and cut and bale hay. To cultivate the soil, a **cultivator** is commonly used. A cultivator can have either shanks or rotary disks. A chisel plow, harrow, or specialized plows can also be used to break up the soil. Harvesting crops requires other machinery. **Combine harvesters** are used to harvest grain crops. They are used in conjunction with grain carts and augers. There are harvesters specialized for harvesting beans, beets, corn, forage, apples, and other crops. Cotton pickers, swathers, mechanical tree shakers, rice hullers, and other machinery are also used to harvest agronomic crops.

Production and Management Practices of Agronomic Crops

There are several methods of managing and producing agronomic crops. Farming agronomic crops is referred to as row-cropping. Traditionally, the soil was plowed, and seeds were planted in rows. Once harvested, the field remained bare until the following year. This system is not sustainable and can lead to soil erosion and soil nutrient loss. Alternate methods of producing agronomic crops are used to improve the health of the soil. **Crop rotation** is a method that produces alternate crops to increase soil health. **No-till** crop management eliminates the tillage of the soil, which increases soil fertility and greatly reduces erosion. **Cover crops**, such as wheat, can be grown when the soil in a conventional system is bare. **Strip cropping** is a production practice in which two crops are grown in alternate strips in the same field.

Importance of Weed and Pest Control in Agronomic Crop Production

Proper pest management is crucial to agronomic crop production. A **pest** is any insect, weed, animal, or disease that can harm a crop and reduce harvest yields. **Animals** that graze, such as deer and rabbits, will consume the leaves and fruits of crops, reducing or eliminating crop production. Birds will consume grains and can impact harvest yields. **Insect** pests can destroy the leaves, roots, and stems of the plant. In large numbers, insects can destroy entire crop fields. **Weeds** are plants that are unwanted and grow among crop plants. Weeds can reduce yields because they compete with the crop plants for nutrients, water, and sunlight. Weeds can also harbor diseases. **Diseases** can spread rapidly in agronomic crops under the right conditions. Diseases cause infection and can greatly reduce yields.

Divisions of Agronomic Crops

The most common crops grown are **cereal grains**. Cereal grains are grasses that are grown for their edible seeds. Wheat, rice, and oats are cereal grains. **Legumes** are crops that grow a seed within a pod and are grown for the seeds. Peas, lentils, and peanuts are legumes. **Sugar crops** are grown for their high sugar content, such as sugarcane. **Oil crops** are grown for their oil content. The oils can be used for biodiesel production, cooking, or animal feed. Soybeans, peanuts, and sesame are grown as oil crops. **Fiber crops** are grown for their fibers, which can be used to make clothing or paper. A commonly grown fiber crop is cotton. **Forage crops** are grown to produce feed for animals. Forage includes many grasses and fodders, such as alfalfa.

Crop Rotation

The main purpose of using a **crop rotation** system is to return nutrients to the soil and reducing the amount of fertilizer used. Green manure adds many nutrients back into the soil. Legumes can be planted after the primary crop is harvested to fix the nitrogen in the soil. Crop rotation systems also reduce pest and disease problems. If the same crop is planted in the same field each year, the pests that affect that crop will build up in the soil and become more of a nuisance each year. Many pests are specialized, and when the crops are alternated, they cannot survive. Soil structure can also be improved by rotating deep-rooted and shallow-rooted plants.

Harvesting Techniques

Harvesting involves removing the mature crops from the field. The harvested crop is gathered and processed before being sold. Traditionally, crops were harvested by hand. Cotton was picked from the plant, and wheat was cut from the field using a sickle before being further processed by hand. Modern farming allows farmers to harvest crops with reduced or minimal manual labor by using machines. **Combine harvesters** can be used to efficiently harvest grain crops. The combine gets its name from its ability to combine three harvesting stages into one. Reaping, threshing, and winnowing were all traditionally performed by hand but can be done rapidly in a combine with minimal effort. **Reaping** cuts the entire grain crop from the field. **Threshing** removes the grain from the plant. **Winnowing** separates the grain from the chaff.

Horticultural Principles

Divisions of Horticulture

Pomology is the science of growing fruit. Pomology can also be called fruticulture. Pomologists study the processes involved in growing, harvesting, and cultivating fruit. **Floriculture** is a branch of horticulture that deals with growing and cultivating flowering and ornamental plants. Floriculturists grow plants that can be used in gardening and provide plants used by florists in floral arrangements. **Landscaping** involves modifying the land around a business or home to improve the aesthetic appeal. Landscaping can involve managing and manipulating turf grasses, gardens, and ornamental plants. **Olericulture** is the science of growing herbaceous vegetable plants. Olericulturists study the production, harvesting, storage, and processing of vegetable crops.

Common Terminology for Horticulture

- **Weeds** are plants that thrive in a location where they are not wanted. A weed can disrupt crop growth and development by competing for sunlight, water, nutrients, and space.
- **Insects** are arthropod, organisms characterized by a segmented body and an exoskeleton. Insects are a common pest for plants; they cause plant injury by direct feeding or cause plant disease by serving as vectors of plant pathogens.
- **Plant Pathogens** are organisms (such as bacteria, virus, or fungi) that cause plant disease and death. Bacteria are prokaryotic, unicellular microorganisms that can cause rots, spots, wilts, cankers, blights, and galls. Viruses are sub-microscopic obligate parasites that can cause discoloration, spots, and rolling of leaves; and curling, stunting, and abnormal coloration of flowers. Fungi are eukaryotic, unicellular or multi-cellular microorganisms that can cause damping off, wilts, die-back, blights, mildew, cankers, leaf lesions, galls, witches' broom, dwarfing, and rosetting.
- **Shrubs** are woody perennial plants, usually broad-leaved, that can either be deciduous (i.e., sheds leaves annually) or evergreen. A shrub is usually lower in stature than a tree and has a relatively greater number of branches located near its base. Shrubs are often planted for their flowers (for instance, azaleas and rhododendrons) or for privacy (evergreen hedges).
- **Bedding plants** are a large group of flowering plant species, usually annuals but also including perennials. Bedding plants are often planted to achieve colorful landscapes during the different seasons of the year. The most popular bedding plants include geraniums, impatiens, petunias, marigolds, begonias, pansies, salvia, and vinca.
- **Cut flowers** are blossoms or inflorescences harvested from an annual or perennial plant and used for decorative purposes. Some examples of cut flowers are sunflower, annual baby's breath, annual statice, lisianthus and zinnia, shasta daisy, aster, yarrow, goldenrod, and peony.
- **Potted Plants**, also called houseplants, are any species of foliage or flowering plants grown in pots or containers for use as decoration indoors (offices and homes), on patios, or, sometimes, in landscapes.

Types of Cultivation for Horticultural Crops

Horticultural crops include fruits, vegetables, and plants that are grown for aesthetic purposes. This wide range of plants creates a wide range of growing methods. **Orchards** are used to grow large fruiting plants such as apple trees. Traditionally, vegetable plants have been grown in fields in suitable conditions. **Greenhouse** growing arose as a way to extend the growing season and grow in otherwise unsuitable environments. Greenhouses allow growers to control the environment and grow plants year-round. **Hydroponics** systems were created to enhance greenhouse growing. Hydroponics involves growing plants without soil, usually in a water and nutrient solution.

Hydroponics systems are highly efficient. **Aquaponics** combines hydroponics and fish farming. The fish fertilize the water for the plants, and the plants put oxygen into the water in return.

Proper Management for Greenhouses, Orchards, Gardens, and Nurseries

There are multiple methods that can be used to produce horticultural crops. **Greenhouses** allow producers to grow crops in areas and climates that otherwise would not be suitable for growing crops. Greenhouses can be used for a variety of plants and can include bedding systems, in-ground planting, hydroponics, and aquaponics systems. **Orchards** are used to grow fruit and nut-bearing trees and shrubs. Most orchards are spaced in a grid pattern, and grass is grown among the trees or shrubs. Orchards grow fruit and nuts at a commercial scale. **Gardens** can refer to food-production plants or flowering plants in landscaping. Gardens used for food production can be grown directly in the ground or in raised garden beds. Gardens are used by individuals to grow food at a small scale. **Nurseries** are businesses that produce young plants. Nurseries can produce bedding plants, young vegetable plants, or young trees and landscaping plants. Nurseries propagate plants and start plants from seed, allowing the buyer to plant older plants that will produce quicker.

Optimal Conditions

An optimum growing temperature can be achieved and maintained in a greenhouse with heaters, ventilation systems, evaporative cooling systems, and roll-up screens or shading materials (paint) to reduce heat from solar radiation. Suitable heaters for greenhouses include space heaters, forced-air heaters, hot-water or steam heaters, and electric heaters (for localized heating). Ventilation systems include roof vents, exhaust fans, and thermostats. Ventilation systems and evaporative coolers keep greenhouses from getting too hot on bright sunny days. Evaporative coolers also provide additional humidity to the greenhouse. Humidity can also be controlled through the use of mist sprays, which can be controlled with a timer. Light intensity and day length can be controlled by artificial lights in the greenhouse. Growers are advised to research the light intensity required by their crops and to adjust the light intensity from artificial sources based on light meter readings.

Common Procedures

- **Transplanting** involves producing seedlings under controlled environment, such as in a greenhouse, and transferring the established plant to a different location, usually outdoors.
- **Hardening off** is the process of conditioning indoor-grown plants for eventual exposure to the outdoor environment. This process involves gradual exposure to the natural elements (e.g., sunlight, wind, precipitation) and gradual reduction in watering for one to two weeks.
- **Pruning** is the judicious removal of senescent or dead leaves or branches of a plant. Pruning is usually performed to control growth, to remove plant parts with localized infection, or to improve the quality or quantity of blooms or fruits.
- **Forcing** is the process of inducing a branch or a bulb to grow or bloom ahead of its natural season. Growth or flowering is induced by exposure to warmer temperatures or artificial light.

Growth Media

Growth media are prepared using various materials or amendments. The common materials for growth media preparation include peat and peat-like materials (e.g., moss, humus or muck), wood residues (e.g., sawdust, bark), agricultural bi-products (e.g., bagasse, rice hulls), sand, perlite, vermiculite, calcined clays, expanded polystyrene, and urea formaldehyde. The amendments used for growth media preparation are primarily chosen based on cost and the cultural requirements of the plants that will be grown on the media. Growth media should possess the following attributes: permeable to water and air; able to retain water and not dry out easily; able to absorb nutrients and supply them to the plant; free of plant pathogens, insects, nematodes and weed seeds; biologically and chemically stable to withstand sterilization; free of organic matter, which can release ammonia upon treatment with heat or chemicals; and, finally, consistency to ensure similar outcome when used in fertilization and irrigation regimes.

Irrigation

The most popular irrigation systems used in greenhouse and nursery production are the overhead and the drip irrigation systems. Overhead irrigation is inferior to drip irrigation because it distributes water unevenly, causing non-uniform plant growth; it creates an ideal humid environment for infection and the spread of disease (through water splash or aerosoles); it uses a greater amount of water (especially in container nurseries); and it contributes to run-off. Drip irrigation, though more expensive to install and maintain, is a more efficient watering system. It uses less water than overhead systems, and uniformly applies water to the growing area. Because water is delivered through tubes on the ground, watering is not affected by the wind or the plant canopy. Drip irrigation does not contribute to run-off, nor does it restrain other nursery activities during operation.

Growth Regulators

Growth regulators in plants are hormones. **Hormones** affect the growth of plants. The four main hormones in plants are: **auxins** (which stimulate cell enlargement), **gibberellins** (which stimulate cells elongation, premature flowering, fruit growth, and breaking dormancy), **cytokinins** (with stimulate cell division), and **inhibitors** (which inhibit seed germination and stem elongation and increase speed of fruit ripening). Stimulants can be used to encourage plants to grow taller. Gibberellic acid can be used as a stimulant. Plants that are too tall can be given retardants, chemical regulators that slow growth. Rooting hormones, such as indolebutyric acid, can be used to encourage new cuttings to create new roots.

Detecting Insects

The key to effective insect management in the greenhouse and nursery is early detection. Early detection provides the grower the opportunity to consider his options and employ the appropriate control measure before the insect damage gets worse. The common methods of detecting insects are: 1) monitoring with the use of sticky traps; 2) inspecting the underside of leaves for the presence of very small insects, insect eggs, larvae, and pupae; 3) beating the leaves to dislodge insects from the plant; and 4) inspecting plants for the common indications of insect damage, such as leaf distortion (i.e., curling), yellowing, stunting, speckling, and webbing. Insect identification guides, extension publications, and extension agents can help growers identify insect pests and determine the appropriate control measures.

Detecting Plant Pathogens

Plant disease is manifested in a variety of ways, and growers should be on the look-out for symptoms of infection. Disease symptoms include wilting, damping-off, rotting, leaf lesions, blight, mildew, canker, galls, leaf distortion, discoloration, yellowing, dwarfing, or stunting. At present, there is a great deal of available literature on the symptoms of disease, their causal agents, and the recommended measures for controlling them. However, if the grower is unsure of the causal agent, a sample of the diseased plant can be sent to a plant disease diagnostician for further analysis. Plant disease diagnosticians employ a variety of methods to observe and identify plant pathogens. Correct identification is critical in determining the appropriate control method.

Controlling Disease

Plant disease is the result of a susceptible host, an aggressive pathogen, and optimal environmental conditions for infection. Plant disease can be prevented by sanitizing the growing area (i.e., removing debris, infected materials, and weeds that may harbor pathogens), and sterilizing the growing media, containers, tools, and implements used in the greenhouse and nursery. Disease prevention also entails the use of disease-free planting materials or disease-resistant plant varieties; crop rotation; insect vector control; proper irrigation and drainage; and the management of environmental factors (i.e., temperature, humidity, aeration, and light) that may support the growth or development of plant pathogens. The application of bactericides and fungicides in the very early stages of infection, and the removal of infected plants from the growing area, may prevent the spread of disease to other plants in the greenhouse or nursery.

Plant Propagation

Plant propagation methods fall into two categories: sexual and asexual. Sexual propagation is achieved through the use of seeds, while asexual propagation is achieved through cutting, layering, dividing, grafting, budding, and tissue culture. Cutting involves separating a leaf, a piece of stem, or a root from a parent plant and allowing the severed material to root. In layering, a new plant is produced by exposing a stem of a parent plant to rooting media and cutting it off once roots are formed. Grafting and budding both involve the union of the stock and the scion, or plant parts from two plants of the same species. In grafting, the cambium layers of the stock and scion are aligned, while in budding, a bud from the scion is inserted into the bark of the stock. Tissue culture involves producing a plant from a piece of bud, stem, or leaf by letting them regenerate on a growing media under sterile laboratory conditions.

Asexual Propagation Methods

The most common methods for propagating plants are cutting, layering, division, and grafting. **Cutting** involves removing a vegetative plant part with a sharp knife from a parent plant. The cutting is treated with hormones to regenerate itself to create a new plant. **Layering** occurs when a stem of a parent plant touches the ground or growing medium and creates roots. The new plant can then be removed from the parent plant. Layering can happen naturally, as in strawberry plants, or with the help of growers to aid the process. **Division** occurs when plants with multiple rooted crowns are pulled or cut apart to create more plants. **Grafting** is a propagation method that joins plant parts to grow one plant and is often used to combine multiple cultivars into one plant.

Greenhouse Structures and Systems

There are several types of greenhouse structures. Greenhouses are categorized by their structure and framework. Post and rafter, A-frame, and Quonset greenhouses, hoop houses, and gutter connected structures are the most common for commercial growers. Lean-to greenhouses are used by individuals and not commercial growers due to the lack of space. Commercial greenhouses are built to stand alone, although they can be connected to one another. **Post and rafter** greenhouses get their name from the simple post and rafter framework. A-**frame** greenhouses are the most simple of the greenhouse structures and are used more by individuals than commercial growers. **Quonset** greenhouses have straight sides with a half-circle top. **Hoop houses** are framed using arched pipes. **Gutter connected** greenhouses have sloped roofs and are connected with a gutter system in between the individual houses. Greenhouses are covered in glazing. There are four main types of glazing available: plastic film, polycarbonate, fiberglass, and glass. Large commercial greenhouses that cover acres are usually framed in steel and glazed with glass panels. Polycarbonate panels and polyethylene film are both popular glazing materials for hoop houses and Quonset greenhouses. Polycarbonate is more expensive and is harder to install, particularly on rounded structures like hoop houses, but is very durable. Polyethylene film is very cheap and easy to install and allows for good light transmission, but will need to be replaced more frequently.

Equipment

Large-scale propagation and maintenance of nursery or greenhouse plants requires the use of specialized structures, equipment, and machinery. Greenhouses require structures (e.g., benches) for holding plants during the growing cycle; equipment for climate control, irrigation, and plant propagation; and machinery for cultivation or mowing, harvesting or digging trees, and loading or transporting materials. Irrigation equipment includes hoses, water wands, feeder hoses, and either drip emitters (for drip irrigation) or spray nozzles (for overhead irrigation). Application equipment includes sprayers, foggers, fog nozzles, and shut-off valves. Propagation equipment includes soil or growth media mixers, sterilization equipment, flat and pot fillers, seeders, and transplanters.

Landscaping Principles

Landscape

Landscape design is design that is dominated by the color green. It is a living design and changes with plants' adaptation, nutrition, and pests. Landscape may require the incorporation of hardscapes such as streets or buildings. Design principles affecting landscape design are order and unity, scale and proportion, and balance and harmony as well as rhythm and repetition. Humans tend to look for order and find it appealing. A well-managed row crop field conveys order and unity. Rhythm and repetition can be seen in golf courses, sand dunes, and water features. Scale and proportion can refer to individual plants or the plants in comparison to a hardscape feature. Balance and harmony can be achieved with colors or plant sizes.

Classifications of Plants Used in Landscaping

- **Turfgrass** is any species of grass planted because of its ability to form dense mats of leaf blades and roots to cover soil surfaces.
- **Annuals** are plants whose life cycle is completed within one growing season.
- **Perennials** are plants whose life cycle spans more than two growing seasons.
- **Shrubs** are woody perennial plants, usually broad-leaved, that can either be deciduous (i.e. sheds its leaves annually) or evergreen. A shrub is usually lower in stature than a tree and has a relatively greater number of branches located near its base.
- **Trees** are woody plants, deciduous or evergreen, that are larger or taller than a shrub and have one or more massive trunks that bear the crown.

Use of Types of Plants in Landscaping

Because turfgrasses are planted to cover exposed soil surfaces for an indefinite amount of time, they should have the ability to establish easily, to adapt to the local climate and climatic variations, and to tolerate drought, salt, shade, wear, pests, and diseases. Annuals are often used as landscape plants because they grow quickly, are easy to maintain, and provide a variety of textures and colors to any landscape during the different seasons of the year. Perennials are chosen not only for aesthetic purposes, but also because they do not require replanting every growing season. The durability of perennials makes them ideal along houses and buildings, as privacy hedges or screens, and for garden borders. Some perennials are used to attract birds or as ornamentals in a landscape. Trees are planted as ornamentals; for protection from wind and sun; for privacy; or to produce attractive and edible fruits.

Landscape Planning

Landscape planning requires the development of a plot plan (i.e. site map) that shows the location and size of all structures present on the lot, including driveways or walkways. Planning also requires a careful analysis of the site, to identify the natural conditions and other features that can influence the choice of plants and the overall design. Site analysis should include information on the local climate, the soil type, the location of utility structures, the architecture and orientation of the house, the existing vegetation, and the surrounding views. Another important step in planning is determining the needs or preferences of the owners; this information is critical in designing a landscape that is not only beautiful but also functional. Information about the site and the owner's needs and preferences will serve as guidelines for choosing and placing plants.

Principles of Design in Landscaping

- **Unity** (also called oneness) is achieved when the components of a landscape fit together to express one main idea or concept.
- **Balance** is the arrangement of components in a given space. Balance can either be symmetrical (i.e., formal) or asymmetrical (i.e., informal).
- **Proportion** is the relationship (in terms of size or dimension) of each component to each other and to the whole landscape.
- **Rhythm** (flow) is achieved when components are arranged or distributed in a given space in such a way that the resulting pattern creates a sense of motion. The repetition of colors, lines, textures, or forms can create rhythm in a landscape.
- **Focal point** (also called emphasis) is achieved by placing a contrasting component among the other components of the landscape.
- **Simplicity** is the ability to express one idea, theme, or concept without too much complexity or ornamentation.

Landscaping Plant Selection

Landscape plants are selected based on their function, appearance, adaptability, and maintenance requirements. While certain plant species are specifically chosen for their ability to provide shade, wind protection, privacy, color, texture, fruit, or scent, the choice is ultimately decided by the plant's ability to adapt to the site conditions. Adaptability ensures that the plant can easily establish itself and thrive under the natural conditions of the site: the intensity and duration of solar radiation, rainfall, soil type, temperature, and air circulation. Plant selection also depends on the level of care that can be provided. It is advisable to select plants that are able to tolerate drought, cold, salinity, shade, insects, plant diseases, human traffic (wear), animals (pets or non-domesticated animals), and pollution. The production of potential allergens and the ability to support wildlife or attract birds or butterflies are also considered when selecting landscape plants.

Landscape Construction

Landscape construction involves hardscaping and softscaping. Hardscaping is the alteration of the ground plane (contour modification) or the flow of water (drainage construction), and the installation of structures like entrances, steps, paths, ramps, water bodies (e.g., ponds, waterfalls), terracing, fences, and barriers. Hardscaping requires knowledge of soil mechanics; soil water retention and movement; surface and subsurface drainage systems; equipment and techniques for contour modification; basic structural design; material selection, detailing and specifications for specific structures; estimation of costs; site preparation; and construction techniques and practices. Softscaping is the installation of plant materials, such as bedding plants, shrubs, trees, and turfgrass. Softscaping requires knowledge of plant materials, the site characteristics (climate, water availability, pest and disease problems in the area), and the owner specifications and preferences.

Considerations When Planting

Planting follows thorough site analysis, consultation with the owner about landscape design and function, species selection, and determination of the level of care or maintenance that can be provided after planting. The site conditions and the level of care to be provided after planting affect the choice of planting material. When planting a tree or a shrub, the site conditions and maintenance capabilities after planting will determine whether a bare-root, root balled and burlapped, or container-grown planting material will be chosen. Site conditions and maintenance capabilities, as well as owner preference, are considered in determining whether small or large planting materials will be planted. The handling and planting procedure, bed preparation, planting depth, and need for support (stakes), anchorage or protection should also be considered.

Care and Upkeep Processes

- **Fertilization** is important for maintaining healthy and beautiful landscape plants. The type and amount of fertilizer and the frequency of application are based on the type of plant, soil nutritional status, and the desired response (for instance, foliage or flower production).
- **Irrigation,** the watering schedule and amount of water to be applied, is determined by the water requirement of the plants, the type of soil, the time of year, and the moisture content of the soil.
- **Mulching** is employed for a variety of reasons, including weed control, conservation of soil moisture, and regulation of soil temperature.
- **Pruning** is essential for aesthetically-pleasing landscape plants. It is done to achieve a desired shape or size, to remove senescent, infected, or injured plant parts, and to stimulate growth or flowering.
- **Pest Management** can be achieved by using plants that are tolerant to common insects and diseases, keeping plants healthy through proper fertilization and irrigation, monitoring pests and diseases, and using mechanical and chemical pest control methods.

Controlling Weeds

Weeds can be controlled, with varying degrees of success, through a variety of physical and chemical means. The physical methods of weed control include soil cultivation, mowing, and mulching; manual removal; selection of a weed-free growing medium; and planting of cover crops. Chemical weed control involves the application of herbicides. Herbicides are classified by: 1) their ability to control weeds during the germination stage (pre-emergence) or at later growth stages (post-emergence); 2) their mode of action, whether contact (kills only the plant part that has been sprayed) or systemic (absorbed by leaves and roots and translocated within the plant); or 3) selectivity (more effective on a particular type of weed or effective on all types of weeds).

Tools and Equipment

- **Seeding and planting-** Tools for preparing the soil for planting include the cultivator, seeder, bulb planter, dibber, all-purpose knife, spade, trowel, and shovel.
- **Cleaning-** Tools for removing leaf litter and plant debris include the rake, leaf blower, vacuum, wood chipper, and mulching lawn mower.
- **Cutting and pruning-** Tools are for trimming or mowing grass and for pruning or shaping landscape plants include the mower, pruning shears, saw, loppers, tree pruners, and hedgers.

- **Irrigation and drainage-** The equipment used for manual or automated watering includes the garden hose, wand, spray nozzles, timer, irrigation valves, underground pipes, sprinkler heads, drip tape, and drip emitters.
- **Pest control equipment-** Common tools and equipment for pest (weeds, insects, plant pathogens) control include the hoe, spray tanks, nozzle, and tips.
- **Fertilizer application-** Tools or equipment used to deliver fertilizer to plant roots or foliage include liquid fertilizer injectors, deep root feeders, spreaders, top dressers, and sprayers.

Care of Equipment and Tools

The tools and equipment used in the installation (planting) and maintenance (pruning, irrigation, fertilization, and pesticide application) of landscape plants need to be cleaned and stored properly after use. Tools that contact soil should be cleaned thoroughly after each use, to remove propagules of insects, fungi, or weeds, which can be spread by the tools during subsequent use. Soil, which can retain moisture, should be removed from the tool surfaces to prevent rusting. Cutting tools that contact plant sap and gums should be wiped clean after use, or disinfected if they came in contact with diseased plant parts. Irrigation systems should be inspected for clogging, leaks, misalignment, or missing parts.

Floral Design Principles

Floral Design

The main principles of floral design are proportion, scale, harmony, rhythm, balance, unity, and emphasis. **Proportion** refers to size relationships among the elements of an arrangement (i.e., flowers, greenery, and the vase or container). The **scale** compares the overall size of the arrangement and its surroundings (i.e., a table centerpiece and the size of the table). **Harmony** refers to creating an eye-appealing combination of textures, colors, and materials. **Unity** of a floral arrangement is achieved through executing all principles of floral design, creating an attractive floral piece. **Rhythm** refers to the visual movement of an arrangement. Rhythm allows the viewers' eyes to wander around the arrangement and hold their attention. **Balance** can refer to the physical balance (weight) or the visual balance (symmetry) of the arrangement. An area of **emphasis** is a focal point and is created with dominant flowers or materials.

Floral Design Elements

- **Color-** the particular wavelength of light reflected by an object. It is used to create a mood or invoke a feeling. The three dimensions of color are hue (the wavelength or location in the color wheel), value (lightness or darkness), and chroma (intensity).
- **Form–** the shape or structure of an arrangement; it is produced when points, lines, and shapes are combined in a composition. Examples of shapes in floral arrangements are triangular, round, horizontal, and vertical.
- **Texture-** the feature of a surface perceived by seeing or feeling. Texture pertains to the quality of being smooth or rough, fine or coarse. Different textures can be used to create a formal or informal floral arrangement.
- **Line** - tall flowers borne close to the stem or elongated greenery. Line flowers or foliage are used to define the shape of a flower arrangement, by giving it height and breadth. Examples of line flowers are gladiola, snapdragons, delphiniums, and cattails. Line foliage includes eucalyptus and grasses.

- **Mass** - large flowers, borne by a single stem. Mass flowers are used as focal points or centers of attraction in floral arrangements because of their size and compactness. Examples of mass flowers are roses, peonies, tulips, hydrangeas, and magnolias.
- **Filler** - clusters of small flowers (or multiple leaves) that are borne on a single stem. Filler flowers are used in the spaces between the line and focal flowers in an arrangement. Examples of fillers include dianthus, baby's breath, statice, asters. Ferns are also used as fillers.
- **Space**- the total area occupied by an object or a floral arrangement. In floral design, the way the objects (of flowers) are distributed in space determines the overall shape of the flower arrangement. Space can also be used to distinguish parts of an arrangement and provide a visual break.
- **Light**- (also known as illumination) used in floral design to provide or enhance visual impact or to create a mood or a feeling in the viewer. Light can be used to focus attention on the entire arrangement or on certain parts.
- **Pattern**- achieved through the repetitive use of color, shape, or texture in a floral arrangement. Pattern is used in floral design to achieve a sense of rhythm or a sense of motion.
- **Balance** is the stability of the composition. Balance, or the sense of being grounded, can be achieved by providing a distinct focal point, such as a large and compact flower (i.e. mass flower).
- **Scale** is the size of the arrangement in relation to the space it occupies. For example, a floral arrangement should be proportional to its container in terms of height and width, or the whole arrangement should be proportional to the size of the room.
- **Rhythm** is the flow or sense of motion in a design. Visual flow is created through the use of pattern or repetition of colors, forms, and textures.
- **Contrast** is achieved when unlike objects are used in a composition. The use of different colors, textures, shapes, and spacing in floral design creates or enhances visual impact.
- **Dominance** is the ability of an object to attract attention or provide interest. Dominance is achieved by using a flower or foliage with a particular color, shape, or texture to draw attention.
- **Unity** is achieved when all the components in a composition create one effect or express one theme or idea.

Color Harmonies

The two types of color harmonies used in floral design are related or contrasting. Two examples of related color harmonies are monochromatic (different tints, tones, and shades of one color) and analogous (neighboring colors in the color wheel). Examples of contrasting harmonies include complementary (colors that are opposite each other in the color wheel), split-complementary (one color and the two colors on either side of the color directly opposite it), triadic (three colors equidistant from each other on the color wheel), and polychromatic (a mix of warm (e.g., red, red-orange, yellow-orange) and cool colors (e.g., blue, blue-green, blue-violet)).

Essential Tools for Flower Design

Some basic tools and materials are required to create and secure flower arrangements. Cutting tools include knives, pruning shears, and scissors for cutting stems, branches, and trimming leaves or thorns. Floral foams, floral netting, and anchor pins are used to hold flower stems in place. These materials are attached to the bottom of containers with waterproof tape, clay, or hot glue. Floral wires are used to lengthen and support stems (i.e., prevent drooping) and also to secure flowers to wreaths. After wiring, floral tape is used to warp the stem, to prevent moisture loss and hide the wire. Floral stem tape is also used to wrap together stems of flowers for corsages, bouquets, headpieces, or boutonnieres. A variety of containers are used in floral arrangements: they include various shapes of vases and bowls that are made of different materials (e.g., glass, plastic, metal).

Harvesting Cut Flowers

Specific techniques for harvesting cut flowers may vary from species to species. Harvesting time also varies according to the species of the cut flowers and the market (e.g. farmers' market, florists, groceries, or internet). Some cut flower species are harvested while the flowers are still closed (e.g., tulips) or when the buds have started to open (e.g., narcissus, hyacinth). Harvesting too early may cause the flowers not to bloom, while harvesting too late (when the flowers are fully open) may shorten the vase life of cut flowers. Harvesting tools include sharp and clean cutting instruments and disinfected buckets or pails. General harvesting techniques for most cut flowers include harvesting at the coolest time of day, placing stems in warm water as they are cut, recutting stems under water, and leaving the harvested cut flowers in hydrating solution for two hours at room temperature before cold storage.

Handling and Storing Cut Flowers

Once cut flowers have been harvested, they should be given water and food and stored at cool temperatures to preserve their quality and ensure a long vase life. Preserving the quality and prolonging their vase life requires keeping stems in water (to prevent wilting) or using anti-microbial solutions instead of plain water (to prevent wilting and control bacterial growth) and storing the cut flowers at 32-38°F with 80-90% relative humidity. In addition to water and anti-microbial solutions (e.g., biocides), there are commercially available hydration solutions (with low pH to enhance water movement through the stems) and holding solutions (formulated with sugars) specifically used to supply the energy needed for flower opening. A technique called pulsing (dipping in sucrose and biocide solution right after harvest) has been used to enhance the quality and vase life of certain cut flower species.

Pest Management and Safety

IPM

Integrated pest management (IPM) aims to control pests while reducing the use of chemicals. IPM requires frequent monitoring of plants. This allows producers to detect pests as soon as they become active. Plants can be closely inspected for pests daily, or traps can be used to monitor for pests. As soon as pests are detected, action is taken to prevent the pest from multiplying. Pests should be treated initially with nonchemical methods. Pests can be removed by hand. Biological controls can be introduced to remove the pest insect. Chemical pesticides should be used as a last resort. If chemicals are used, they should be used to treat only affected plants. The reduced amount of chemicals used in IPM systems greatly reduces environmental pollution and also saves producers money.

Cultural, Biological, Mechanical, and Chemical Controls

Cultural pest control involves manipulating the environment to reduce the likelihood that pests will become active. It can also implement preventative practices to prevent pests. An example of cultural pest control would be growing pest-resistant varieties. **Biological** controls use other organisms to remove pests naturally. Pest insects can be removed by using that insect's natural predator. The predator feeds on the pest, eliminating the pest. Aphids can be removed by introducing lacewings or ladybugs. **Mechanical**, or physical, pest control simply removes the pest or the part of the plant that is affected. Insects can be removed by hand, and diseased plants can have affected leaves or stems cut off. **Chemicals** can be used as a last resort of pest control. Pesticides such as herbicides, fungicides, and insecticides can be used to eliminate pests.

Pesticides

Pesticides are chemicals that are used to remove pests from plants. Pests can be in the form of insects, weeds, or fungi or any other organism that can harm plants. **Herbicides** are chemicals that are used to kill pest plants, or weeds. There are selective herbicides and nonselective herbicides. **Insecticides** control pest insects. The insects are killed either by coming into contact with the chemical or by swallowing the chemical. **Fungicides** are used to control fungi that cause disease. They must come into contact with the fungi to be effective and can be used as a preventative. **Miticides** are used to eliminate mites and ticks. The ticks and mites must come into contact with the chemical for it to be effective. **Molluscicides** eliminate slugs and snails. Molluscicides are usually prepared as a bait that then poisons the slugs and snails. Rodenticides are used to remove mice and rats. They are usually used as bait and then poison the rodents. **Nematocides** remove nematodes and are applied as a fumigating spray.

Safe Pesticide Use

Pesticides are chemical poisons used to kill pests and can be dangerous if used improperly. To use pesticides safely, the label must be read. The label contains all of the directions and precautions that should be followed to prevent harm. Ensure that the pesticide is the proper substance for the intended use. Have clean water and detergents available in case of spills. Wear protective clothing, including gloves and respirator if necessary. Avoid getting concentrated chemicals on the skin. Wear goggles to protect the eyes and gloves to protect the hands. If a chemical gets onto skin or clothing, wash immediately. Do not inhale or ingest a chemical, including fumes, dust, or mist. Do not eat or smoke while applying pesticides. Only apply pesticides in favorable weather conditions to avoid rain washing the pesticide away or wind spreading the pesticide. Some pesticides can be applied only within certain temperature ranges. Store and dispose of chemicals properly. Clean up thoroughly after using pesticides. If pesticide has been ingested, immediately call a doctor with the label in hand.

Safety Hazards Related to Plant Production Systems

There are many safety hazards related to plant production. Chemicals are used in plant production, and many of them are toxic or poisonous to humans. Contact with skin and mucous membranes should be avoided. Caution should be taken to avoid breathing them in. Plant hormones used in plant production can make people sick, and contact with them should also be avoided. Propagating plants often involves hormones and sharp tools, both of which should be handled carefully to avoid injury. Landscaping work often uses power tools that should be used carefully to avoid severe wounds or dismemberment. Lawnmowers should be used only with the safety guards in place. Greenhouses may require chemical treatment for pests, and treatment should be done carefully due to the enclosed space. Heavy equipment is one of the most dangerous aspects of agricultural work and is often used in large plant production systems. Heavy equipment should be used only by trained individuals.

Hazardous Plant Classifications

A **noxious** plant is a plant that has been designated, by the US Department of Agriculture or another agricultural authority, as a plant that is hazardous to crops, humans, livestock, or ecosystems. Many noxious plants are invasive; some are native. A common noxious plant is the thistle. **Invasive** plants are plants that are not native and adversely impact the surrounding ecosystem. Invasive plants can disrupt ecosystems by dominating the region due to the lack of natural controls. A common invasive plant is kudzu. A **poisonous** plant is a plant that produces toxins that discourage herbivores from consuming them. Poisonous plants contain parts that can cause illness, injury, or death to humans or animals. A common poisonous plant is poison ivy.

PPE

There are several types of **personal protective equipment** (PPE) that should be used in plant production. Plant production often requires the use of chemical pesticides, herbicides, and other chemical controls. These chemical compounds are harmful to humans and can inflict injury through the skin, mucous membranes, respiratory system, or ingestion. To prevent injury from plant production chemicals, PPE can be used. Gloves can be worn when mixing or handling chemicals to prevent skin contact. Goggles or face shields can be used to prevent chemicals from getting into the eyes. Occasionally respirators can be used to prevent inhaling chemicals. Plant production also requires the use of sharp objects such as knives, scalpels, pruners, and other sharp hand tools. Heavy gloves can be worn to protect the hands from injury.

MSDS

A **material safety data sheet** (MSDS) contains information about potential health hazards, chemical ingredients, physical characteristics, control measures, and safe handling procedures for hazardous chemicals. An MSDS must identify the material, manufacturer, and an emergency manufacturer telephone number. The MSDS will also identify the hazardous ingredients and possibly the percentage concentration of each substance. The chemical name for the substance is listed along with the OSHA Permissible Exposure Limit and the Threshold Limit Values. The MSDS will state the chemical's appearance, odor, boiling point, vapor pressure, specific gravity, evaporation rate, flash point, extinguishing media, fire and explosion hazards, reactivity data, health hazard data, and spill and leak procedures as well as control measures to reduce or eliminate hazards.

Chapter Quiz

Ready to see how well you retained what you just read? Scan the QR code to go directly to the chapter quiz interface for this study guide. If you're using a computer, simply visit the online resources page at **mometrix.com/resources719/osatagred** and click the Chapter Quizzes link.

Agricultural Mechanics

Biotechnology in Agriculture

Major Biotechnological Innovations

Through **biotechnology**, scientists are able to incorporate modern genetics into food production. **Genetically modified organisms** (GMOs) are used in a multitude of ways. There are strains of GMOs that have increased yields, herbicide tolerance, and insect resistance. The "Round-Up Ready" crops are GMOs that are resistant to herbicide sprays. This allows producers to spray entire fields and not harm the crop plants while killing all of the weeds in the field. New strains of GMOs are constantly being created to serve different functions. Producers living in drier areas that are prone to drought can purchase drought-resistant crops. GMOs can also be created to increase the nutritional value of a crop. In many Asian countries rice is a staple in the diet. In these same countries, vitamin A deficiency is a common problem. There are now strains of GMO rice that produce vitamin A to prevent the deficiency.

Advantages of Advances in Biotechnology to Local Producers

Biotechnology allows smaller producers to keep up with the large commercial producers. In the past, smaller producers were subject to the elements and environmental conditions. These producers might not be able to afford the irrigation systems that large producers could in times of drought. If a pest came through the area, a small producer could lose an entire crop. Biotechnology allows small producers the ability to purchase drought-resistant, herbicide-resistant, and pest-resistant strains of plants. Small producers also often fill niche markets. Genetically modified crops that are more flavorful or colorful and have a longer shelf life appeal to the markets of small producers. With biotechnology, small producers can offer consumers a higher-quality product.

Major Legal and Ethical Issues Surrounding the Adoption of Biotechnology

Biotechnology has great potential to be helpful, especially in the medical field. Biotechnology also has potential to be misused, leading to health problems, discrimination, inequality, and even lethal war tools. **Cloning** is a biotechnology often discussed in ethical debates. There are two main groups of cloning: research and reproductive. Research cloning involves cloning somatic cells for research purposes and is generally accepted. Reproductive cloning involves creation of a new life and is universally rejected in humans. **Genetic trait selection** has been used in agriculture for decades. **Genetically modified organisms** (GMOs) have the potential to increase yields and nutritional value of many foods. Genetic modification of humans has the potential to prevent genetic diseases, such as cystic fibrosis. There is fear that genetic modification in humans could lead to genetic enhancement.

Social and Cultural Issues Related to Agricultural Biotechnology

Genetically modified organisms (GMOs) have had DNA from a non-related species transferred into their genes with biotechnology. Many consumers are wary of the effects of consuming genetically modified foods. The genes that are transferred can come from other plants, animals, bacteria, or viruses. The long-term effects of GMOs are still unknown and have led to several states starting to require labeling of GMOs on food products. Consumers are also wary of products from livestock that have been treated with **antibiotics** and **hormones**. There has been an increase in antibiotic-resistant bacteria, and many people believe that antibiotics given to livestock as preventatives are part of the cause. Many consumers claim that growth hormones used can speed the development of antibiotic-resistant bacteria as well as increase the risk of health issues, including cancer.

Economic Impact of Biotechnology

The economic impact of biotechnology in agriculture is both immense and multisourced. A large percentage of the market consists of genetically modified crops. These crops often have higher yields and longer shelf life. Genetically modified crops reduce pesticide use (and costs) as well as the use of herbicides. The use of herbicide-tolerant crops has allowed reduced and no-tillage production, saving fuel, chemical, and soil restoration costs. Some biotech crops reduce greenhouse gas emissions from less fuel use and increased soil carbon storage from reduced tillage. The economic impact of biotechnology in agriculture is estimated to be in the hundreds of billions of dollars.

Environmental Issues Related to Agricultural Biotechnology

Biotechnology in agriculture can quickly become issues in environmental discussions as agriculture is so closely associated with the environment. Many crops develop undesirable plants (weeds) that grow among them. These plants are undesirable to farmers as they compete for sunlight, water, and nutrients with the crop plant. Enough weed growth can stunt crop growth, so farmers often spray their fields with herbicides. Many crops are herbicide tolerant so the entire field can be sprayed. This method of spraying can create spray drift or runoff. It can also lead to weeds that develop a resistance to herbicides, requiring stronger and stronger chemicals. Farmers also have problems with insect infestations. The solution has been chemical pesticides. Chemical pesticides are not selective and kill all insects, including beneficial pollinators, such as honey bees. The honey bee population has been affected tremendously by chemical pesticides.

Hazards in Biotechnology Labs

There are many possible hazards in a biotechnology lab. Chemicals are a major hazard commonly found in a laboratory setting. Chemicals can cause skin irritations, chemical burns, eye irritation, or can even cause severe illness or death. It's important to understand the safety hazards of working with chemicals. When mixing two chemicals together, never breathe in the fumes or lean over the reaction to avoid harm. There are often hot surfaces or open flames in a laboratory setting. Hot plates and the open flame of a Bunsen burner can cause burns. When working in a lab, long hair should be tied back to avoid catching it on fire. There are often other hazards in a biotechnology lab such as radiation, sharp objects such as knives and syringes, and potential pathogens.

Genetic Engineering, Cloning, and Stem-Cell Research in Agriculture

Agriculture is faced with the difficult task of feeding a rapidly growing population with ever-decreasing resources and arable land. Technologies such as genetic engineering, cloning, and stem-cell research can help farmers and agriculturists reach these goals. **Genetic engineering** is the manipulation of an organism's genes using biotechnology. **Genetically modified organisms** (GMOs) can have increased production, result in increased tolerance to abiotic factors such as heat or drought, and can alter the composition of food to be more nutritious. **Cloning** can be used to create superior breeding stock. Farmers can clone their best breeding animals to upgrade their herd quality. This allows farmers to increase yields and productivity. **Stem-cell research** has the potential to create bigger, stronger crops and more productive livestock. Stem-cell research has both agricultural and biomedical applications.

Purpose of GMOs in Agriculture

Genetically modified organisms (GMOs) create a huge advantage in the struggle to feed the growing population. GMO crops can be genetically modified to give farmers an advantage. Crops can be created with genes that allow them to be drought-, pesticide-, and herbicide-resistant. This allows farmers to spend less money taking care of the crops and getting a higher yield. Crops can also be modified to have longer shelf lives so that they can be shipped further distances without spoiling. GMO crops exist that have increased flavor, various textures, and even different colors so that farmers can sell more easily in niche markets. GMOs can also be used to provide higher-quality nutrition. Crops can be modified to produce nutrients or vitamins that they would not typically produce. Rice has been modified to produce vitamin A to help prevent vitamin A deficiency in many Asian countries where vitamin A deficiencies are common.

Food Science Industry, Safety, and Regulation

Trends and Developments in the Food Products and Processing Industry

Trends affect the way that food products are created, processed, and marketed. A recent trend that is gaining traction is the **buy local** trend. This idea involves purchasing produce and foods from local farmers either on site, at farmer's markets, or through community share programs. The buy local trend provides consumers with the freshest produce and food products while allowing them to see who produces the food and where it is produced. The idea of **free range** entails allowing animals the opportunity to graze freely on pasture. Many consumers prefer to purchase free-range eggs rather than eggs that are produced by hens in commercial hen houses. **Irradiated beef** is beef that has been treated with radiation. The radiation kills pathogens that may be on the meat that could make consumers sick. Irradiated beef has a longer shelf life than un-irradiated beef because pathogens such as E. coli and salmonella have been eliminated.

Dietary Trends Affecting the Food Industry

Dietary trends affect the way that food is created, processed, and marketed. **Low-fat** products are created and marketed to consumers interested in cutting back on the amount of fat intake. These products have much of the fat content removed. **Sugar-free** products are also popular for consumers who want to decrease the amount of added sugar they ingest. Sugar-free products are often naturally sweetened or sweetened with a sugar replacement such as aspartame. **Gluten free** is a fairly new trend that stemmed from the allergy to gluten in people with Celiac disease. Gluten is an elastic substance that is created when wheat flour is mixed with water. Some consumers believe that gluten found in breads can cause inflammation. There is a growing market for gluten-free products. As scientists and nutritionists continue learning about the effects of foods on the body, trends will continue to change regarding the food industry.

Major Industry Organizations That Affect Food Products and Processing

The Congressional committees responsible for food safety are the Agriculture Committee and Commerce Committee in the House; the Agriculture, Nutrition and the Labor and Human Resources Committee in the Senate; and the House and Senate Agriculture, Rural Development and Related Agencies Appropriating Subcommittees. The **Food and Drug Administration** oversees both domestic and imported foods with the exception of meat and poultry products. The **Food Safety and Inspection Service** ensures meat and poultry products are safe, wholesome, and correctly labeled. The **Environmental Protection Agency** establishes tolerance levels for pesticide residues of food commodities or animal feed. The **National Marine Fisheries Service** inspects seafood products. Other groups involved in the food products industry include the AMS, APHIS, CDC, ATF, and state and local regulatory groups.

Regulation of the Food Products and Processing Industry

The responsibility of safeguarding the commercial food supply falls under the **United States Department of Agriculture** (USDA) and the **US Food and Drug Administration** (FDA). The FDA oversees food processing, tests for environmental contaminants, sets levels of pesticides that can be used on crops, checks levels of pesticide residue, and regulates food labeling. Food products must be labeled with a **country-of-origin label** stating where the product was raised and produced. The product must also have a **nutrition label** that shows the calories, serving size, ingredients, and caloric breakdown. The USDA also requires **inspections** that are done through the Food Safety and Inspection Service (FSIS). FSIS inspectors ensure that animals being used for food are healthy and free of disease or illness and that the processes used to prepare the food items are clean and sanitary.

HACCP and Other Major Food Safety Practices

The United State Department of Agriculture (USDA) has adopted the **Hazard Analysis Critical Control Point System** (HACCP). This is a tool used to prevent foodborne hazards. HACCP focuses on problem prevention, and the HACCP is used by food companies to determine their "critical control points." These are areas in which hazards can be prevented, controlled, or eliminated. Usually a series of steps is created to manage the critical control points. Effective record keeping is a major component of the HACCP process. HACCP is required in the meat and poultry industry by the USDA, the low-acid canned food industry, and juices by the Food and Drug Administration. Inspections are also performed by the Food Safety Inspection Service in the meat, poultry, and egg industries to prevent foodborne illnesses.

Controlled Features in the Processing of Food

Preventing foodborne illnesses begins with proper food storage and food-handling procedures. A properly controlled environment prevents the growth, survival, and spread of pathogens that cause illness. There are six factors that affect growth of bacteria: food, acid, temperature, time, oxygen, and moisture. Bacteria require food to survive, and moist, protein-rich foods such as meat, eggs, and dairy products provide a rich environment for bacterial growth. Acidic foods such as lemon juice or vinegar prevent bacterial growth. Bacteria grow rapidly in the danger zone (4°C–60°C). Bacteria require time to grow, so extended time with proper conditions facilitates growth. Aerobic bacteria require oxygen to multiply, whereas anaerobic bacteria grow in oxygen-free conditions. Bacteria also require moisture to grow and multiply rapidly in moist foods. Bacteria growth can be prevented with a time–temperature relationship. Bacteria can be killed by reaching a certain temperature for a certain amount of time.

Grading of Food Products

The United States Department of Agriculture created grade labels to distinguish among degrees of food quality. Canned and frozen vegetables can be graded as Grade A, Grade B, and Grade C. Grade A vegetables are top quality in terms of tenderness, appearance, flavor, and uniformity. These are best used for attractive special dinners or lunches. Grade B vegetables are very good quality although more mature and less tender than Grade A. Grade C vegetables are not as uniform or colorful and are generally more mature. These are best suited in soups, stews, and casseroles. Meat products can be given grades of prime, choice, select, standard, commercial, and utility. Prime, choice, and select are used to create retail cuts of meat. Standard, commercial, and utility are used to create manufactured meat products.

Methods by Which Value Can Be Added to Agricultural Commodities

Value-added agriculture involves taking a raw agricultural commodity and changing it to create a new product. This can be done by packaging, cooking, cooling, drying, processing, or any other process that alters the original raw commodity into something new. Value-added products generate higher returns for producers. New market opportunities are also created, especially in high-demand niche markets. Livestock producers can produce table-ready cuts of meat rather than slaughter ready animals. Dairy producers can produce cheese or ice cream instead of just milk. A wheat farmer could produce flour or even bread instead of just grain. Value-added products can also be simple, such as bagged lettuce mixes or braided garlic.

Processing Techniques

Fermentation is a process using bacteria or yeast to add shelf life, increase palatability, or process food to make nutrients more available. Fermentation is the result of anaerobic respiration from the bacteria or yeast cells. **Homogenization** is a process used to eliminate creaming in milk. The milk is forced through a homogenizer with tiny openings. These small openings break up the fat particles and keeps them permanently separated. **Pasteurization** is the process of heating milk or another substance up quickly and then quickly cooling it. This destroys bacteria and enzymes that cause milk to spoil. **Preservation** techniques are used to lengthen the shelf life of food products. This could include drying, freezing, salt-curing, or other methods meant to increase the time the food will not spoil. **Meat fabrication** is the process of taking an entire animal carcass and breaking it down into cuts that the consumer will purchase such as steaks, roasts, and chops.

Aseptic Technique

Aseptic technique is the method used to prevent contamination in a lab. Asepsis refers to the condition in which no living disease-causing pathogens are present. Aseptic technique minimizes the spread or inoculation of pathogens. All supplies and reagents used during a procedure must be clean and sterile. Hands must be washed before and after handling any culture even if gloves are worn. Cell cultures should be worked one at a time with sterile equipment to avoid cross-contamination from occurring between cultures or tissue samples. The overuse of medications such as antibiotics to kill pathogens should be avoided and unnecessary if proper aseptic technique methods are used.

Safety Equipment for Laboratory Experiments

Lab coats can be worn to prevent chemical spills or stains from getting onto street clothes. Don't wear lab coats or clothes that have loose or bulky sleeves as these can get in materials or catch on fire. Long hair should be tied back. Closed-toed shoes are necessary, and shoe covers may be required. Safety googles can be used in some instances to avoid eye irritation. Always be aware of the eye wash station in the lab. If chemicals get into your eyes, rinse them at the eye wash station. Be aware of where the lab's emergency shower is. If chemicals are spilled on you, rinse yourself under the emergency shower.

Safe Handling of Laboratory Materials, Chemicals, and Equipment

When working in a laboratory, the work space should be uncluttered to give plenty of room to prevent spills or accidents. Equipment should be washed and dried before using. When disposing of chemicals or potentially hazardous materials, pay attention to the labels. Some substances should be disposed of in a biohazard waste container. Substances should be washed off the skin immediately to avoid skin irritations or burns. Hot glassware should be handled with tongs or heat-resistant gloves. Long hair and loose clothing should be tied back to avoid exposure to chemicals, hot surfaces, or open flames. Don't reach over an open flame when working in a lab. Some chemicals require working with under a vented, hooded area.

Mechanical Principles in Agriculture

Hydraulics

Pascal's law says that when there is an increase in pressure at any point in a confined fluid, there is an equal increase at every other point in the container. Hydraulics systems use an incompressible fluid, usually oil or water, to transmit forces from one location to another within the fluid. There are two main types of hydraulic systems: single acting and double acting. A **single-acting** cylinder has one port for oil, and a spring retracts the piston. Single-acting cylinders have only pushing power. A double-acting cylinder has two ports that push and pull the piston. A **double-acting** cylinder therefore has pushing and pulling power. A cylinder can be identified as single- or double-acting by looking at the number of ports.

Pneumatics

According to Pascal's law, when there is an increase in pressure at any point in a confined gas, there is an equal increase at every other point in the container. Pneumatic systems work similar to hydraulic systems. The difference between the two is that pneumatic systems use compressed gas (usually air, nitrogen, or other inert gases) rather than a liquid as in hydraulic systems. A compressor pumps air into a receiver, which holds large amounts of compressed air until the pneumatic system needs it. Air can carry dirt, water, and other contaminants, so filters are used in pneumatic systems to clean the air. Pneumatic pressures tend to be lower than those of hydraulic systems and can be made with lighter-weight material such as aluminum rather than heavy steel.

Basic Metals

Carbon steel is used in construction of buildings, pipelines, and other commercial construction projects. Carbon steel can be categorized into four basic grades that are determined by the percent carbon content. **Mild steel** has between 0.05% and 0.3% carbon. **Medium carbon steel** has between 0.3% and 0.6% carbon. **High-carbon steel** contains 0.6% to 1.5% carbon. Tool steel is commonly made of high-carbon steel because of its durability. If the carbon content is over 2%, the metal is considered **cast iron**. **Stainless steel** is a corrosion-resistant iron alloy that commonly contains 10.5% or more of chromium along with other added elements to give it specific properties. **Copper** is used for electrical transformers and wire because of its high conductivity and resistance to corrosion. **Bronze** is made by combining copper with another metal (usually tin). **Brass** is a soft metal commonly recognized by its similar appearance to gold and is created by combining copper and zinc.

Horsepower for Engines, Equipment, and Electrical Motors

Simply defined, **horsepower** measures the rate at which work is being done. Horsepower units originated from the rate of work that a single horse could perform. After experimentation, it was found that a single horse was capable of 33,000 ft-lbf of work per minute.

$$\textbf{Power} = \textbf{work/time}$$

$$\textbf{Work} = \textbf{force} \times \textbf{distance}$$

$$\text{Therefore, } \textbf{Power} = (\textbf{force} \times \textbf{distance})/\textbf{time}$$

Horsepower of electrical motors, engines, and equipment is calculated from speed and torque. RPM and the in-lbf measurements can be fit into the equation:

$$\textbf{Horsepower} = (RPM \times in - lbf)/63{,}025$$

The number 63,025 is a constant when torque units are in in-lbf. If torque units are in ft-lbf, simply substitute the ft-lbf for the in-lbf in the equation, and use 5,252 as the constant.

Conduction, Convection, and Radiation

Heat can be transferred in three different ways: conduction, convection. and radiation. Thermal energy being exchanged by two systems through dissipating heat is known as heat transfer. **Conduction** occurs when heat is transferred through direct molecular collision. Fast-moving (hot) particles collide with slow-moving (cold) particles. This causes the slow-moving particles to speed up. **Convection** occurs when a gas or liquid is heated and then dissipates. Molecules expand and rise when heated. Convection occurs when a gas or liquid is over a heated surface. The gas or liquid then carries the thermal energy with it. **Radiation** occurs when electromagnetic waves carry thermal energy from an object.

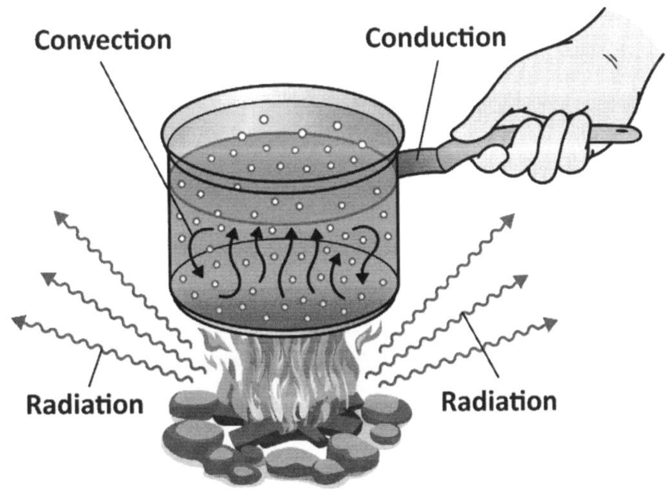

Oil Viscosity and Lubrication

Viscosity measures an oil's resistance to flow. The temperature of an oil affects the oil's viscosity. Oil provides a lubricating film between moving parts in an engine. Proper **lubrication** is necessary for an engine to last. An oil with the proper viscosity will protect engine parts from wearing. Oil viscosity will help determine how much oil an engine uses (especially in cold weather) and the low-temperature oil flow to the engine. Generally, the lowest-viscosity oil is used that will support the required load. Viscosity indexes measure how fast the viscosity changes with temperature changes. Viscosity of oils are measured using either the Kinematic or Saybolt system. The Society of Automotive Engineers (SAE) records engine oil viscosities and defines the requirements for SAE viscosity grades.

Common Electrical Terms

An ampere, or **amp**, is a unit used to measure electrical current. Amperage draw can be calculated by dividing watts by volts. **Volts** are used to measure electrical voltage. Voltage can be calculated this way: volts = amps x resistance. **Ohms** are units used to measure electrical resistance. Ohm's law states current is equal to voltage divided by resistance. The equation to calculate ohms is: ohms = voltage / resistance. A **watt** is a measure of electrical power. For electrical systems, power =

voltage x current. **Kilowatt hours** (kWh) are used to measure electricity use in residences. One kWh is equivalent to the energy used if a single 1,000-watt appliance ran for one hour. An electrical **conductor** is any material or item that allows the flow of electricity. The opposite of a conductor would be an insulator. **Resistance** defines the measure of an object's opposition to electricity flow. Resistance is measure in ohms. A **transformer** transfers electricity from one electrical circuit to another.

Information on Motor Nameplates

A motor nameplate contains information needed when repairing the motor or purchasing replacement parts. It contains information such as amperage, voltage, horsepower, wattage, and rpm. **Amperage** can be found next to the AMP in the nameplate. Amps are given as a full load amp rating, which gives the rate the motor will consume power at 100% of the rated load. **Voltage** information can be found beside the VOLTS label. Motors are designed to be run at the voltage labeled. **Horsepower** information can be found beside the HP label on the motor nameplate. Horsepower measures the mechanical output of a motor. A motor nameplate may not include information regarding **wattage** information. However, wattage can be easily calculated using the equation: watts = amp x volts. **Rpms** can be found next to the RPM label on the nameplate. Rpm describes the shaft speed of the motor. The motor nameplate can also include the serial number, design letter, service factor, efficiency, frame size, and torque values.

Grounding and GFCI

Electricity in wiring systems uses current that can cause electrical shocks. Electrical systems want to ground, or get rid of the current, and return to equilibrium. This is usually achieved in a circuit through the neutral wires. However, if the electrical circuit is damaged, the current can pass through metal, wood, or people to return to equilibrium. A **grounding** system provides an alternate grounding option in case the circuit becomes damaged. Grounding wires provide an alternate pathway for the current to reach the ground. **Ground-fault circuit interrupters (GFCI)** can be used to offer additional grounding protection. GFCIs will sense ground faults and shut the power off to the circuit before damage can be done.

Ohm's Law

Ohm's law was discovered by George Ohm and describes the relationships between voltage, amperage, and resistance. Ohm's law states that the current flowing through a conductor is proportional to the voltage between the ends of a conductor. Ohm's law can be calculated with the equation: $\boldsymbol{R = V/I}$ with R being resistance in ohms, V being voltage, and I representing current. Ohm's law can be rearranged to find voltage using the equation $\boldsymbol{V = IR}$. Ohm's law can also be rearranged to calculate current using the equation: $\boldsymbol{I = V/R}$. Ohm's law can be used to calculate power using the equation: $\boldsymbol{P = VI}$. Once power is calculated, the total amount of energy used in Joules (watt-seconds) can be calculated with the equation: **electrical energy** (in Joules) = **power x time** (in seconds).

Electrical Diagrams

Electrical circuit diagrams are used to show the actual electrical connections and components of a circuit. They can be referred to as circuit diagrams, electrical diagrams, or wiring diagrams.

Electrical diagrams are used frequently in construction and maintenance fields. The following diagrams are commonly used to indicate components of electrical circuits.

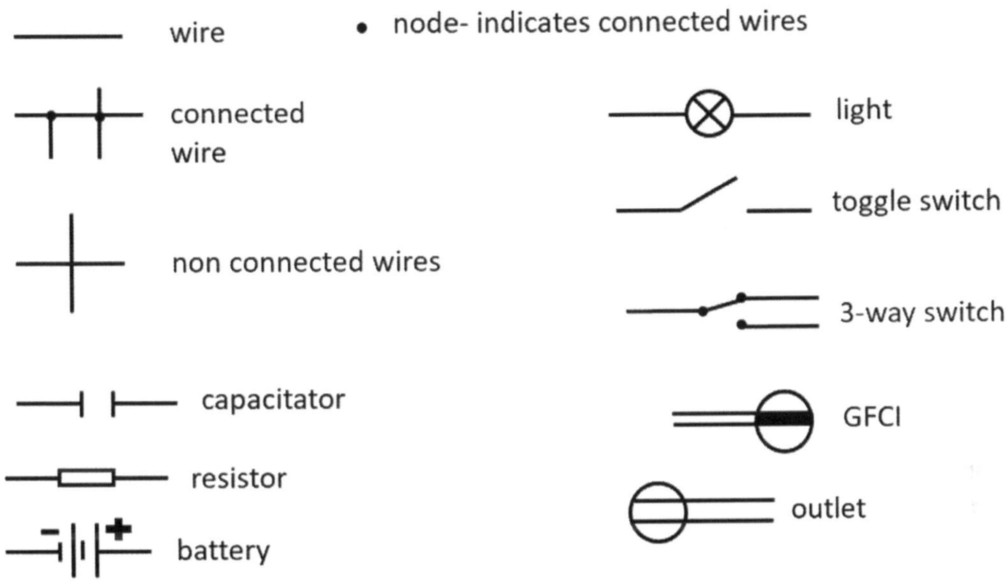

AC and DC Circuits

There are two types of electrical current: **alternating current** (AC) and **direct current** (DC). Electrical current refers to the flow of electrons in a circuit. The main difference between AC and DC is the direction of flow. If the two were graphed, DC would be a straight line because it always flows in the same direction. AC would look like a wave on a graph because it switches directions periodically. AC switches back and forth between positive and negative currents. Receptacles would be examples of AC circuits. The current coming through the receptacle must travel long distances, and AC travels more efficiently. Batteries are an example of DC circuits. Batteries have a positive and negative pole because the current runs in one direction.

Conductors and Insulators

Conductors are materials that allow electrons to flow freely from particle to particle. Conductors allow electricity to flow freely. Most metals are good conductors and allow current to flow freely. Conductors have loosely bound outer electrons that are free to move, allowing electrical current freedom to pass through. Conductors are generally good heat conductors as well. **Insulators** are materials that prevent electrons and electricity from flowing freely. Most nonmetal substances such as rubber, wood, glass, and plastic are insulators. Insulators have a high resistance to electrical current flow because the outer electrons are tightly bound. A receptacle in the home is a good example of using both conductors and insulators. Inside the receptacle, the outlets are metal that come in contact with the metal prongs. This allows the current to pass through. The outside of the outlet is covered with plastic to prevent electrocution.

Agricultural Energy Sources and Tools

Energy Sources

Mechanical energy is the result of kinetic energy and potential energy. **Kinetic** energy is motion, and the more motion an object has, the higher its kinetic energy (i.e., rivers or wind). **Potential**

energy is energy stored that has the potential to be released (i.e., compressed spring). Potential and kinetic energy can be converted into mechanical energy with windmills, generators, turbines, and so on. **Thermal** energy, or heat, is created by an object's internal molecular movement. Steam engines can transform thermal energy into mechanical energy, and thermal power plants can transform it into electricity. **Chemical** bonds store energy between atoms in a molecule. Exothermic chemical reactions break the bonds and release the energy. **Combustion** is an exothermic reaction. During combustion, oil, gas, or coal convert energy into heat and light, which can be captured and turned into mechanical or electrical energy.

Benefits and Costs of Energy Sources

When comparing energy sources, it's important to note costs, environmental impact, climate impact, and energy output. **Wind power** is an energy source that requires large amounts of land, available wind, and up-front costs. In suitable areas, wind farms can create clean energy with no carbon dioxide emissions. Land surrounding windmills can be used as farmland. **Hydropower** requires large financial investment up front. Hydropower plants also create significant change to surrounding ecosystems. Hydropower is clean with essentially no emissions and provides large-scale energy production. **Solar power** has been expensive, but the costs are decreasing. Solar power is dependent on sunlight; therefore, solar energy production is intermittent. Solar energy is also clean and relies on the unlimited resource of sunlight. **Nuclear power** has significant up-front costs and must manage high-level waste for a long time. Nuclear power has low carbon dioxide emissions and produces large amounts of energy. **Coal power** plants emit large amounts of carbon dioxide, and coal mining has negative environmental impacts. Coal power is reliant on fossil fuels, which are a limited resource.

Basic Operating Principles of an Electrical Motor

An **electric motor** converts electrical energy into mechanical energy. Electric motors can be explained by Fleming's Left-Hand rule, which states "whenever a current carrying conductor is placed inside a magnetic field, a force acts on the conductor in a direction perpendicular to both the directions of the current and magnetic field." Electric motors create magnetic fields. Between the poles of a magnetic field, a rotor spins to generate force in the form of rotation. Electric motors can be powered by either direct current (DC) or alternating current (AC). DC electric motors are powered by sources such as batteries. AC electric motors are powered by being plugged in.

Gears and Pulleys

A **pulley** is a simple machine that is used to reduce a workload. A pulley is a wheel with a groove or rim that a cord fits in. The wheel and axle of the pulley reduce the amount of force needed to lift an object. Fixed pulleys stay in one place. Movable pulleys move with the object that is being moved or lifted. Fixed pulleys and movable pulleys can be combined to create compound pulleys. **Gears** are another simple machine used to reduce workload. Gears are wheels that rotate around their center and have grooved teeth. Gears can also be referred to as cogs. Gears fit together with their teeth. Therefore, when one gear moves, the attached gears also move. A driver gear is the gear that causes the other gears to move. When two or more gears are connected, it is called a gear train. The last gear of the gear train that is being moved is called the driven gear. The gears between the driver gear and the driven gear are called idlers.

Gear Reduction and Multipliers

Gears can be used to reduce output speed or increase the torque of an electric motor or engine. **Gear reduction** refers to the speed of the rotary machine. The rotary speed is reduced by dividing it by a gear ratio greater than 1:1. This is done by using a smaller gear with less teeth interlocking and driving a bigger gear with bigger teeth. Gear reduction increases torque by multiplying the torque by the gear ratio. There are two ways to calculate the gear ratio. Gear ratio can be calculated by the equation: gear ratio = number of teeth on output gear / number of teeth on input gear. It can also be calculated with the following: gear ratio = diameter of output gear / diameter of input gear. No power is lost in gear reduction, although some efficiency is lost. Gear reduction decreases the input speed, and **multipliers** increase input speed. A 2:1 gear reducer would take a 2,000-rpm motor and make it turn 1,000 rpm.

Transfer of Power or Energy from a Motor to an Implement

Energy or power is produced with a motor (either compression, spark ignition, or electric). The power is transferred from the motor through a shaft to a coupling, gear box, chain, or pulley system. The power take-off (PTO) is used to transfer an engine's mechanical power to a piece of equipment, such as an implement. PTOs allow implements to function without their own motor or engine. PTOs can be crank-shaft driven, tractor style, or truck transmission style. Tractor PTOs can be driven with the transmission. This style of PTO functions only when the clutch is engaged, and when the clutch is pressed in, the PTO does not function. PTOs essentially take rotary power from the motor and convert it into hydraulic power, when it can then be turned into either a rotary force or mechanical force depending on the need. The PTO then transfers power to the implement through the PTO shaft.

Basic Maintenance and Adjustments of Internal Combustion Engines

Internal combustion engines must be maintained properly to function without issue. Engine maintenance can be directly related to the engine's life span. Each internal combustion engine will have slightly varied recommended maintenance routines. All internal combustion engines will require clean fuel, clean air, and proper lubrication to run correctly. Oil should be checked frequently. Oil levels should be maintained. Old oil that looks dark or dirty should be replaced. The oil filter should be replaced each time the oil is changed. Air filters need to be changed routinely, especially in dusty environments. Spark plugs and wires that are faulty can cause engine misfires and should be replaced routinely. Adjusting an engine may involve calibrating or balancing the carburetor, adjusting the idle speed, and adjusting the ignition timing. Newer motors make some adjustments on their own but may need occasional additional adjusting and tuning.

Small Gas Engine Parts

The largest part of the gas engine is the **cylinder block**. The cylinder block is where the cylinders are bored. The **cylinders** are the part of the engine where fuel combustion takes place. Cylinders are round, bored-out tubes where pistons work. **Pistons** are cylindrical pieces of metal that move up and down inside of the cylinder. Pistons have a ring around the top called a **piston seal** that keeps the combustion chamber sealed off. **Rods** connect the pistons to a crankshaft. The **crankshaft** rotates in a circular motion, working to move pistons up and down the cylinders. **Spark plugs** provide the spark so that the fuel can be ignited. The **carburetor** mixes fuel with air to produce combustible gas. The **camshaft** is a large rod with a gear on one end that raises and lowers valves. The **flywheel** maintains the speed of the running engine. The **fuel tank** holds the fuel that is used to run the engine.

Four-Stroke Cycle and Two-Stroke Cycle

There are two main types of gasoline-powered engines: two-stroke and four-stroke engines. Simply put, a two-stroke engine performs combustion and the exhaust cycle in two strokes of the piston, whereas four-stroke engines require four piston strokes. A **four-stroke** engine goes through four steps. The piston is moved down by fuel combustion (power stroke). The piston moves back up to push exhaust out (exhaust stroke). The piston moves back down to pull fuel in (intake). The piston moves up again to restart the cycle (compression stroke). The power stroke has to be strong enough to move the piston through two cycles. In a **two-stroke** cycle, the processes are combined. The power stroke also releases exhaust. The compression stroke and intake are also combined. This creates the possibility that fuel can escape, decreasing efficiency. Two-stroke engines typically require oil to be mixed with the fuel.

Spark-Ignition Engine Operation

An internal combustion engine uses the chemical process of combustion (burning fuel) to release energy. In a spark-ignition engine, gasoline is commonly used as the fuel source. In a gasoline engine, gas is mixed with air in the carburetor. There are four main processes that need to take place: fuel intake, compression, combustion, and exhaust. The combustible fuel and air mixture from the carburetor is brought down into the cylinder during the intake piston stroke. The piston then compresses the fuel and air mixture. A spark provided by the spark plug ignites the fuel. The ignition and burning of the fuel is called combustion. Combustion releases energy and forces the piston back down in the power stroke. Exhaust is released, and the cycle starts over again.

Compression Engine Operation

Diesel engines are compression ignition engines. Diesel is injected into the combustion chamber above the piston. Diesel engines do not use a spark to ignite the fuel. Instead, the diesel is ignited with compression and hot air. Temperatures inside of the combustion chamber can range from 400 degrees Celsius to 800 degrees Celsius. During the suction stroke, clean air is pulled into the cylinder. The piston moves up the cylinder and compresses the air tightly. This causes the temperature of the air to rise. Injectors then spray diesel into the combustion chamber. The diesel, coming into contact with the hot air, instantly ignites and forces the piston down. As the piston moves up, exhaust is released, and the process restarts.

Fuels Used in Internal Combustion Engines

There are two main types of internal combustion engines: spark ignition and compression ignition. Both types are usually powered with fossil fuels. Commonly, these are petroleum-based fuels. Petroleum-based fuels include **diesel**, **gasoline**, **petroleum gas**, **jet fuel,** and **propane**. Spark-ignition engines commonly use gasoline as a fuel source. Compression ignition engines use diesel fuel. Petroleum-based fuels are not the only options. Coal can also be transformed into gasoline and diesel using the Fischer-Tropsch process. **Biofuels** are used as a source of renewable fuel. **Ethanol** is derived from corn and is added to gasoline. **Biodiesel** can be used in compression ignition engines. Biodiesel is created using crops that have high triglyceride oil concentrations, such as soybeans. Spacecraft engines use **hydrogen** as a fuel. Hydrogen, methanol, liquefied petroleum gas, paraffin, and tractor-vaporizing fuel can be used in engines with modifications.

Engine Displacement

Engine displacement can be defined as the swept volume of pistons inside the cylinders. Engine displacement impacts an engine's power and fuel efficiency. Engine displacement is calculated using the bore, stroke, and number of cylinders. The bore refers to the diameter of the cylinders. The stroke is the measure of distance the piston travels. As the crankshaft rotates, pistons move up and down in a circular motion. Although the individual cylinder volume changes, the overall engine volume remains the same due to the reciprocation of all cylinders. The equation for calculating engine displacement is: **engine displacement = $\pi/4 \times (\text{bore}^2) \times$ stroke x number of cylinders**. Engine displacement can be expressed in liters, cubic inches, or cubic centimeters.

Hand Tools

Tape measures are used to take either straight measurements or circumference measurements. **Framing squares** are L-shaped tools used for framing and making angles. A **ripsaw** is a handsaw that has chisel-shaped teeth used to make cuts with the grain of wood. A **crosscutting saw** is a handsaw that has teeth facing both the front and back of the saw used to make cuts against the grain of wood. A **coping saw** is a smaller, fine-bladed handsaw that is used to make curved, irregular, or fine cuts. A **level** is a wooden or aluminum bar that has transparent tubes with air bubbles. Levels are used to determine if an object is level. A **hand plane** is used to smooth or shape the surfaces of wood and has a flat blade underneath a handle. Planes are pushed against the surface of the wood to create cuts. A **chisel** is a hand tool used to remove shavings of wood. **Mallets** are used to strike other hand tools without damaging handles. **Hammers** are used to secure fasteners like nails. **Files** and **rasps** are used to create and smooth curves and holes. **Screwdrivers** are used to apply or remove screws.

POWER TOOLS

Air compressors store compressed air that can power tools or fill air tanks or tires. **Grinders** can be used to cut through metal or tile and can be used to polish. A band saw is a large, upright saw that has a long, stationary blade that allows for harder cuts. A **belt sander** is a handheld sander that can quickly sand large areas. **Circular saws** are named for the disc blades that rotate in a round motion. Circular saws make straight cuts. **Drills** can be used to replace handheld drills and screwdrivers. **Impact drivers** add an in-and-out force to a spin and can loosen stuck screws and nuts. A **jigsaw** is a small saw with a fine blade used to make intricate cuts. **Lathes** are used to create symmetrical objects on a rotating axis. Other commonly used power tools include table saws, routers, reciprocating saws, nail guns, drill presses, rotary tools, planers, and miter saws.

ELECTRICAL WIRING TOOLS AND SUPPLIES

Circuit testers and meters can be used to check the voltage of a circuit. They are used to verify the power supply is off before electrical work is performed. **Wire strippers** are used to cut electrical wires and remove insulation from wires. **Lineman's pliers** are used to cut, bend, or twist electrical wires. **Diagonal pliers**, often called side-cutters, are used to cut wires. **Electrical tape** can be used to repair wires, or colored electrical tape can be used to identify individual wires. When working with conduit, a **conduit bender** is used to bed the conduit. Electrical work will often require various types of screwdrivers, drills, and saws. Any tool that is used on electrical circuits should be insulated properly for safety.

PNEUMATIC SHOP EQUIPMENT

Proper maintenance and use of pneumatic tools keeps the tools in good working condition. Preventative maintenance involves preventative measures to ensure the tool remains productive. Pneumatic tools require clean, dry air to function properly. Filters, regulators, and lubricators keep the tool lubricated, clean the air, and maintain the proper air pressure. Pneumatic tools should be used at their rated pressure (usually 90–100 psi). Wear parts should be lubricated frequently to minimize wear and tear. Pneumatic tools function using shop air that is collected in **air compressors**; therefore, air compressors are necessary and should be well maintained. Pneumatic tools like **impact drivers** (wrenches) are connected to the compressor with air hoses, which should be in good condition and rated for compressed air.

HAND TOOL AND POWER TOOL MAINTENANCE

Hand tools such as screwdrivers, hammers, and pliers require maintenance to keep them in good working condition. Hand tools should not be stored in the environment. They should be stored in dry areas. Hand tools should be wiped clean after use. Chisels or other hand tools used for striking can create rough or bent edges. These can be ground smooth for proper function. Hand tools can be coated with lubricating oil to prevent rust. Power tools also require maintenance. Power tools should be wiped down after each use. Exhausts and intakes should be cleaned periodically to prevent buildup. Filters need to be changed routinely. Power tools should be stored away from dust and moisture. Inspect power cords for damage, and replace or repair damaged cords. Moving parts need to be lubricated to reduce wear and tear. Batteries should be used frequently and charged to full capacity and then removed from the charger.

Mechanical Safety Regulations and Hazards

Safety Procedures with Electricity and Electrical Wiring

When working with electricity or electrical wiring, it is important to take proper precautions to avoid an electrical shock. Do not use damaged electrical equipment such as frayed cords or electrical equipment with missing insulation. Avoid water, and do not touch electrical wiring or equipment with wet hands. Turn off the main breakers when working on receptacles. Take steps to ensure the breaker is not turned on until the receptacle work is complete. Use insulated tools only when working with electricity. Heed warning signs or tags on energized parts or electrical equipment. Insulated rubber gloves and goggles should be used when working on electrical circuits. Use an electric tester to ensure wiring is not live before working. Do not use metal ladders when performing electrical work.

Proper Safety Procedures When Dealing with Power and Energy Sources

Hands should always be clean and dry when working with power and energy sources and equipment. Water is a conductor, so hands, clothing, and tools should be dry. Appropriate clothing and personal protective equipment should be used to prevent accidental harm to hands, the head, or the body. Tools and equipment should be in good condition and not damaged. Avoid using tools on power or energy sources that are not properly insulated. Unplug tools or equipment that are not being used. Equipment that has recently been used should be allowed to cool off before covering. Identify and verify possible embedded electrical circuits before drilling, digging, or cutting into the ground or walls. All safety regulations of the work space should be followed.

Importance of Proper Laboratory Safety

Safety in the agricultural mechanics laboratory provides good working habits and a safe working environment for students. The overall goal of safety procedures in the agricultural mechanics lab is the safety of everyone in the lab. Tools, equipment, and facilities should also be protected. Safety rules and procedures should be created and followed. Following safety rules decreases the chance that accidents will occur. When safety rules are not followed, accident incidents increase. Tools and equipment used in the agricultural mechanics lab can be extremely dangerous and lead to burns, cuts, dismemberment, and even fatal wounds. Some general rules of safety for an agricultural mechanics lab include the following: eliminate running or horseplay in the lab; report damaged or broken tools or protective equipment (including personal protective equipment and tool or equipment safety guards); wear eye protection, ear protection, and dust masks as needed; no working without the teacher present; and proper tool and equipment use and handling should be followed at all times.

SDS

Safety data sheets (SDSs) contain the same general information that material safety data sheets (MSDS) possessed. SDSs detail information about the properties of chemical substances. The SDS is broken into 16 sections. The first section provides identification of the chemical and its recommended use. Section two identifies hazards and associated warnings. Section three identifies the composition and detailed information on ingredients including chemicals, substances, and mixtures. Section four identifies first-aid measures. Section five details recommendations for fire-fighting measures for fires caused by the chemical. Section six includes accidental release (spills, leaks, etc.) measures and cleanup practices. Section seven provides information about safe handling and storage practices. Section eight details exposure controls and personal protection. Section nine identifies physical and chemical properties. Section ten details reactivity hazards and chemical stability. Section 11 lists toxological information and health effects. Sections 12 through 16 are not mandatory but may include ecological information, disposal considerations, transporting information, regulatory information, and other information.

OSHA Regulations

Occupational Safety and Health Administration (OSHA) regulations are intended to promote the safety of workers. Agricultural operations are considered dangerous and are covered by OSHA's Agriculture, General Industry, and General Duty clause standards. Potential hazards in the agricultural mechanics laboratory should be labeled using OSHA lab safety colors and conspicuous warning signs. Personal protective equipment should be utilized at all times to reduce the risk of injury. Students and workers must be trained to comply with OSHA regulations to reduce injury incidents. This includes proper storage and handling of chemicals, power tools, and other hazardous objects commonly found in the agricultural mechanics laboratory.

OSHA Regulations Regarding Laboratory Safety Colors and Uses

The Occupational Safety and Health Administration (OSHA) requires workplace hazards to be identified and visibly marked. This includes the agricultural mechanics laboratory. Boundaries and warnings can be indicated using a color code. The colors of tape and signs identify the type of hazard present. The color code is intended to reduce accidents. Red is used to mean danger or stop, such as an emergency exit. Fluorescent orange or orange-red indicates a biosafety hazard, such as a sharps container. Yellow means caution (i.e., FLAMMABLE). Orange indicates a warning such as moving parts. Green identifies safety areas such as first aid kits or eye rinse stations. Blue represents information (bulletin boards). Black, white, yellow, or a combination of black with white or yellow can be used to demonstrate boundaries for traffic areas or stairways. Magenta or purple on yellow means radiation caution, such as X-ray rooms.

Proper Storage of Compressed-Gas Bottles According to OSHA Regulations

The Occupational Safety and Health Administration (OSHA) requires proper storage, handling, use, and inspection of compressed gases. OSHA requires the **Compressed Gas Association** (CGA) guidelines for compressed gases to be followed. Compressed gas cylinders should be stored based on their hazard class and identified with a conspicuous sign. Bottles should be stored in dry, well-ventilated, well-drained, and fire-resistant areas. Temperatures should not exceed 125 degrees Fahrenheit. Storage areas should protect compressed gas bottles from damage. Oxidizing gases should be kept at least 20 feet from flammable gases or combustible materials. Storage areas must have fire protection equipment. Compressed gas cylinders should be inspected regularly for signs of corrosion, denting, or gouges.

Storage and Disposal of Hazardous Materials

Proper storage and disposal of hazardous materials reduces the chance of accidental injury and limits negative health and environmental impacts. Hazardous waste materials are harmful or contain harmful substances and can cause injury. Pesticides, paint, fuels, and other chemicals are hazardous waste. The **Environmental Protection Agency** (EPA) has guidelines for proper disposal of hazardous wastes. The **Resource Conservation and Recovery Act** (RCRA) established regulations for basic hazardous waste management to properly identify, store, and dispose of hazardous waste. Fuel containers should be stored in well-ventilated areas away from potential flame sources. Waste fuels can be disposed of at hazardous waste drop-off sites. Pesticides should be stored according to the label and are usually disposed of with clean sweep programs, which are pesticide disposal programs. Paint can be disposed of in hazardous waste drop-off sites.

Potential Safety Hazards in the Agricultural Mechanics Laboratory

Most work performed in an agricultural mechanics laboratory is dangerous. Injuries can easily occur if eyes, ears, hands, arms, feet, and legs are not protected properly. Eyes and the face can be injured by spills of toxic chemicals, hot liquids, molten metals, gas fumes, and flying pieces of wood, metal, or dust. Heavy equipment such as saws or routers can be loud enough to damage hearing. Sanding, painting, and welding can release toxic particles into the air. Long hair and loose clothing can easily become tangled in equipment. Steel-toed boots can offer foot protection from falling objects. Leather gloves and aprons can shield the body from excessive heat or abrasion. Other causes of injury in the agricultural mechanics laboratory include falling, electrical contact, exposure to fire, or striking against an object.

Agricultural Construction and Fabrication

Safety Practices Associated with Building Construction

There are many health and safety risks involved in building construction; therefore, safety practices are necessary. Chemical, physical, biological, and ergonomic risks are found frequently in construction. Any worker on a construction site should be aware of all hazards and prepared to prevent accidents. Workers should prevent fall injuries by using proper protective gear such as personal fall arrest systems. Hard hats and sturdy, nonskid boots should be worn in construction sites. Stairways, ladders, and scaffolding should be used safely and as intended. Tools should be hoisted onto scaffolds or ladders once the worker has stopped climbing. Personal protective equipment should be used to protect the eyes and face. Chemicals such as lead, mercury, or asbestos can be found in construction sites; therefore, workers should be familiar with reading safety data sheets.

Reading and Interpreting Project Plans for Agricultural-Structure Projects

Project plants for agricultural-structure projects are similar to blueprints of homes and commercial structures. Agricultural-structure projects can include simple projects such as pole barns or hay barns, chicken coops, grain silos, or more intensive structures such as milking parlors, swine barns, or large greenhouses. Project plans are usually presented with an orthographic view. An orthographic view is comparable to a floor plan of a home when viewed from above. The view shows all measurements and walls, doors, windows, exits, and fixtures such as sinks or toilets. Project plans will also often include an elevation view. An elevation is a side view of the structure from the outside. Project plans can also include views from the front and rear outside of the structure. All project plans should have scales or measurements of structures used to construct the project.

Importance of Slope, Elevation, and Grades in Site Preparation

A little bit of slope can be both functional by draining water away from the structure as well as aesthetically pleasing. Moderate slopes (those less than 10%) are easy to build on and help drain water without too much surface runoff and erosion. About 15% to 20% of slopes will require more grading to build upon. Slopes greater than 20% require extensive cut and fill groundwork, which are both costly and risky. Erosion and drainage are issues that are commonly involved with steep slopes. Grading keeps unwanted water away from a structure by changing the slope of an area. A grid system can be used to calculate the elevation of points on the grid. These points can then be adjusted accordingly to create a level pad for the structure's foundation. Slope, elevation, and grades should be created in such a way that water drainage occurs without pooling around the structure. These should be adjusted in ways that minimize soil disruption.

Types and Designs of Buildings

There are numerous types of buildings, each with various designs for the intended use. Homes can take on many different styles themselves, from apartment buildings, condominiums, and townhouses to single-family homes and even earthen homes. Retail buildings often include a storefront for selling items and a warehouse for storing products and materials. Airports, schools, town halls, hotels, movie theaters, restaurants, gas stations, and other business and government buildings are designed with specific functions in mind. Agricultural structures can include dairy parlors, silos, barns, hay storage buildings, workshops, meat-processing facilities, run-in sheds, chicken coops, and stores. Each of these structures can vary in their design to meet the needs of the intended use. For example, barns built to raise chickens are different than the barns used to feed and house dairy cattle. The two would not function well if the intended animals were swapped. Each building is designed to meet the needs of the intended space in a way that is functional and profitable.

Construction Materials

One of the most important (and often overlooked) aspects of building construction is the selection of quality building materials. Construction materials commonly used are wood boards and studs, concrete and steel rebar, steel beams, metal siding, bricks, wood siding, vinyl, paints, and roofing materials. Building materials should be durable. Durable materials will last longer and better stabilize the building. Check the stiffness and strength of materials. Materials should be strong enough to hold up to the intended use. Consider tensile, compressive, and shear strengths of the possible materials. Never use materials that are worn, warped, or otherwise aged in new construction projects. The cost of materials should also be considered, but the budget should still allow for quality materials.

Bill of Materials

A **bill of materials** (BOM) is a list of raw materials, components, and assemblies required to construct a product. A bill of materials is used to calculate the cost of building a structure and can be used to order the materials required to complete the project. A bill of materials should include parts, components, and material names and descriptions. The descriptions should briefly explain to the reader the material's purpose in the project. The parts and materials should also have a listed quantity needed. Vendors or suppliers of materials should be included. The unit cost for each part, component, and material should be included. The total cost of materials can then be calculated and should be included. A bill of materials should be laid out in a way that is both easy to read and understand.

Framing Terminology

An **A-brace** is a temporary brace that is used to hold a wall upright during framing. It is shaped like an A and provides support. A **bottom plate** is a horizontal framing board that is the lowest horizontal board in a wall. **Ceiling joists** are horizontal framing boards that the ceiling materials are fastened to. **Cripple studs**, or cripples, are vertical framing boards that are above and below windows, doors, and headers. **Headers** are horizontal framing boards above windows, doors, or openings in a wall to support the cripplers above it. **Joists** are horizontal framing boards that support ceilings and floors. **Rafters** are framing boards used in the ceiling. **Studs** are framing boards used to make up walls. Wall insulation is installed between wall studs, and wall materials are fastened to the studs.

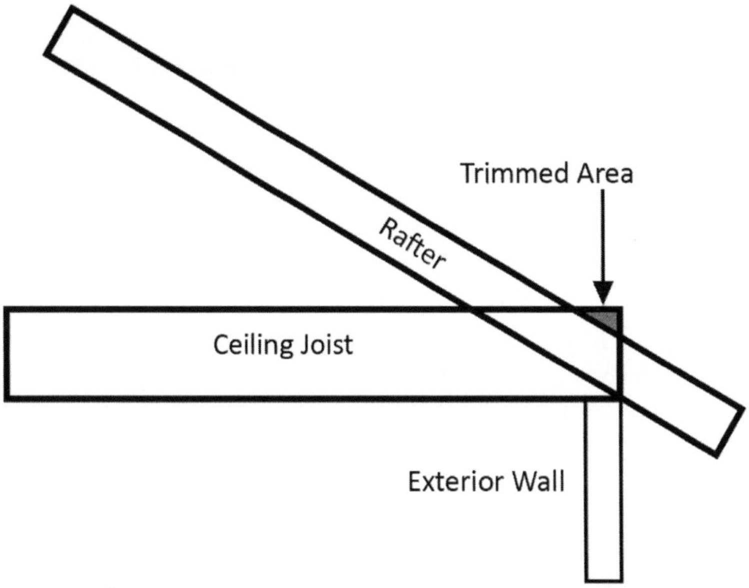

Walls, Supports, and Siding Used in Agricultural Buildings

Bearing walls are load-bearing walls and can hold weight from roofs, ceilings, or floors above. Load-bearing walls offer support to other walls, floors, and ceilings. Without enough support, structures will collapse. **Nonbearing walls** do not support weight from floor framing, roofs, or ceiling joists. **Cavity walls** are walls built with two layers and a space between the two layers. They are used to prevent water penetration to the internal surface of the wall. **Partition walls** are nonbearing walls used to break a large space into smaller spaces. Agricultural buildings can be covered in many siding materials. Wood materials are commonly used and include plywood, tongue-and-groove siding, wafer boards, board-and-batten siding, and beveled wood siding. Metal, vinyl, and asphalt siding materials are also used. Metal corrugated siding, aluminum siding, and vinyl siding can be used. Many older structures were covered in asphalt shingle siding, but that is not commonly used on new structures.

Heating, Cooling, and Ventilation of Agricultural Structures

Agricultural structures often contain perishable goods or live animals. Either way, proper heating, cooling, and ventilation are necessary. Ventilation provides fresh air into a structure. Ventilation requires sufficient openings to allow stale air out and fresh air to enter. Wind and thermal buoyancy drive natural ventilation. Openings at the roof allow hot, stale air to exit, whereas side openings allow fresh air to enter. Fans can add mechanical ventilation when natural ventilation is not adequate. Many agricultural structures that require temperature control are also metal buildings. Metal buildings can be insulated to maximize heating and cooling efforts. Livestock barns may require complete HVAC systems to be installed. Large fans and misting systems can also be used to cool large livestock barns.

Metal Shop Safety Procedures and Equipment

Metal shops contain many potential hazards and dangerous tools. Safety rules should be followed at all times. Machines in motion should never be left unattended. Machines should not be used without the safeguards in place. If safeguards are removed for tool servicing, they should be replaced immediately after and before being used. Brushes or other tools should be used to remove metal chips or shavings, not bare hands. Safety goggles or face shields should be worn to protect the eyes and face. Sturdy, nonslip boots should be worn to protect the feet. Metal should be handled with leather gloves. Proper clothing should be worn (no shorts, no loose clothing, etc.). All metal fabrication tools should be used for their intended uses only. Welding helmets should be worn during welding to protect the eyes from the welding light. Respirators, heat-resistant clothing, and aprons should be used as needed to protect the body.

Types of Welding

Shielded metal arc welding (SMAW) is a type of stick welding. An electric current forms an electric arc between the welding rod (stick) and the metals to be joined. SMAW is commonly used to weld iron and steel. **Gas metal arc welding** (GMAW) is also called metal inert gas (MIG) welding. A shielding gas along the wire electrode heats the two metals to be joined. MIG welding is the most common industrial welding process. **Flux-cored arc welding** (FCAW) is an alternative to MIG welding. FCAW has fast welding speeds and is portable, making it a common choice in construction. **Tungsten-inert gas** (TIG) welding is used to weld together thick sections of steel and other nonferrous metals. TIG welding uses a tungsten electrode. **Oxy-fuel welding**, or oxyacetylene welding, uses oxygen to heat base metals and a filler metal. **Brazing** joins two metals by using a filler metal and is often used when combining dissimilar metals. Oxy-fuel welding and brazing both utilize a torch to weld.

Common Welds

There are six common types of welds that can be used to combine metals. **Fillet** welds are used to combine two perpendicular base metals. The metals are not usually cut before a fillet weld. A **groove** weld is used to create a strong connection between two base metals. The sides of the base metals are grooved to allow full penetration of the filler metal. **Tack** welds are used to anchor joints before welding longer joints. Tack joints must be reheated to prevent cracking as the permanent weld is created. **Multipass** welds are used to fill large joints when one weld will not fill it. The joint is filled using a series of overlapping passes. **Plug** welds can be used to join two overlapping metals together. Holes are drilled into the top plate, into which filler metal is deposited to join the metals. A slot weld is similar to a plug weld. A **slot** weld utilizes longer openings into which filler metal is deposited.

Common Welding Joints

The five most common welding joints include the tee joint, the edge joint, the corner joint, a lap joint, and the butt joint. **Tee joints** are formed when two base metals form a 90-degree angle. The edges of the weld lie in the center of a plate to create a T shape. **Lap welding joints** occur when two base metals overlap onto one another. **Edge joints** are used to connect sheet metal with flanging edges. **Corner joints** are used when two base metals make a 90-degreee angle at the edge of one component to create an L shape. A **butt welding joint** can also be called a square groove weld. Butt joints are used to join two adjacent flat pieces that are parallel and side by side.

Arc Welding Procedures and Terminology

Arc welding joins two metal pieces together using a flux-covered electrode that is melted and becomes the filler material joining the two base metals. After a bead is laid, a brush or chip should be used to remove the slag from the bead. **Slag** is the leftover melted flux material from the electrode. The position of the electrode affects the shape of the weld bead. There are two positions: **work angle** and **travel angle**. The work angle creates a 90-degree angle between the electrode and horizontal. Travel angle is a 15- to 30-degree angle from the vertical and the electrode. The American Welding Society (AWS) numbering system gives information about a welding rod. The numbering system includes a letter prefix and a four- or five-digit numbering. The prefix E signifies an arc welding electrode. The first two (or three in a five-digit number) digits describe minimum tensile strength. The next digit indicates the position, and the last two digits indicate the coating and recommended current. Arc welding uses **polarity** and can be performed as alternating current (AC) or direct current (DC). Direct current can be either positive or negative. The polarity used is determined by the rod used.

Proper Metal Cutting Practices

Many metals are used in metal shops and require a variety of cutting methods. The methods used will depend on the type of metal being cut and the amount of precision needed. To cut metal by hand, **hand shears** and **hacksaws** can be used. Cutting metals by hand is best performed on thin, pliable metals such as thin aluminum. **Grinders** can be used to cut metal when a smooth edge is needed. **Lathes** use an extremely sharp edge to cut metal and can be precise. **Punches** use sharp edges and large amounts of pressure to cut through robust metals. **Water jets** combine water and abrasives to cut metals that cannot tolerate being heated. **Oxyacetylene torches** use a flame to burn through metal. **Plasma cutters** create an extremely hot flame to cut through metal and can be precise. **Laser cutting** uses an intense beam of light to melt through and cut metal.

Oxy-Fuel Welding Procedures and Terminology

Oxy-fuel welding uses compressed oxygen and a fuel (usually acetylene) to produce an extremely hot handheld flame. The gases are compressed and held in separate tanks. The tanks are then held onto a cart. The gases are released from the tanks through regulators and into hoses. The gases are then fed into the torch body, where they are combined. Welding tips can be fit into the torch body. To ignite the flame, acetylene should be opened slightly before a striker is used to light the flame. Acetylene should be adjusted until a clean flame that is touching the tip of the torch is achieved. Then the oxygen can be turned on. Oxygen will change the flame from yellow to blue and create three visible cones within the flame. Adjust the oxygen until only two flames are visible. There are seven oxy-fuel welding positions: the forehand, overhead, horizontal, flat, fillet, backhand, and vertical.

Cold Metal Work

Cold metal work refers to deformation of metals below the recrystallization temperature (usually at room temperature). There are benefits to cold metal working: increased strength, dimension control, improved surface finish, no heat involved, and more easily reproduced parts. There are four major types of cold metal working: squeezing, bending, shearing, and drawing. A common type of **squeezing** is seen in cold rolling. Steel is often cold rolled, a process that forces the steel between rollers to reduce the thickness. Cold **bending** uses rollers and shaping tools called dies to bend steel and other metals. Pipes are often bent using cold bending. Thin metals can be cut using **shearing**, or die cut, processes. Shearing uses a punch and dies to press out pieces of sheet metal into plates, rods, or other shapes. **Drawing** uses tensile force to pull (draw) metal through a die to stretch it into a certain shape or thickness.

Safety Practices for Plumbing

Plumbing work usually involves pipes, which can contain pressurized water or sewage, so it is important to follow safety procedures. One of the first things to do when performing plumbing work is to shut off the water supply to prevent pressurized water from spraying out. Safety glasses can prevent pressurized water, sewage, or other contaminants from getting into the eyes. Gloves should be worn to avoid contact with chemicals or germs. When using chemicals, always read and follow the directions and cautions on the label. If gas is smelled while performing plumbing work, immediately turn off the gas supply, and notify the gas company. Plumbing work can involve cutting or drilling of pipes. Make sure that the pipes being cut or drilled are the correct ones before working. Do not hold the pipe where the cut is being made to avoid cutting the hands. Leather gloves can be worn to protect the hands while cutting, and latex gloves can be worn underneath to prevent contaminants from getting onto the skin.

Plastic Pipe Fitting Process

Plastic pipe is the most commonly used pipe in plumbing, with **polyvinyl chloride** (PVC) being one of the most common. Plastic pipes can be cut with almost any type of saw, including handsaws. Fittings such as tees or unions are used to assemble a system. Pipes should be measured to maximize the surface areas that will cement together. This will ensure a water-tight seal. Once the pipe is cut, the rough edges (**burrs**) need to be removed to create a clean, smooth surface. Pipes should be dry fitted and tested before being cemented due to the fast drying time of pipe cement. PVC primer cleans and prepares the surfaces to ensure a solid bond. The surfaces that will be cemented should be primed, then liberally coated with a layer of pipe cement. This should be done one joint at a time. The cemented joint should be twisted to ensure the cement is spread around the entire joint. The cemented joint should be dry enough to release in about 30 seconds.

Sweating Copper Pipe

The process of **sweating copper pipe** is the process of fitting together copper pipes and creating a sealed joint. Copper pipes should be measured and cut to the proper length using a copper tube cutter or saw. The rough edges (**burrs**) around the cut ends need to be removed using a file or wire brush. A copper cleaning brush should be used to clean the end of the pipe and the inside of the fitting. The copper needs to be cleaned until it is bright and shiny. Soldering paste can then be applied to the end of the copper pipe and the inside of the fitting. The two are joined together. A propane torch is used to heat the joint. Once the joint is warm, the propane torch is used to apply solder to the joint to create a water-tight seal. Excess solder should be cleaned off using a rag.

Protecting Water Pipes Against Freezing

There are several ways to prevent water pipes from freezing in cold temperatures. Exposed pipes will freeze faster than protected pipes. Pipes can be wrapped with pipe insulation. All crawlspace and attic pipes should be insulated. Pipes can also be wrapped in heat cables or heat tape. Air leaks can allow enough cold air in to freeze pipes and should be sealed. An indoor valve can be used to drain water from outside faucets to prevent freezing. When outside temperatures are below freezing, faucets can be turned on to trickle warm water to prevent freezing. Cabinet doors can be opened to expose pipes to warm air. Water systems can be shut off and drained to prevent freezing in instances where pipes may be exposed to freezing temperatures while unattended for long periods of time.

Plumbing Materials and Common Joints

Plumbing materials include acrylonitrile butadiene styrene (ABS), brass, copper, chlorinated polyvinyl chloride (CPVC), and polyvinyl chloride (PVC). **ABS** is commonly used in waste and sewage systems. ABS is a black plastic. **Brass** is used for potable water and is resistant to heat. **Copper** is less commonly used due to the cost and the sweating (fitting) process required. **CPVC** is used to carry both hot and drinking water. **PVC** can be used to carry many water systems except hot water. Common fittings include adapters, caps, elbows, tees, and wyes. **Adapters** are fittings threaded at both ends used to connect pipes of two different sizes. **Caps** are used to cap pipe ends. **Elbows** are used to create a bend in a system. Generally, elbows are 90-degree or 45-degree angles. **Tees** create a 90-degree branch in a system. **Wyes** are generally used in drainage systems and have a 45-degree branch.

Agricultural Technology and Applications

GIS and GPS

A **geographic information system** (GIS) is a software program that combines and utilizes information. **Global positioning systems** (GPSs) use satellites and receivers on Earth to determine location relative to the Earth. GISs can utilize information gathered from GPSs, data collected through research or surveys, and other sources to create extremely detailed data about a location or area. GISs allow users to create maps that can contain layers of information. Census data (city information, population, gender, family size, etc.), topography, vegetation cover, soil types, animal populations, disease outbreaks, climate data, and more can be analyzed and mapped using GIS. This allows users to view multiple sets of data compared to location at a particular time.

Use in Precision Agriculture

Global positioning systems (GPSs) and geographic information systems (GISs) are tools that can provide farmers and producers with real-time data collection and accurate position information. **Precision agriculture** uses GPS and GIS to collect geospatial data about soil, animal, or plant requirements that are more specific than traditional methods ever were. This allows producers to apply site-specific treatments. Precision agriculture allows producers to apply site-specific treatments rather than applying a wasteful, uniform treatment over a widespread area. Precision agriculture allows producers to micromanage their farms, increasing production and reducing environmental impacts. GPS, GIS, and remote sensing can be used to gather and analyze information about land and water. GPS and GIS integration help producers manage pests more effectively and use less chemicals and soil amendments.

Applications of GPS Technology in Agriculture

A global positioning system (GPS) is used in many ways to increase farmer productivity and efficiency. GPS is used in precision agriculture to enhance farming efficiency. Producers utilizing GPS technology see higher production rates with lower input costs and labor. GPS systems can map field boundaries, roads, irrigation, property lines, or areas affected by disease or pests. Aircraft sprayers (crop dusters) use GPS data to accurately cover fields. Traditionally, aircraft relied on human flaggers to indicate fields. GPS also allows aircraft sprayers to target specific problem areas, reducing chemical use and chemical drift. GPS systems can be used to ensure even seeding and fertilizer dispersion. Conventional seeding and fertilizing involved broadcast spreading over a large area. Precision plowing uses GPS to create precisely spaced furrows.

Potential Applications for Computer-Controlled Technology

Agriculture uses technology such as sensors, drones, geographic information system (GISs), global positioning systems (GPSs), self-driving tractors, and other computer-controlled technology to make farming more efficient and sustainable. In greenhouses, temperature, light, humidity, and irrigation can be controlled using technology. Sensors can determine if ventilation is required and automatically open or close vents and louver systems. Computer numerical control (CNC) machines are automated machines that can rapidly produce metal parts that would otherwise be produced by hand using grinders, lathes, mills, and a variety of metal-working methods. New technology, such as the driverless tractors, allow farmers to work in multiple places simultaneously. Automated equipment increases efficiency and reduces costs, wastes, and labor.

Land Area in Acres and Location from Diagrams or Legal Description

Acreage can easily be calculated if a property's measurements in square feet are known. To determine square feet, multiply the property's length in feet by the property's width in feet. One acre is equal to **43,560 feet**. Divide the square feet of the property by 43,560 to get the property size in acres. **Plat maps** can be used to identify land features. Plat maps have a scale that correlates to actual property measurements. The **metes and bounds system** begins the description at a corner. The property lines are described and circle back to the starting point. The **township and range system** uses a grid system. There will be two intersecting lines: an east-west base line and a north-south meridian line that intersect the entire territory. Plat maps and parcel maps are found in county clerk offices. The system used (either metes and bounds or township and range) are determined by the county.

Basic Surveying Procedures and Equipment

Land surveying is used to determine the relative positions of points regarding the Earth and locating them in the field. Surveying begins with equipment and method selection and determining field point locations. Measurements are taken in the field and recorded. The recorded measurements are used to determine locations. The information is then plotted as a map or plat. Plane surveying assumes a flat, horizontal surface. Geodetic surveying takes the Earth's true shape and curvature into account. There are several types of surveys: boundary, control, engineering, photogrammetry, topographic, route, and hydrographic. Horizontal distance can be measured by tapes, EDM and global positioning system (GPS) methods. **Gunter's chain** is used to measure distance and is a 66' long chain. A **transit** is used to measure horizontal and vertical angles. **Total stations** can measure horizontal distance and slope distance.

Calculating Slope, Elevation, and Grades

Slope measures steepness and is expressed as a percent, degrees, or a ratio. To calculate percent slope, divide the rise (change in elevation) by the run (distance between points) and multiply by 100. Slope = (rise/run) x 100. **Elevation** is the height above average sea level. Elevation can be found by using a benchmark, which is a permanent reference point (i.e., fire hydrant, curb, etc.). The benchmark has a known elevation. Therefore, elevation can be calculated. First, the height of instrument must be calculated using the equation: backsite + benchmark elevation = height of instrument. Once the height of the instrument is known, elevation can be calculated using the equation: height of instrument – foresite = elevation. **Grading** is the modification of existing land for construction or drainage. A grade is calculated to determine the amount of cut and fill required.

Chapter Quiz

Ready to see how well you retained what you just read? Scan the QR code to go directly to the chapter quiz interface for this study guide. If you're using a computer, simply visit the online resources page at **mometrix.com/resources719/osatagred** and click the Chapter Quizzes link.

Environmental Science and Natural Resources

Ecological Principles and Environmental Systems

Organic and Inorganic Compounds

The main difference between organic and inorganic molecules is the presence of carbon. **Organic compounds** contain carbon and usually hydrogen (to form hydrocarbons), whereas most inorganic molecules do not contain either carbon or hydrogen. A few exceptions can be seen in carbon monoxide and carbon dioxide, both of which are inorganic. Organic molecules are closely associated with living things. Organic molecules include nucleic acids, proteins, carbohydrates, lipids, and enzymes. All of these molecules are required by cells and living things to grow, survive, and reproduce. **Inorganic compounds** include salts, metals, and other elemental compounds. Most molecules are produced by living organisms, whereas inorganic compounds occur in nature.

Carbon Cycle

Carbon drives photosynthesis; is a major component in nutrients such as fat, protein and carbohydrates; and provides energy in the form of hydrocarbons. All of these characteristics make it imperative to understanding the **carbon cycle**. Carbon is involved in a multitude of processes and steadily moves through the carbon cycle. In the atmosphere, carbon attaches to oxygen to create carbon dioxide. Plants breathe in carbon dioxide and use it during photosynthesis to create a carbon-containing molecule called glucose. The carbon becomes part of the plant. Animals consume the plant, consuming the carbon. Dead organisms and waste materials containing carbon decompose and become part of the soil, eventually creating carbon-containing fossil fuels. When we burn fossil fuels, carbon is released into the atmosphere. Carbon is also released into the atmosphere by animal respiration, plant respiration, and even root respiration.

Water Cycle

The **water cycle** explains the process and changes that water molecules go through in the atmosphere. Water goes through precipitation, condensation, evaporation, and transpiration. **Precipitation** occurs when water falls from the atmosphere to the Earth's surface. Precipitation can occur in the form of rain, sleet, snow, or hail. Precipitation contributes to streams, rivers, surface runoff, and groundwater. Water on the Earth's surface, especially in oceans, lakes, and other large bodies of water, is warmed by sunlight. When it warms enough, it changes from a liquid to a gas in a process called **evaporation**. Once enough water evaporates, it gathers in the atmosphere, where it cools and condenses, forming clouds. This **condensation** process is also contributed to by transpiration. **Transpiration** is the process of plants releasing water into the atmosphere through their leaves.

Nitrogen Cycle

The **nitrogen cycle** is a complex biogeochemical process that explains how nitrogen changes through multiple forms. Nitrogen changes during five major processes: nitrogen fixation, nitrogen uptake through growth of organisms, nitrogen mineralization through decay, nitrification, and denitrification. All nitrogen changes are greatly affected by microorganisms, especially bacteria. **Nitrogen fixation** is the process that converts dinitrogen into ammonium. Nitrogen fixation occurs through bacteria, lightning, hot lava flows, and forest fires. Ammonium is taken up by plants or microorganisms to create organic, nitrogen-containing molecules during **nitrogen uptake**. When organisms die, they decay. During decay, organic nitrogen is converted back to ammonium through **nitrogen mineralization**. The ammonium can be taken up again or further transformed into nitrate during bacterial **nitrification**. During **denitrification**, nitrate or nitrite can be converted to dinitrogen or nitrous oxide gas by bacteria.

Types of Ecosystems

Biomes are terrestrial ecosystems that extend over a large geographical area. **Ecosystems** describe areas that have common features and include both living and nonliving characteristics. Within ecosystems, it is important to note that features can vary widely (i.e., Southeastern US forests and Pacific Northwest coastal forests). There are six major types of ecosystems: forests, grasslands, deserts, tundras, and freshwater and marine ecosystems. **Forests** include tropical, temperate, boreal, and taiga ecosystems. They are typically warm, have high moisture and are characterized by lush, dense, tree-covered areas. **Grasslands** include prairies, savannas, and steppes. They are usually found in temperate or tropical regions, are semi-arid, and dominated by grass species. Grazing animals are common in grasslands. **Deserts** are characterized by their low amount of annual precipitation (<10 inches/year), sand dunes or rocks, and sparse vegetation. Animals must be highly adapted to desert conditions to survive. **Tundras** are snow covered, treeless, cold ecosystems. Many have permafrost and brief springs and summers. The two aquatic ecosystems are characterized by the presence of water and can be split into two types: marine and freshwater. **Marine** ecosystems have a high salt concentration and **freshwater** has a low salt content.

Biotic and Abiotic Factors That Define an Ecosystem

Both abiotic and biotic factors are included in defining ecosystems. **Abiotic factors** are the nonliving components of an ecosystem. They include physical and climatic factors such as sunlight, precipitation, temperature, wind, water, soil, storms, fires, and even volcanic activity. **Biotic factors** occur as a result of abiotic factors and adapt accordingly to survive. Biotic factors include plants, fungi, animals, and microorganisms. Biotic factors impact both their environment and other species. Abiotic factors can relocate living things when storms or geographical changes take place. Biotic factors can also prevent or change how abiotic factors serve their purpose. An example of this can be seen in a heavily forested area when the forest canopy blocks sunlight from reaching the forest floor.

Wetlands

Wetlands are areas of land where water covers the soil either all year or most of the year. Wetlands include places such as bogs, swamps, mangroves, and salt marshes. Wetlands are a crucial part of the natural environment. They protect shores from wave activity, acting as a buffer to prevent erosion of coastal areas. Wetlands reduce the impact of flood waters. The dense root and vegetation of wetlands acts a sponge and spreads the flood waters out over a large space. Wetlands also absorb pollutants and improve the water quality. They provide unique habitats for a wide range of life, including many species unique to wetlands. They provide nurseries for young marine and freshwater species. Wetlands are extremely productive ecosystems and can be compared in that regard to coral reefs and rainforests. Wetlands help maintain global climate by storing carbon in the plants and soil rather than releasing it as carbon dioxide, which contributes to global warming.

Succession in a Forest

Ecological succession, or **succession**, refers to the change of species in an ecological community over time. Succession in forests is usually caused by some form of disturbance due to forest fires, severe wind events, or logging. Forest succession is a type of secondary succession because the succession follows the disruption of an already existing community. Opportunistic species, such as the black cherry tree, create large quantities of seeds to colonize the empty space. Once they have produced a closed canopy, shade-tolerant species become established under the opportunistic species. Succession has many intermediate stages, and species can act as opportunistic or tolerant based on the circumstances.

Relationship Between a Species and its Habitat

Both the general habitat and the characteristics of the habitat determine the species found within the habitat. Animals require food, water, shelter and space. Food sources could be plants, seeds, insects, or other animals. Food sources could be scarce or plentiful. Water sources could also be scarce, such as in a desert, or abundant near a lake or river. Wildlife need cover for many life functions such as nesting, escaping predators, or seeking shelter from the elements. Animals also need space, and generally the larger the animal, the more space it requires. Species have unique ecosystems or habitats that they are suited to live in. Animals that are forced out of their natural habitats are forced to either adapt rapidly to survive or die out.

Food Web

A **food web** is an interconnection of food chains. Food webs combine food chains within an ecosystem as the trophic levels often exhibit some overlap. Food webs are typically shown as an image. Food webs can also be called **consumer-resource systems** and can illustrate how the trophic levels interact and exchange resources such as oxygen, carbon dioxide, or nutrients.

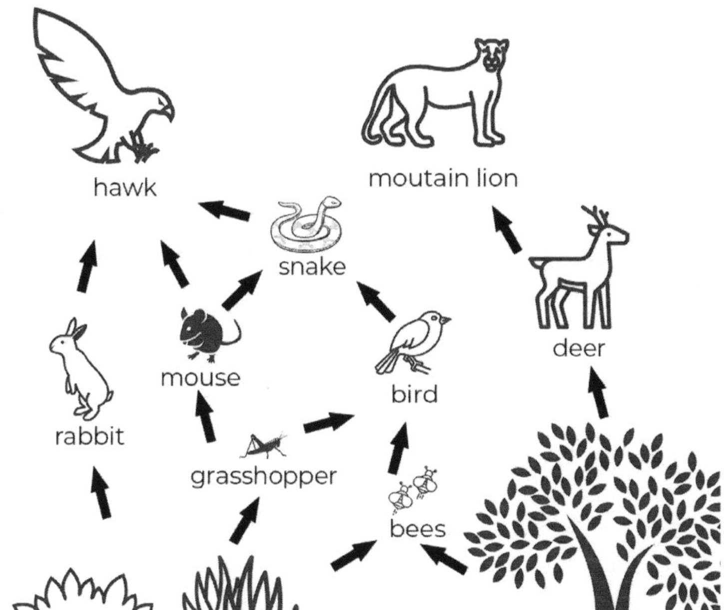

Indicator Species

Indicator species serve as ecological monitoring tools. Their existence, nonexistence, or general health and well-being in an environment can indicate the health of an ecosystem. Scientists can predict how changes in an environment can affect other species more difficult to study. Indicator species can give clues about food, water, climate change, or disease in an environment. Indicator species should be species that are always present in a habitat in large quantities, making them easily located to study. Indicator species should also be sensitive to change and react consistently to environmental changes. Frogs are a commonly used aquatic indicator species because their skin is moist and highly permeable, allowing pollutants to enter their bodies. Lichens can also be used as indicator species to monitor air quality as they are sensitive to heavy metals and acid rain.

Population Growth and Carrying Capacity

As a population grows in an environment, it experiences **exponential growth**. Exponential growth is the rapid population growth over a short period of time. Resources in an environment are limited, so exponential growth cannot be sustained. Population growth begins to level out in what is called **logistic growth**. Once population growth is more restricted and the population is stabilized, it reaches its **carrying capacity**. Carrying capacity is the population size that an environment can sustain or carry. Carrying capacity of an environment depends on species and resources available. Carrying capacity can have chaotic fluctuations caused by disease or natural disasters. Cyclical fluctuation of carrying capacity is normal and is called the **stable limit cycle**.

Renewable and Nonrenewable Resources

Nonrenewable resources are resources that are available in limited quantities usually due to the large amount of time required to replenish them. Many scientists agree that nonrenewable resources are resources that are not replenished within a human lifetime. Nonrenewable resources include fossil fuels, coal, and natural gas. These are energy-dense resources but limited in supply. **Renewable resources** are replenished naturally over short periods of time. The general consensus is that renewable resources are replenished or capable of being replenished within a human lifetime. Renewable energy resources include wind, water, solar, geothermal, and biomass. Plants, animals, air, water, and nutrients are all renewable resources. They may move or go through cycles, but they do not run out or become depleted.

Point and Nonpoint Source Pollution

The difference between point and nonpoint pollution is that **point source pollution** has a single, easily identifiable source. **Nonpoint source pollution** is caused by multiple pollutants from multiple sources, which may not be easily identified. A coal-burning power plant that releases sulfur dioxide into the air would be categorized as a point source pollution. A pipe that empties waste water from a water treatment facility would also be considered point source pollution. Smog within a city is caused by many sources, including cars and industrial processes, so identifying the direct causes is more difficult, making it an example of nonpoint source pollution. Fertilizer runoff is another example of a nonpoint source pollution. Because nonpoint source pollutions are hard to identify, from an environmental standpoint, nonpoint source pollution is more difficult to remedy and is a common issue in air and water pollution.

Biomagnification

Biomagnification is a term used to describe biological magnification. Biomagnification explains the increase of contaminated substances or chemicals that takes place in food chains. These substances include heavy metals such as mercury, pesticides such as DDT, and polychlorinated biphenyls (PCBs) compounds. These toxins are ingested by organisms because their environment is polluted. These toxins build up inside the organism's cells. When the organism is consumed by another organism higher in the food chain, the toxins gradually become concentrated higher in the food chain. This is a repetitive process and occurs across the food web. Therefore, toxin loads are most concentrated at the higher trophic levels of the food chain.

Ecosystem Management

Federal Agencies Responsible for Environmental Regulation

The **Environmental Protection Agency** (EPA)'s mission is to protect human and environmental health. The EPA was established in 1970 and is responsible for researching effects and mandating the use of pollutants. The EPA regulates the manufacturing, processing, distribution, and use of chemicals as well as sets the limits of pollutants that can be found in food, animal feed, and water. The **Natural Resources Conservation Service** (NRCS) was formerly known as the Soil Conservation Service (until 1994). The NRCS mission is to improve, protect, and conserve natural resources on private land. NRCS focuses primarily on agricultural lands and is a resource available to farmers. The **Bureau of Land Management** (BLM) was created in 1946 when the General Land Office and the Grazing service were combined. BLM lands include more than 247.3 million acres located primarily in the western states. The BLM' mission is to sustain the health, diversity, and productivity of the public lands for the use and enjoyment of present and future generations.

Significant Legislative Milestones Related to Natural Resources

The **Clean Air Act** was passed in 1963 and has since been amended several times. The Clean Air Act is designed to control and minimize air pollution. It covers vehicle emissions, industrial pollution, toxic air pollution, acid rain, ozone depletion, and other air quality issues. The **Clean Water Act** was passed in 1972 and is a federal law that aims to minimize water pollution (not to be confused with the **Safe Water Drinking Act** that maintains groundwater standards). The Clean Water Act aims to restore and maintain the chemical, physical, and biological integrity of bodies of water by preventing pollution as well as maintaining wetlands. The **National Environmental Policy Act** of 1969 promotes the enhancement of the environment and created the President's Council on Environmental Quality. The **National Forest Management Act** of 1976 requires the US Forest Service to develop plans for national forests, set standards for timber sales, and create policies to regulate timber harvesting to protect national forests from permanent damage.

Impact of Federal Regulations on Agriculture Production

Agriculture has the potential to affect the surrounding environment; therefore, many environmental regulations directly or indirectly impact agriculture. Many regulatory actions including air, water, energy, and pesticides directly affect agriculture. The **National Ambient Air Quality Standards** aim to reduce emissions and pollutions, including dust. **Water rights** are not largely regulated by the federal government but instead are regulated by state governments. Concentrated animal feeding operations must receive federal permits to prevent release of sediment, nutrients, pathogens, and pests into the water supply. Federal government regulates pesticide use by requiring registering and restricting agricultural use. The **Environmental Protection Agency** can regulate pesticide use that has the potential for spray drift. Spray drift can cause environmental impacts that would potentially cause harm to endangered species, thus violating the **Endangered Species Act**.

Preservation and Conservation

Both preservation and conservation involve some degree of protection. These two practices are closely associated, but the way they are carried out differs. **Conservation** generally refers to the protection of natural resources. **Preservation** is usually associated with the protection of buildings, objects, and landscapes. Conservation involves the sustainable use and management of natural resources such as wildlife, water, air, and earth deposits. Preservation attempts to maintain present conditions of natural resources or ecosystems. One of the major differences between the two is that conservation allows for use of natural resources but in a way that is sustainable and does not waste. Preservation seeks less human-involved management.

Reforestation

Reforestation involves reestablishing wooded ecosystems that have been depleted usually through deforestation. Reforestation can help mitigate climate change because forests act as a major carbon sink. Trees have abundant roost systems that can help keep soil in place. Soil productivity is increased because soil erosion is minimized. Forests help filter and regulate the flow of water, largely due to the canopy leaves that intercept and slow water fall to the ground. Plants and trees remove nutrients from the soil and water, reducing nonpoint source pollutants from reaching groundwater. Forests that are eradicated through deforestation may take decades or centuries to reestablish, if ever. Planting trees in a deforested area speeds up the establishment and can allow for future harvest. This sustainable practice ensures there are forests available in the following generations.

Methods Used to Limit Erosion and Runoff

Riparian buffers are strips of trees, shrubs, and grass that exist between cropland and water sources such as streams or rivers. The vegetation in the buffer acts as a sponge to soak up excess nutrients that would become runoff. The dense root systems of the buffer hold soil in place and can prevent soil erosion and flooding. **Wind breaks**, occasionally called shelter belts, are linear plantings of trees and shrubs planted around crop fields or pastures. Windbreaks reduce wind erosion of light-textured soils. Crop fields can also be planted in **cover crops** to reduce erosion and nutrient runoff between plantings. **Reduced tillage** and **no-tillage** practices reduce soil erosion and nutrient runoff also. Both cover crops, and reduced or no-tillage methods leave vegetation in the ground that holds soil in place and soaks up nutrients.

Best Management Practices

Best management practices is a term used to describe methods or techniques used in agriculture, natural resources management, and environmental sciences to reduce negative impact on the environment and reduce pollution. **Stocking rate** refers to the number of animals that can be sustained on a specific area for a specific amount of time. Too many animals in a confined area such as a pond or pasture will rapidly decimate the food supply and other resources. Proper livestock stocking improves the production of the livestock and reduces the impact on surrounding wildlife habitat. When proper stocking rates are used, wildlife and livestock can live in the same habitat. For endangered species, critical habitat is crucial for their survival. **Critical habitat** is habitat that includes specific areas that have physical or biological features that are essential to the conservation of the species. When critical habitat is conserved, many endangered species see an increase in population.

Population Sampling Techniques

A **population** is a group that is being researched to be understood (i.e., white-tailed deer in a specific county or the top 8" of soil in a certain area). The **sample** is the organisms or items actually collected and measured. **Quadrat sampling** is a tool useful for studying biodiversity in an environment. A series of premeasured quadrats, usually squares, are placed in a habitat of interest. The species within the quadrat are identified and recorded. **Electrofishing** is a fish sampling tool that is used to gather fish populations. An electrofishing boat produces an electric field and temporarily stuns the fish, allowing them to be collected and measured. Radio tracking determines information about an animal through the use of radio signals. **Radio tracking** is commonly used in national parks and requires the live capture of an animal and attaching a collar or device to them. The tracking device then sends or receives radio signals to alert researchers about the location of the animal.

Rotational Grazing

Rotational grazing is the practice of moving grazing livestock between pastures or paddocks as needed or on set time intervals. One of the major benefits to rotational grazing is increased forage production. Rotational grazing prevents **overgrazing**, which involves animals consuming grasses repetitively. Overgrazed grasses lose the ability to recover from grazing. Another advantage to rotational grazing includes increased soil fertility, therefore reducing the need for purchased fertilizer while increasing forage growth. Forages on rotational grazing have an increased resistance to drought due to the healthier root masses. There is also an increase in organic matter in the soil along with the increase in forage, which leads to increased water absorption by the soil. This in turn, means there is decreased surface runoff. More grazing areas will be available throughout the year if managed properly. Rotational grazing limits the need for feed during times of drought, controls less-desirable plants, improves animal management, decreases animal internal parasite loads, and creates a system of forage management that works more closely with the surrounding ecosystems.

Common Forestry Harvest Techniques

Silviculture is the management of wooded areas and involves systems of harvest and regeneration. **Clear-cutting** involves removing an entire stand of trees with no preference to age or type. After clear-cutting, trees can be replanted or left to naturally regenerate. **Seed tree harvesting** includes removing a majority of trees but leaving large, mature trees that can provide seed to reestablish the stand. The seed trees can be removed later. **Shelterwood** is a partial harvest method that allows new trees to grow under maturing trees. The shelterwood can be removed later. **Select cutting**, or thinning, involves removing individual or groups of trees to allow natural regeneration. Select cutting can be a single tree or group tree selection.

Preemergence and Postemergence Herbicides

Herbicides are chemicals used to prevent or stop unwanted plant (weed) growth. The two groups of pesticides are preemergent and postemergent herbicides. **Preemergent herbicides** are used to prevent plant growth. Preemergents can be applied directly to the soil in either a liquid or granular form. The preemergent herbicide coats the outsides of seeds and suffocates the seed, preventing it from growing. Preemergents can be used earlier in the year to prevent unwanted growth. Preemergents are not effective on perennials because they do not emerge from seeds. **Postemergence herbicides** are used on plants that have started to grow. Postemergence herbicides enter the plant system and travel down the plant stalk and into the root system. Postemergence herbicides are only effective on plants that have growth but, applied late in the year, can prevent seeding.

Selective and Nonselective Herbicides

Selective herbicides are commonly used to kill weeds in lawns and are used by homeowners. They kill weeds and not surrounding plants. Selective herbicides kill specific weeds. Some target broadleaf weeds such as dandelions or thistles, whereas others target grass-type weeds. Selective herbicides that target grass-type weeds would not be suitable choices to use in lawns. **Nonselective herbicides** kill all plants that they come into contact with. They can be used to clear an entire lot and are often used by landscapers. They can also be used to kill weeds along fence rows or weeds growing in cracks in sidewalks or driveways. Because these herbicides kill all plants they come in to contact with, care must be taken to treat only the undesirable plants.

PPE and Safety Procedures Related to Environmental and Natural Resources

For environmental and natural resources health exposures, the use of **personal protective equipment** (PPE) and safety precautions refers to general contact control practices. Boots or heavy shoes, protective gloves, and potentially protective headgear should be used to prevent potential injury against debris or sharp objects. Disposable exam gloves should be worn when there is a possibility of skin contact. Dust masks prevent dust from entering the mouth or nose. Goggles, face shields, and safety glasses prevent particulates from entering the eyes. Biohazard clothes and shoe coverings should be worn when hazardous substances can cause contamination. A respirator should be worn when airborne particles, infectious disease, or mold spores are present.

Importance of Hunting, Fishing, and Outdoor Recreation to the Economy

There are millions of Americans who hunt, trap, fish, and spend recreational time outdoors each year. These outdoor enthusiasts spend billions of dollars annually on noncommercial hunting, fishing, trapping, and outdoor recreation expenses. Hunting, trapping, fishing, and outdoor recreation activities create hundreds of thousands of jobs in the United States. The economic impact of hunting, trapping, fishing, and outdoor recreation is expected to increase as more people seek outdoor adventures. Revenue generated by hunting, trapping, fishing, and outdoor recreation also impacts the conservation and preservation portions of the economy. Much of the revenue generated purchasing licenses, park passes, and other fees is put into conservation and preservation efforts, easing the expenses that the government and organizations must spend to finance these efforts.

Contributions of Natural Resource Management to the National Economy

Renewable and nonrenewable natural resources as well as environmental and ecosystem services are an integral part of creating real wealth within a nation. Natural resources and environmental services provide natural capital that can be used to create other forms of revenue. Natural resources provide employment opportunities and create the livelihoods of citizens. The need to use these resources sustainably also creates additional employment opportunities in natural resources management and environmental service sectors. The government also creates jobs in these sectors to ensure that environments are preserved and natural resources are used sustainably as these are the foundation for long-term economic development.

Conventional and Alternative Energy Sources

Conventional energy sources include the fossil fuels such as coal, oil, and natural gas. These energy sources are burned to utilize energy. Coal must be mined, whereas oil and natural gas are drilled for. Burning these fuels releases strong pollutants into the atmosphere and has contributed immensely to global climate change. **Alternative energy sources** include solar, biomass, and wind power. Solar energy is harnessed by collecting solar energy on a panel. Solar energy is being utilized on solar energy farms and on the tops of rooftops in cities across the world. Biomass is an energy source that uses plant and animal waste products to create energy. The biomass is burned, which raises similar questions about air pollution as burning fossil fuels. However, biomass is sustainable as it involves burning renewable resources. Wind power involves harnessing the power of the wind through large windmills. Wind is a renewable resource, and windmills are a truly clean energy source. Wind farms can also be used to raise livestock or crops as there is ample open space around the windmills.

Environmental Impacts of Energy Production

All forms of energy production have an environmental impact. The utilization of **fossil fuels** for energy has significant environmental impacts. To extract fossil fuels, they must either be mined or drilled for. Mining underground and on the surface involves removing huge volumes of rock and relocating it, effectively altering two ecosystems. Drilling for fossil fuels can reduce the surrounding water quality by releasing toxic chemicals and heavy metals. Burning fossil fuels is what releases energy. This also releases greenhouse gases, contributing to global warming. Capturing **wind power** is a clean alternative as it releases no pollutants or emissions. **Solar power**, another clean alternative, requires extensive land space and contributes to habitat loss. The components used to create solar panels contain potentially harmful chemicals. **Hydroelectric energy** is also clean but greatly alters habitats in the surrounding aquatic and terrestrial environments.

Products Derived from Natural Resources

There are countless products that can be derived from natural resources. The following products can be derived from timber or wood sources: wood, sap, fiber, aspirin, acetone, charcoal, oils, resin, pulp, veneers, yeast, glycerin, lignin powder, glucose, xylose, poles, essential oils, and fruits and nuts. Each of these products can be used for countless products. Fuel is considered a resource and is created through natural gas, fossil fuels, or coal. Fish and wildlife are commonly hunted, trapped, or caught as a food source. Medications, skins, and furs can also be used from fish and wildlife. Plants other than trees provide numerous products as well including fibers, medications, oils, food, housing, building materials, heating, and cosmetic and aesthetic products.

Effects of Urban Sprawl on the Environment

Urban sprawl is a term used to describe the outward growth of cities. Urban sprawl occurs when the population of a city outgrows its limits and spreads into the outlying areas. An obvious effect of urban sprawl is the change from wildlife habitat to low-density land use. Many species of wildlife cannot survive in urban settings and are forced to move elsewhere. This usually results in a decrease in the species' population. This also results in a decrease in biodiversity of that area. Urban sprawl also creates increased air pollution from car exhaust, power facilities, and industrial processes. There is a significant increase in runoff in cities when compared to rural or undeveloped land. Much of the land in cities is under pavement, and pavement does not absorb runoff but allows it to readily flow across the surface. Increased runoff lowers water quality and creates erosion problems.

Chapter Quiz

Ready to see how well you retained what you just read? Scan the QR code to go directly to the chapter quiz interface for this study guide. If you're using a computer, simply visit the online resources page at **mometrix.com/resources719/osatagred** and click the Chapter Quizzes link.

Foundations of Agricultural Education

Leadership Principles and Skills

Importance of Personal Leadership Development

Personal leadership development is a process unique to each person and his or her personality. Core values, personality traits, and personal strengths and weaknesses help determine a person's leadership style. An autocratic leader has complete control over all decisions. Visionary leaders see things others cannot and unite others to work toward a vision. Democratic leaders respect the opinions of others and share in labor with them. Maslow's hierarchy of needs breaks human needs into five categories starting with the most basic needs: physiological, safety, love and belonging, esteem and accomplishment, and self-actualization and achieving one's potential. Maslow explained that leaders tend to be self-actualizing, and successful leaders work to meet the hierarchical needs of others.

Forms of Leadership

Authoritarian leadership is a leadership style in which the leader holds all authority and makes all decisions. **Democratic** leadership gives the leader the final say in decisions, but subordinates can contribute, and communication is encouraged. **Situational** leaders must change their leadership style to accommodate their subordinates. **Transformational** leaders work by motivating and empowering subordinates. **Visionary** leaders motivate others to work toward a common goal or vision. **Facilitative** leaders guide subordinates only as much as needed to be successful. **Laissez-faire** leadership is not usually effective and gives all authority to subordinates. **Transactional** leaders give subordinates expectations and reward them when the orders are followed.

Team-Building Skills

The ability to work successfully in a team setting is an important trait for students and potential employees to have. One of the most important skills is effective communication. Communication on a team is more than stating an opinion or giving advice. Effective communicators are also effective negotiators, influencers, and advisors. Effective communication relies on the ability to listen to others, so good communication usually means strong interpreting skills also. Working on a team can be frustrating, so team members who can motivate other members will lead to a team that performs better. The ability to encourage and inspire other team members will bring the team closer and allow for higher productivity.

Positive and Negative Attributes of a Leader

Positive traits of a leader encourage communication and growth of a group. A positive leader is fair and does not show favoritism. A negative trait would be a leader that is quick to show favoritism. A good leader is knowledgeable about his or her job and its expectations. A bad leader is not knowledgeable or acts like he or she is when he or she is not. A good trait for a leader to have is honesty and trustworthiness. A bad trait for a leader to have is to be dishonest or not trustworthy. A good trait for a leader to have is good communication skills. Good leaders are approachable, listen to concerns, and have strong interpersonal skills. Bad leaders have poor communication skills and can be considered rude or uncaring. Good leaders often make fast, good decisions that have positive impacts. Bad leaders will avoid making a decision, delaying them, or shirk the responsibility of making decisions. Good leaders are able to bring teams or committees together to reach a common goal, whereas bad leaders tend to drive teams apart.

Importance of Ethics in Leadership

Ethics are the moral reasons or principles that are used to guide decisions. Good leaders should have strong ethics and a good sense of doing the right thing and being fair. Leaders that put an emphasis on ethics are called ethical leaders. Ethical leaders put the common good in front of other decisions. They are able to motivate others to live and function at a higher standard of ethics. If the leader of a team, committee, or business is ethical, then the organization itself is also ethical. If the leader is not ethical and performs acts that he or she should not perform, then this tends to trickle down the ladder and can affect all members or subordinates. There is a saying that "good ethics is good business" because ethics have a profound impact on how well businesses are run and how well they perform.

Review Video: Ethical and Professional Standards
Visit mometrix.com/academy and enter code: 391843

Effective Communication Skills

Effective communication skills are imperative for any team member, leader, or employee if he or she wants to be successful. One of the best ways to be a good communicator is to be a good listener. **Listening** allows us to understand the other person's viewpoint, which is critical in effective communication. **Nonverbal** communication is also powerful when it comes to being an effective communicator. The body posture, facial expressions, and eye contact can all give clues to how someone is feeling. Paying attention to nonverbal cues can give hints as to what someone is thinking. To be considered a good communicator, one must be approachable. Approachable people are friendly and empathetic. **Verbal** communication should be clear and concise. When verbally communicating, convey the message and be done. **Written** communication can be taken in different views, so it is important that written communication is well thought out and conveys the message clearly and respectfully. Written communication is often appreciated by superiors and can be done via email.

Techniques to Improve Communication Skills

The best ways to improve communication skills are to practice them. To improve listening skills, the best thing to do is to spend time listening to other people. When talking, people want to know they are being heard. Do not act distracted or uninterested. To improve reading skills, practice reading daily. Work up to reading slightly more difficult materials. Writing can also be improved by doing it daily. When writing something important, such as an email to a superior, type it, and save it as a draft. Later, read it with a fresh mind, and make sure that it conveys the right message. When speaking, maintain good body posture and a positive attitude. Pause before speaking, and make sure the message comes out clearly, not the first thing on the mind. Nonverbal communication includes the body posture, hand gestures, and facial expressions. Keeping a positive attitude will help convey positive verbal communication.

Determining Validity and Reliability of a Source

When performing any type of research, it is important that sources used are valid and reliable. There are two types of sources: firsthand and secondhand. Firsthand sources in the scientific community include data collected for a person's own research project. Secondhand sources can be sources such as books, newspaper articles, magazines, census data, or scientific journals. It's important to be able to recognize the difference between factual information and opinion. Many magazines, newspapers, and other media include significant amounts of opinion. When researching, the best bet is to use peer-reviewed scientific journals. These are articles that were written by researchers and peer reviewed for accuracy before being published. Peer-reviewed articles include an easily identifiable author (or authors), a date published, and a bibliography. A bibliography details and sources that the researches used and includes information about those sources.

Scientific Method

The scientific method is a method developed and used by scientists to perform scientific research. The method is the same across the globe, ensuring that scientists are performing valid experiments. The first part of the scientific method includes asking a question or making an observation (which leads to a question). The researcher can then come up with a hypothesis. A hypothesis is an educated guess. The hypothesis can then be tested using an experiment. The experiment yields data, which is recorded and analyzed. The data can either prove the hypothesis correct or it can prove the hypothesis incorrect. If the experiment proves the hypothesis incorrect, the hypothesis must be altered. Another experiment can be performed to test the new hypothesis. No matter the outcome of the experiment, it must be reported. This allows other scientists to see the data and perform experiments related to the same experiment without having to perform the experiment again.

Career Development

Careers Within the Agriculture, Food, and Natural Resources Career Cluster

The agriculture, food, and natural resources career cluster focuses on both traditional agriculture studying and working with land, air, plants, and animals. It also focuses on nontraditional agriculture in areas of agricultural technology and renewable energy sources such as wind and solar power. There are seven career pathways in the Agriculture, Food and Natural Resources Career Cluster. The agribusiness pathway employs the business side of agriculture: financing, marketing, and distributing agricultural goods and commodities. The animal systems pathway includes careers that involve animals and can include careers such as veterinarians, animal scientists, and livestock producers. The environmental service pathway employs people that are interested in preserving the environment. The food products and processing systems pathway is a cluster dedicated to food production, preservation, and processing. The natural resources systems pathway is a cluster for careers that focus on the natural world and natural resources. Careers in the natural resources cluster would include foresters and geologists. The plant systems pathway includes careers that are dedicated to plants. Careers include row crop farmers and plant geneticists. The power, structural, and technical systems pathway employs people who are interested in how machinery works and repairing machinery. Careers in this cluster would include agricultural engineers, welders, mechanics, and windmill constructors.

Specific Skills and Education Needed for Career Pathways

There are seven career pathways that are available for agricultural education students. Students can learn skills in animal systems; plant systems; natural resource systems; environmental systems; food products and processing systems; power, structural, and technical systems; and agribusiness. Each pathway requires different skill sets. Animal systems require knowledge about animals, nutrition, and disease. Plant systems require knowledge about plant processes such as photosynthesis, nutritional requirements, growing conditions, and propagation methods. Natural resources systems require knowledge about natural resources including air, water, soil, and renewable and nonrenewable resources and how to manage them sustainably. Environmental systems require knowledge about ecosystems, wildlife, and pollutants. Food products and processing pathways require knowledge about how food is raised or grown, processed, preserved, and cooked. Power, structural, and technical systems pathways require knowledge about machinery, power, construction, and engineering principles. Agribusiness pathways require knowledge about business management, marketing, and financing.

Agricultural Careers Available to Students in an Agricultural Education Program

There are numerous agricultural careers available to agriculture students. Students should narrow their interests down to one or two career pathways: animal systems, plant systems, natural resource systems, environmental systems, food products and processing, and power, structural, and technical systems as well as agribusiness systems. The following are examples of careers available in each pathway:

- Animal systems—dog groomer, veterinarian, zookeeper
- Plant systems—plant geneticist, greenhouse grower, landscape architect
- Natural resource systems—forester, park ranger, conservationist
- Environmental systems—environmental scientist, ecologist, environmental policy maker
- Food products and processing systems—nutritionist, food chemist, meat inspector
- Power, structural, and technical systems—welder, machinist, agricultural engineer
- Agribusiness systems—farm appraiser, market analyst, grain and livestock buyer

Developing a Career Plan

A career plan maps out short- and long-term career goals and steps to take to achieve those goals. The first step to creating a career plan is to determine career options. Personal interests, skills, values, and strengths can help determine possible career paths. For example, someone interested in animals may want to consider jobs in the animal science or veterinary fields. The list of options can be narrowed by job shadowing, researching, talking to professionals in the field, volunteering, or completing internships. Career options should be prioritized to suit personal interests and skill sets. Suitable careers can be compared to each other. Career options should be weighed against personal skills, strengths, and weaknesses.

Meeting Career Goals

A career plan maps out short- and long-term career goals and steps to take to achieve those goals. Once career options are identified and narrowed, the process of working toward those goals can begin. Ideally, there should be one or two career options. This allows the individual to narrow work specifically for the career goal. This can help students determine classes to take or colleges and majors to consider. The career goals should be realistic, and other considerations should be made. Will there be a demand for this career, and what are the necessary qualifications to be successful? Specific, measurable, attainable, realistic/relevant, and time-bound (SMART) goals should then be developed for the short term and the long term. Employment should also be in line with the long-term career goal. A student interested in wildlife and fisheries should try to find employment opportunities related to that field to build experience.

Components Related to Job Preparation

Achieving career goals and landing a dream job can be difficult, especially in career fields that have low demand or are saturated with new potential workers. Potential employees can set themselves apart by being well prepared for the employment process. A résumé is essential to applying for jobs and being offered employment. A prepared résumé shows employers that the applicant is serious about the application. Résumés should include work and school history, contact information, and any relevant experience. References should also be included or typed up in a separate document. All references should be made aware that they are being used as references. If an interview is requested, it is imperative to arrive on time (or early) and be well prepared. Research the company ahead of time, and write down questions to ask the interviewer. When approaching the interviewer, the interviewee should shake hands and stand until directed to be seated. The interviewee should have good posture and avoid nervous habits. After the interview, a note thanking the interviewer for the interview can be mailed.

CDEs

Career development events (CDEs) are competitions that students can participate in through the Future Farmers of America (FFA). CDEs allow students to practice and hone skills that will be used in later careers. Students perform many of these competitions as a team; therefore, they learn valuable teamwork skills. CDEs can be held at the local, state, and national levels. Students must work and study hard to be successful in CDEs at any level. Students can participate in multiple CDEs. There are numerous CDEs offered at the national level, with more offered at the state and local levels. Some examples of CDEs include: Parliamentary Procedure, Livestock Evaluation, Agronomy, Land Evaluation, Poultry Evaluation, Dairy Cattle Evaluation, Environmental Science, Forestry, Prepared Public Speaking, and Milk Quality and Products as well as Agribusiness Management.

Components of Agricultural Education Programs

Comprehensive Agricultural Education Program Components

The three components of a comprehensive agricultural education program are the agricultural classroom and laboratory experiences, Future Farmers of America (FFA) experiences, and the supervised agricultural experience (SAE). These three components are necessary to create a comprehensive agricultural education program. The student gains knowledge about agricultural processes in the classroom and lab. FFA allows students to compete in competitions and practice building teamwork and leadership skills. The SAE teaches students about working in a chosen career field, finances, and record keeping as well as employment skills. The three components of a comprehensive agricultural education program are often illustrated as follows:

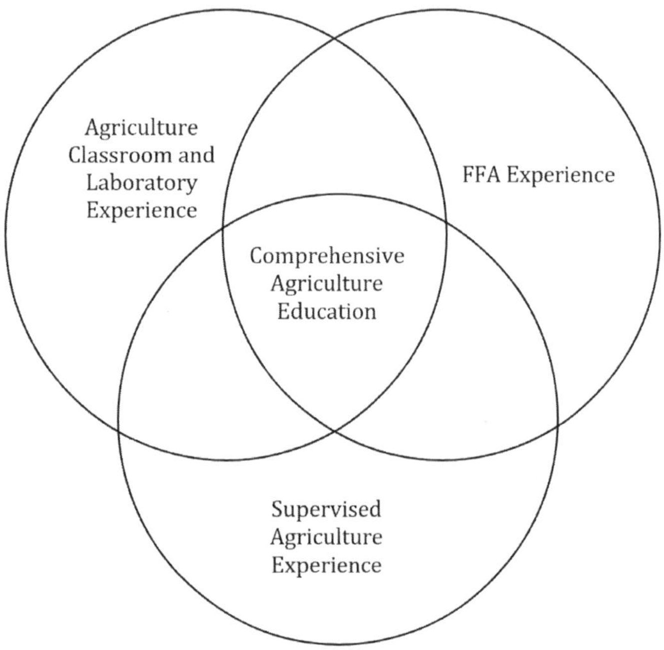

Scope and Sequence for a Secondary Agricultural Education Program

Agricultural education programs in secondary schools are meant to prepare students for success in the field of agriculture after graduation. The secondary agricultural education program seeks to not only instill students with a knowledge of agriculture but also create tomorrow's leaders. A successful agricultural education program includes the agricultural classroom and laboratory and Future Farmers of America (FFA) membership and experiences as well as a supervised agricultural experience (SAE). Secondary agriculture programs are often developed as a pathway that students can take. The different concentrations in agriculture make up the pathways. Students can choose to focus in animal systems, plant systems, agribusiness systems, natural resources systems, environmental systems, food products and processing, or power, structural, and technical systems. Each pathway begins with the Agriscience course, which is used to introduce first-year agricultural education students with the many areas involved with agriculture in the hopes that they will choose a pathway that interests them. After the initial course, students take courses that are gradually more complex along their pathway. For example, a student interested in plant science would take the following courses: ninth grade, Agriscience; 10th, Plant and Soil Science; 11th, Principles of Hydroculture; and 12th, Greenhouse Management.

Advisory Committee

An advisory committee comprises members of the community that meet regularly and discuss the agricultural education program. The advisors are members of the community who are involved with local agriculture. The committee can be composed of employees of local businesses, local postsecondary agriculture educators, farmers and producers, extension agents, or any other community members who could offer reasonable input. The purpose of the committee is to provide the advisor(s), school administration, and school board members with input into the local agriculture opportunities. The committee can offer advice as to the current curriculum and if it meets the needs of current employment opportunities. Committee members can inform the advisor about current and upcoming employment opportunities and skills required to land jobs. They can also update advisors on new technology, equipment, or methods that are being used in the agriculture industry.

FFA

Mission Statement, Motto, Ceremonies, and Salute

The Future Farmers of America **(FFA) mission statement** is: FFA makes a positive difference in the lives of students by developing their potential for premier leadership, personal growth, and career success through agricultural education. The **FFA motto** is: Learning to Do, Doing to Learn, Earning to Live, Living to Serve. During meetings and conventions, the FFA officers will perform the opening and closing ceremonies to officially begin and end the meetings. The president, vice president, secretary, sentinel, reporter, treasurer, and advisor all have speaking roles in the ceremony. At the end of the opening ceremony, the president asks the members the question "FFA members, why are we here?" to which all members stand and reply "To practice brotherhood, honor agricultural opportunities and responsibilities, and develop those qualities of leadership which an FFA member should possess." During the closing ceremony, all FFA members present will stand and recite the Pledge of Allegiance together.

Creed

I believe in the future of agriculture, with a faith born not of words but of deeds—achievements won by the present and past generations of agriculturists—in the promise of better days through better ways, even as the better things we now enjoy have come to us from the struggles of former years.

I believe that to live and work on a good farm, or to be engaged in other agricultural pursuits, is pleasant as well as challenging; for I know the joys and discomforts of agricultural life and hold an inborn fondness for those associations which, even in hours of discouragement, I cannot deny.

I believe in leadership from ourselves and respect from others. I believe in my own ability to work efficiently and think clearly, with such knowledge and skill as I can secure, and in the ability of progressive agriculturists to serve our own and the public interest in producing and marketing the product of our toil.

I believe in less dependence on begging and more power in bargaining; in the life abundant and enough honest wealth to help make it so—for others as well as myself; in less need for charity and more of it when needed; and in being happy myself and playing square with those whose happiness depends upon me.

I believe that American agriculture can and will hold true to the best traditions of our national life and that I can exert an influence in my home and community that will stand solid for my part in that inspiring task.

Types of Membership

There are four types of membership within the National Future Farmers of America (FFA) Organization. The four membership types are active, honorary, collegiate, and alumni. **Active** memberships are for students in grades 7 through 12 who are actively enrolled in secondary agriculture programs. To become an active member, students must be enrolled in at least one agricultural course, pay chapter dues, be interested in FFA and agricultural activities, and remain in good conduct standing with chapter, local, state, and national FFA. **Honorary** membership is reserved for individuals who have made significant contributions to the FFA and agricultural education. **Collegiate** memberships are for students enrolled in two- or four-year postsecondary schools. Collegiate memberships are through the college's FFA chapter. **Alumni** memberships are reserved for former active members, collegiate members, honorary members, or agricultural education supporters.

Historical Moments and Figures

The following are major historical moments and figures of the Future Farmers of America:

- 1917—Smith-Hughes Act provides financial support of secondary agriculture education.
- 1925—Virginia agricultural educators Henry C. Groseclose, Harry Sanders, Walter S. Newman, and Edmund C. Magill organized the Future Farmers of Virginia, which would serve as the model for the Future Farmers of America (FFA).
- 1928—FFA is established in Kansas City, MO.
- 1929—National blue and corn gold colors adopted.
- 1930—National FFA creed, written by E. M. Tiffany is adopted.
- 1933—Blue corduroy jacket is adopted as official dress.
- 1935—New Farmers of America (NFA) is created for African Americans.
- 1965—NFA merges with FFA.
- 1969—FFA opens membership to girls.
- 1971—National FFA Alumni Association is created.
- 1991—Chapters from US Virgin Islands and Guam are chartered.
- 1994—Corey Flournoy is elected as the first African American national FFA president.

Constitutional Officer Positions and Duties

Future Farmer of America (FFA) officer positions include the following: president, vice president, secretary, treasurer, reporter, sentinel, and advisor. The **president** represents the chapter, engages in meetings, and appoints committees. The **vice president** coordinates committee work, assumes the duties of the president when absent, and maintains a chapter file. The **secretary** prepares the meeting agenda, records meeting minutes, and is responsible for chapter correspondence. The **treasurer** collects dues, prepares membership rosters, and maintains accurate records. The **reporter** publishes a chapter newsletter, acts as photographer, and plans public information programs. The **sentinel** helps maintain order during meetings, keeps the meeting room comfortable, and involves the community with activities. The **advisor** supervises members and informs them. The parliamentarian, historian, and chaplain are optional officer positions.

Degrees

The **Discovery** Future Farmers of America (FFA) degree is a local degree awarded to students enrolled in agriculture for at least part of the year and are paid FFA members. It is symbolized with a discovery pin. The Green Hand degree is awarded to first-year high school FFA members and serves as the basic local degree. It is symbolized with a bronze pin. The **Chapter** FFA degree is a local degree awarded to students in their second or third year of FFA. Students must have an active SAE. It is represented with a silver pin. The **State** FFA degree is awarded at the state level. It requires at least 24 months of membership. Students must hold an office at the chapter level. It is symbolized with a golden chain above the name on the jacket. The **American** FFA degree is the highest degree awarded and is awarded at the national level. Students must have 36 months of FFA membership, be a high school graduate, have a strong SAE, and exhibit strong community involvement and leadership skills. It is symbolized with a golden chain with a key at the end.

Program of Activities and Committee Structures

The **Program of Activities** (POA) outlines the proposed activities for a Future Farmers of America (FFA) chapter for the year. The POA is available for students, educators, board members, FFA advisors, and the community to view planned FFA events throughout the year. The Program of Activities is broken down into student development, chapter development, and community development sections. **Committees** are used to divide the work set forth in the POA into manageable sections. Committees are created to accomplish goals, and each FFA member should serve on at least one committee. Committees can be split up in various ways but are commonly split up to cover standards set forth in the POA. These include the following: leadership, healthy lifestyles, career success, scholarship, personal growth, chapter recruitment, financial, public relations, cooperation, support group, economic development, environmental and natural resources, human resources, citizenship, and agricultural promotion.

Basic Parliamentary Procedural Motions Described in the FFA Manual

Opening and closing ceremonies come from the latest edition of the Future Farmers of America (FFA) manual. Opening ceremony opens the meeting for discussion and is followed by items of business. Any items of business from the Program of Activities are opened up for discussion. To present an item of business, a member stands and addresses the president with the item of business and present a proposal. Another member can second the proposal. The proposal can be opened for debate. Members can vote on items of business where the one-person-one-vote rule applies. Privileged motions include adjourn, recess, and raising a question of privilege. Incidental motions include appeal, suspend the rules, point of order, division of the assembly, and parliamentary inquiry. Subsidiary motions include lay on the table, commit or refer, postpone to a certain time, previous question, amend, limit or extend debate, and postpone indefinitely. Motions bringing an item of business before the chapter include take from the table, reconsider, and rescind. The closing ceremony concludes the meeting.

Proper Presentation and Disposal of a Main Motion

The purpose of a main motion is to present an item of business for consideration and action by the chapter. Only one main motion can exist at a time. While a main motion is pending, a subsidiary or incidental motion that arises must be disposed of before the main motion can be considered. A subsidiary motion can dispose of a main motion. A main motion may not interrupt a speaker, must be seconded, is debatable and amendable, must have majority vote, may be reconsidered, and ranks last in pertinence. The president will ask, "What is the next item of business?" The member addresses the president, and the president acknowledges the member. The member presents the main motion, and another member seconds it. The president states the main motion and opens the floor for debate. A vote is taken in which majority vote has to occur for the motion to pass. Members in favor of the motion say "aye" and those opposed say "no." The president then recites the outcome of the vote.

Purpose of Parliamentary Procedure in an FFA Meeting

Parliamentary procedure is based on democratic principles. When groups of people come together to discuss items important to them, there is often much discussion. Democratic discussions can be effective if performed correctly, which is where parliamentary procedure comes in. Parliamentary procedure provides all members with an equal right to debate. Parliamentary procedure also allows members to vote on items of business, and only majority vote items prevail. Parliamentary procedure ensures that all members are given equal consideration and prevents any one group from becoming overly powerful. Parliamentary procedure can be thought of as a code of ethics for conducting a meeting.

FFA Award Programs

There are numerous ways that students can be recognized in Future Farmers of America (FFA). Degrees are awarded at the chapter, state, and national levels. At the local level, students can receive the Discovery and Green Hand degrees. The degree given at the state level is the state degree. The degree given at the national level is the American degree. Students can complete applications to receive degrees and will receive them if the minimum requirements are met. Proficiency awards can be given to students that are proficient in their SAE area. The proficiency awards are competitive, and the students are competing against other students in the same category at the state and national levels. Star awards are given to outstanding national degree recipients. Chapters can also win National Chapter awards for outstanding success. FFA has partnered with multiple agribusinesses to offer scholarship opportunities for FFA members. Students complete a competitive application and can receive scholarships from companies such as John Deere, Bayer, and Chevrolet.

SAE

Purpose

A supervised agricultural experience (SAE) is one of the three components of a strong agricultural program. An SAE is a project that is performed outside of the normal class period. The SAE allows the student to explore an agricultural interest further. Students develop an SAE with the assistance of the advisor if needed. SAEs not only allow students to explore interests but give the student experience in a field also. An SAE is a required component in an agricultural education program. SAEs can teach students valuable skills that they would not learn in the classroom. Students learn responsibility, data collection, bookkeeping, communication, and other coveted skills that they can use in their careers, even if they do not pursue a career in the field that their SAE was in. If students pursue a career related to their SAE project, then they will have gained valuable skills that are specific to that career type. For example, if students are interested in owning a landscaping business, they can start cutting grass as an SAE. They can grow their customer group while learning more about landscaping and running a business.

Types

There are six types of supervised agricultural experiences (SAEs): Entrepreneurship, Placement, Research, Exploratory, Improvement, and Supplemental. **Entrepreneurship** SAEs involve a student-run business. The students start a business and is paid (i.e., mowing yards or opening a dog-sitting business). **Placement** SAEs place a student in employment (can be paid or volunteer) to practice skills in a career field. **Research** SAEs involve students performing research about an agricultural topic that they are interested in (e.g., fertilizer effects on corn crops). **Exploratory** SAEs give students the opportunity to explore fields of agriculture that they are interested in. **Improvement** SAEs are more similar to community service projects. Students can create improvement projects to improve their community (e.g., building a playground). **Supplemental** SAEs are performed along with the main SAE. For example, if a student worked at a wildlife rescue for a placement SAE, he or she may want to research the wildlife rehabilitation rates or methods as a supplemental, research SAE. SAEs can fall into one of the following career areas: animal systems, agribusiness systems, environmental service systems, food products and processing, natural resources, plant systems, and power, structural, and technical systems.

Development

The first step in developing a supervised agricultural experience (SAE) program is to identify interests. Students should complete an SAE resource inventory to help determine resources available for the SAE project. The student can then narrow some SAE opportunities. A long-term plan for the SAE should be developed and should detail expected skills and experiences gained from the SAE. An SAE budget should be created. The SAE should be thoroughly discussed with the student's parents. Students should also create a list of supplementary skills and experiences that will accompany the SAE project. The scope of the SAE project should be increased annually. This will allow students to be eligible for advanced Future Farmers of America (FFA) degrees. Projects should include a detailed budget, partners, and name and size of the business (if entrepreneurship) as well as detailed activities for the calendar year.

Student Advancement and Awards

Students must have an active supervised agricultural experience (SAE) to receive the chapter degree. Students seeking a state degree must have exceptional SAE projects. Students seeking the national degree must also have exceptional SAE projects. SAEs can also earn students awards in proficiency. Proficiency awards are given to students with outstanding SAE projects. Students can win proficiency awards at the state and national level. Proficiency awards are accompanied with reward money. Currently, approximately $4 billion per year is awarded to students annually for SAE projects. Proficiency awards are given in 51 national proficiency areas. Proficiency award areas are broken down into entrepreneurship areas, placement areas, combined (both entrepreneurship and placement) areas, and research areas. Within each area the awards are broken down further into agricultural systems.

Basic Financial Record-Keeping Skills

Financial record-keeping skills are an excellent life skill that a supervised agricultural experience (SAE) can teach. Financial record-keeping skills are necessary for an SAE to be successful. Financial records can be used to make management decisions and illustrate the cash flow within a business. Students are better able to manage finances when they can see where money is earned and where it is spent. Good records can be used to show financial growth from year to year. Any business that makes money is required to report the income to the federal government and pay taxes. Good financial records can be used to gather information for tax return forms. SAE awards and degree applications will require proof that an SAE is successful and profitable. Financial records can act as proof of income and expenses for awards and applications.

Chapter Quiz

Ready to see how well you retained what you just read? Scan the QR code to go directly to the chapter quiz interface for this study guide. If you're using a computer, simply visit the online resources page at **mometrix.com/resources719/osatagred** and click the Chapter Quizzes link.

OSAT Practice Test

Want to take this practice test in an online interactive format?
Check out the online resources page, which includes interactive practice questions and much more: **mometrix.com/resources719/osatagred**

1. Which is the correct National FFA mission statement?

a. The National FFA Organization is dedicated to making a positive difference in the lives of students by developing their potential for premier leadership, personal growth, and career success through agricultural education.
b. The National FFA Organization is dedicated to making a positive difference in the lives of students by developing their potential for premier academics, personal development, and lifetime success through agricultural education.
c. Learning to do, doing to learn, earning to live, living to serve
d. The National FFA Organization strives to develop competent and assertive agricultural leadership as well as increase awareness of the global and technological importance of agriculture and its contribution to our well-being.

2. A cattle rancher wants to eliminate horned animals from her Hereford operation. She breeds a polled cow to a horned bull. The bull has sired both polled and horned offspring in the past. Calculate the percent chance that the calf resulting from this breeding will be polled.

a. 0% chance of being polled
b. 25% chance of being polled
c. 50% chance of being polled
d. 100 % chance of being polled

3. Under what conditions would a student be eligible to receive an American degree?

a. A student who is a graduated National FFA member
b. A student in the 11th grade who has been active for three years
c. A student who has received a Chapter degree
d. A student with a National Proficiency Award finalist application

4. The Agricultural Marketing Service utilizes voluntary vegetable grading. A tomato that is free from decay and freezing injury, has sunscald but is not seriously damaged by it, is mature, and is misshapen would be most likely classified into which category?

a. US No. 1
b. US Combination
c. US No. 2
d. US No. 3

5. There are four levels of membership within the National FFA Organization. Which is available to students at postsecondary schools with active FFA chapters?

a. Alumni
b. Collegiate
c. Citizen
d. Honorary

6. Herbicides are used to prevent or stop unwanted plant growth. A landscaping company is starting a job in late spring that requires them to start Bermuda lawns in a recently renovated assisted-living community. They want to start seeding Bermuda in early summer. Which would they most likely use?

a. A selective herbicide
b. A nonselective herbicide
c. A broadleaf postemergence herbicide
d. A pre-emergence herbicide

7. What does the acronym SAE stand for?

a. Supplemental agricultural experience
b. Supervised agricultural experience
c. Supervised agriscience experiment
d. Supplemental agriscience experiment

8. The National FFA Organization adopted colors to represent the organization. Which of the following correctly explains the reason behind the colors chosen?

a. Red, white, and blue were chosen as the colors to represent the FFA. FFA is a national organization; therefore, the colors of the United States should also represent the FFA.
b. Corduroy blue and harvest yellow were chosen as the colors of the FFA. FFA official dress includes a blue corduroy jacket for both males and females, so corduroy blue was a fitting choice. Harvest yellow represents the yellow of golden wheat fields and corn fields, both representative of agriculture.
c. National blue and corn gold were chosen as the colors to represent the FFA. National blue was chosen as it is the blue on the American flag and represents that FFA is a national organization. Corn gold represents agriculture in all states as corn is grown in every state.
d. Royal navy and bumblebee yellow were chosen as the colors for FFA. National blue represents the blue on the American flag, indicating that FFA is a national organization. Bumblebee yellow represents the hard work that bees contribute to agriculture, reminding us that agriculture requires hard work and dedication.

9. Select the list of courses that students would take in an agricultural education program if they were interested in learning how the economics of forestry in the United States are related to the economics of other business types, such as crop sciences, landscaping, or paper products?

a. Plant and Soil Science, Animal Science, Agribusiness, and Nursing
b. Natural Resources, Environmental Science, Chemistry, and Wildlife Biology
c. Agribusiness, Agriculture Economics, Natural Resources, and Greenhouse Management
d. Agricultural Engineering, Agricultural Mechanics, Criminal Justice, and Agriscience

10. Choose the correct National FFA motto.

a. Learning to do, doing to learn, earning to live, living to serve
b. Practice brotherhood, honor agricultural opportunities and responsibilities, and develop those qualities of leadership that an FFA member should possess.
c. I pledge allegiance to the flag of the United States of America, and to the republic for which it stands, one nation under God, indivisible, with liberty and justice for all.
d. I strive to establish and enhance my skills through agricultural education to enter a successful career.

11. The following items are the human needs represented in Maslow's triangle. Order the needs correctly beginning with those that should be met first and ending with the needs met last.

I. Esteem
II. Physiological
III. Self-actualization
IV. Love and belonging
V. Safety

a. I, III, V, IV, II
b. I, II, III, IV, V
c. III, I, IV, V, II
d. II, V, IV, I, III

12. Choose the following symbol from the National FFA emblem that has the incorrect meaning.

a. The owl, long recognized for its wisdom, symbolizes the knowledge required to be successful in the industry of agriculture.
b. The plow signifies labor and tillage of the soil, the backbone of agriculture and the historic foundation of our country's strength.
c. The rising sun serves as a reminder of our freedom and ability to explore new horizons for the future of agriculture.
d. The cross section of the ear of corn provides the foundation of the emblem, just as corn has historically served as the foundation crop of American agriculture.

13. What is the purpose of a lesson plan?

a. Lesson plans are used to give instructional facilitators a guide to the curriculum pacing in a classroom.
b. Lesson plans are given to students to show them what they will be learning.
c. Lesson plans are not a useful tool for teachers and should be used only when requested by administration or instructional facilitators.
d. Lesson plans help the teacher outline the lesson and stay on task.

14. During a National FFA opening ceremony, the following statement is made: "Thank you. FFA members, why are we here?" Which constitutional officer position is responsible for making that statement?

a. Advisor
b. Vice president
c. Sentinel
d. President

15. During a chapter meeting, students present a motion to host a cookout. What is the next step of parliamentary procedure to take place after a main motion is presented?

a. The motion is seconded.
b. Members debate the motion.
c. The chair states the motion.
d. The chair puts the question and members vote.

16. A Future Farmers of America (FFA) chapter decides to volunteer in a soup kitchen over the holidays. Which section of the chapter's program of activities should this be added to?

a. Student development
b. Chapter development
c. Community development
d. Amendments

17. Students completing National FFA degree requirements are presented with pins. Which pin is presented to a first-year FFA member?

a. Bronze emblem pin
b. Gold emblem pin
c. Gold key and chain pin
d. Silver emblem pin

18. Which is NOT a requirement to establish a new National FFA chapter in the continental United States?

a. Contact the state supervisor of agricultural education.
b. Contact the National FFA Center located in Indianapolis, Indiana.
c. Receive approval from the local school board administration.
d. Develop a chapter constitution and a program of activities.

19. The acronym COLT stands for which of the following?

a. Combined officer leadership training
b. Chapter officer luncheon training
c. Chapter officer leadership training
d. Combined officer luncheon training

20. Explain the purpose and importance of a course syllabus.

a. A course syllabus is used to give exact dates of tests and due dates of assignments for students. This allows students much more time to prepare for upcoming graded work.
b. A course syllabus introduces the course material. It should be two to three in-depth pages introducing the main ideas of the course.
c. A course syllabus is used to give parents a list of required materials and explain where any fees or dues associated with the course will go. The course syllabus also outlines any school dress code policies or rules of the school.
d. A course syllabus is intended to give students a brief overview of the course and estimated timelines of sections covered. The syllabus should also include materials required and contact information for the teacher.

21. A school administration recommends that teachers incorporate learning styles in lesson planning for special education students. Explain the idea that he or she is suggesting.

a. He or she is suggesting incorporating whole child learning, which is a teaching style that encourages students to learn and apply knowledge and skills through an engaging experience.
b. He or she is suggesting incorporating flipped learning, which involves transformational leadership, global engagement, poverty, and equity, redefining student success as well as teaching and learning.
c. He or she is suggesting differentiated instruction, which is a style of teaching in which educators divide their time, resources, and efforts to teach students of various backgrounds, readiness levels, skill levels, and interests.
d. He or she is suggesting incorporating project-based learning. This is a style of teaching in which students review introductory materials at home prior to a new lesson, then perform in-depth reviews or hands-on projects in the classroom.

22. According to Gardener's Multiple Intelligences theory, there are at least seven ways that students can learn. Choose the intelligence type with the correct explanation.

a. Visual-spatial: Students have a strong wisdom of body and ability to control physical motion.
b. Audial: Students have a strong ability to understand a concept just by listening to the teacher.
c. Linguistic: Students have a strong ability to use spoken or written words.
d. Intrapersonal: Students have a strong ability to communicate effectively with others and develop relationships.

23. The Model of Hierarchical Complexity uses 16 stages to create a framework that organizes patterns of human development. A child who can solve problems using empirical evidence, algebra, or logic would fall into which stage of development?

a. Formal
b. Nominal
c. Primary
d. Sensory

24. Teachers can use Bloom's Taxonomy or Webb's Depth of Knowledge to format questions that require the student to express a deeper level of understanding of the content. Which question example falls into the evaluate category of Bloom's Taxonomy?

a. Why is it important to study energy conservation?
b. Plan and conduct an experiment to test the effect of exercise on heart rate.
c. What are possible sources of error in the experiment?
d. List the steps of the scientific method.

25. A new teacher is set up with a mentor teacher when he is hired. The mentor teacher invites the new teacher to observe the classroom at the end of the year. He realizes that the students are extremely well-behaved and the focus is entirely on the content being taught. He also notices that the classroom next to his mentor teacher's classroom is quite the opposite: the teacher struggled to maintain control of the classroom, much less teach content. The mentor teacher likely has a ______________ type of leadership in her classroom, whereas the teacher next door likely has a __________________ type of leadership in her classroom.

a. democratic; authoritarian
b. authoritarian; Laissez-faire
c. Laissez-faire; servant
d. servant; charismatic

26. A new farmer setting up his farming business with his brother is looking over options for managing their business. He's worried about protecting his personal assets in the long run but wants to make decisions for the business. Which business type should he consider?

a. Corporation
b. Sole proprietorship
c. Cooperative
d. Partnership

27. The owner of an apple orchard business has noticed a decline in profits for the last few years. After speaking with a business consultant, the owner has decided that the orchard needs to specialize or diversify its available products. The orchard company sells only Fuji apples, applesauce, and apple cider. The owner wants to try both diversifying and specializing products. Explain how he or she can achieve both diversification and specialization at the same time.

a. The orchard is currently limited to selling three products. The company needs to add more products to the line. The owner can market dehydrated apples, apple preserves, apple pie filling, or even apple cider vinegar.
b. The orchard is selling products from only one type of apple: the Fuji apple. The company needs to add a variety of apple trees, such as Granny Smith, Golden Delicious, and Gala apples to the orchards. The products sold now can incorporate the different types of apples.
c. The orchard should focus on one product. By focusing on one product, the owner can create a higher-quality product. The owner should perform a market analysis to indicate which of the three current products should be the focus of the orchard's production.
d. The orchard currently specializes in Fuji apples and should market Fuji apple products. The owner can then diversify the product line to include multiple products created using Fuji apples. The orchard can sell Fuji apples, dehydrated Fuji apples, Fuji applesauce, and canned Fuji apples

28. The law of diminishing returns is a concept in economics used to describe the effects of output with input factors. Which point in the graph indicates the point of diminishing returns?

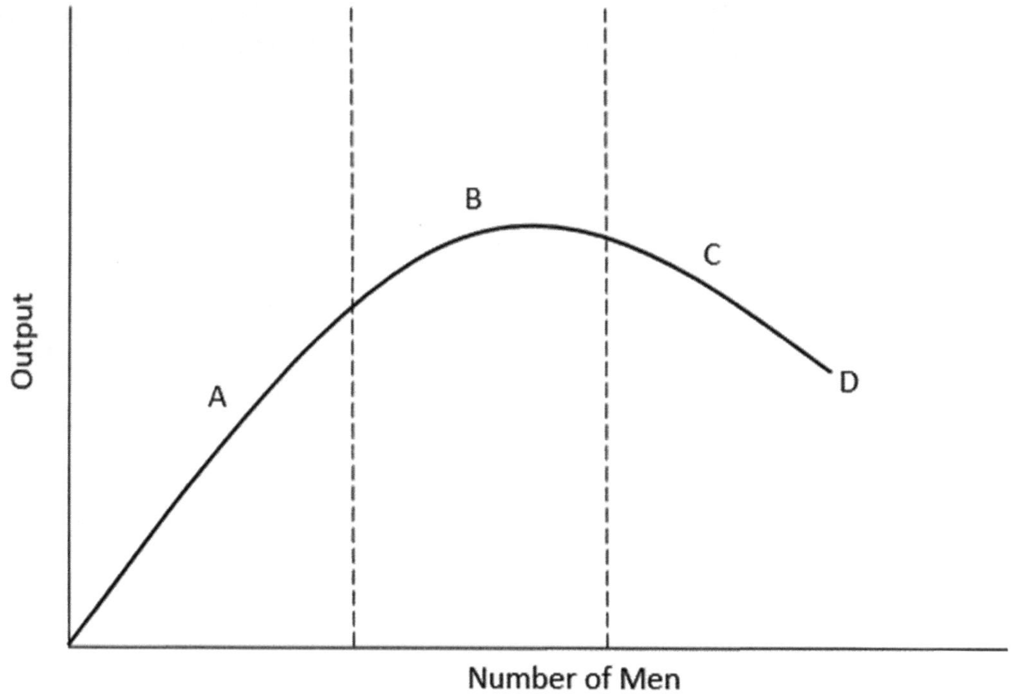

a. A
b. B
c. C
d. D

29. A cotton mill owner wants to know his equity in the business. According to his balance sheet for the previous year, the warehouse premises are valued at $1 million, the factory equipment is valued at $1 million, and inventory is valued at $800,000. Debtors owe the business $400,000. The balance sheet also indicates that he owes the bank $500,000, creditors $800,000, and the wages and salaries owed stand at $800,000. Calculate his owner's equity.

a. $1.1 million
b. $2.7 million
c. –$1.6 million
d. –$800,000

30. Futures contracts are mainly used by hedgers, speculators, and arbitrageurs and play a pivotal role in the market of agricultural commodities. Which statement is incorrect?

a. Hedging is a means to control or eliminate risk and is used by those that are averse to taking risks.
b. Speculation depends on risk in the hope of making good returns and is used by those who are not afraid to take risk to seek a larger profit.
c. Speculation is used to minimize or eliminate the probability of substantial loss of profits due to movements in the price of the underlying asset.
d. Arbitrage involves the simultaneous buying and selling of an asset to profit from small differences in price.

31. A business owner is interested in expanding the product line that her business sells. She wants to make sure that her business has the funds to expand the product line. Which calculation would be the most useful for her?

a. Enterprise budget
b. Free cash flow
c. Capital expenditures
d. Net income

32. Risk is involved with any business and can affect agribusinesses even more. A crop farmer wants to reduce the risk in his business. Which is NOT a way he can reduce risk?

a. Try different production practices.
b. Invest in crop insurance.
c. Incorporate new technology into production.
d. Eliminate contract production to increase flexibility.

33. A first-year cattle farmer is completing an enterprise budget. He sold 80 cows for a total of $60,000. He spent $15,000 on feed, pasture management, and veterinary expenses. He spent an additional $20,000 on machinery repair. During this first year, he paid off his $30,000 farm loan that was used to purchase cattle. He also paid $25,000 on machinery and land loans and insurance. He suffered a $5,000 equipment depreciation fee. Calculate his return above total costs.

a. $25,000
b. –$60,000
c. –$35,000
d. $55,000

34. There are two types of accounting that can be used: single-entry and double-entry methods. Which is an example of an incorrect entry using the double-entry method?

a. Sales revenue of $500 would be entered into the balance sheet account called "cash" and into the income statement sheet called "revenue."
b. A $1,000 computer purchase would be a $1,000 debit to decrease your income statement "technology" expense account and a $1,000 credit to increase your balance sheet "cash" account.
c. When a business borrows money from the bank, the assets will increase by the loan amount, and the liabilities will also increase by the loan amount.
d. Goods purchased for resale will increase the assets and decrease the "cash" account.

35. Balance sheets are useful tools for businesses. The balance sheet is one of the most basic fundamentals of business accounting. Which of the following statements is not true about balance sheets?

a. The balance sheet equation is: net income = revenues – expenses.
b. The balance sheet equation shows what a company owns, what a company owes, and what stake the owners have in the business.
c. Claims on the company assets are separated into two categories: liabilities and equity.
d. Assets are the resources that the company has to use in the future such as cash, accounts receivable, and fixed assets.

36. Large businesses and corporations often use stocks and shareholders to limit liability and increase worth. Which item is NOT correctly defined?

a. A stock is a unit into which the capital worth of a corporation has been divided.
b. A dividend is money distributed to a stockholder as his or her share of the company's profits.
c. A resource is an item that controls or directs a business operation.
d. Capital is a collection of valued resources made by people and used for production.

37. Businesses have both fixed and variable costs. An example of a fixed cost would be ________, whereas an example of a variable cost would be _________.

a. raw materials; rent
b. labor; shipping
c. advertising; depreciation
d. insurance; commission

38. Commodities futures are commonly used in agricultural commodity markets. Commodities futures are agreements to buy or sell a raw material at a specific date in the future at a particular price. Which description of agricultural commodity futures is correct?

a. Buyers of food, energy, and metal use futures contracts to fix the price of the commodity they are purchasing to increase the risk that the prices will go up.
b. If the price of the underlying commodity goes up, the buyer of the futures contract loses money. He or she gets the product at the lower, agreed-upon price and must sell it at the lower price.
c. Commodity sellers use futures to guarantee the best possible market price. Commodity prices fluctuate daily. Futures allow sellers to take advantage of the highest price point.
d. If the price goes down, the futures seller makes money. He or she can buy the commodity at today's lower market price and sell it to the futures buyer at the higher, agreed-upon price.

39. Agricultural economics focuses on the economic side of producing, marketing, and selling agricultural commodities. Due to the growing population and decreasing resources available, a focus on intensive production and sustainability has emerged. Which explanation is false?

a. Intensification is the term used to describe more intensively using current land. This is often resulting from increased application of non-land inputs, technology change, or a combination of the two.
b. The allocation problem is solved by asking people what they would pay for certain commodities and then cost fixing at the consumer recommended price.
c. Extensification is using more land for crop and livestock production.
d. The philosophy of scarcity states that we run into scarcity because as a society we have unlimited wants but limited resources and therefore must efficiently allocate resources.

40. Plants can be classified into two main types based on their structural features. Which of the following does not correctly explain the classification?

a. Monocots have one cotyledon, whereas dicots have two cotyledons.
b. The root system of monocots is a taproot system, whereas the root system of dicots is fibrous.
c. Monocot floral parts exist in multiples of threes, whereas dicot floral parts exist in multiples of four or five.
d. The vascular bundles of monocots are arranged in complex patterns, whereas the vascular bundles of dicots are arranged in a ring.

41. Plants use the process of photosynthesis to store energy. What is the equation for photosynthesis?

a. $6CO_2 + 6H_2O \rightarrow C_6H_{12}O_6 + 6O_2$
b. $CO_2 + H_2O \rightarrow CH_2O_3 + O_2$
c. $C_6H_{12}O_6 + 6O_2 \rightarrow 6CO_2 + 6H_2O + ATP$
d. $CO_2 + 4H_2S + O_2 \rightarrow CH_2O + 4S + 3H_2O$

42. Which of the following best describes the relationship between photosynthesis and respiration in plants?

a. Photosynthesis creates usable sugar in the form of glucose that the cells can utilize. Respiration is the process of the cells using glucose to perform cellular functions.
b. Respiration creates types of energy for cells. Photosynthesis is the process of breaking the energy down into usable adenosine tri phosphate (ATP) that the cell can use.
c. Photosynthesis creates glucose that the cells can use to create energy. Respiration is the process of breaking the glucose down into ATP that the cell can use.
d. Respiration occurs before photosynthesis takes place and pulls in carbon dioxide into the plant. Photosynthesis is dependent on respiration to provide the carbon dioxide needed for photosynthesis to take place.

43. A grower has a 9' x 128' bench over which he wants to suspend supplemental high-intensity discharge (HID_ lighting that is 400W. The plants that will be grown on the bench perform best with a light intensity of 8600 lux or 800fc. The effective flux of the HID lights is 38,400 lumens. Calculate the number of lights the he will need to cover the growing bench.

a. 30
b. 55
c. 3
d. 24

44. A nursery business is adding greenhouses to expand the amount of plants that they can offer. They have decided to use hoop houses framed with aluminum pipes. Explain the covering that would be best suited to cover their greenhouses.

a. Glass would be the best suited to cover their greenhouses. Glass is resilient and lasts a long time, ensuring that they get the most value for their money spent. Clean glass also allows maximum light transmission.
b. Polycarbonate panels would be the best choice to cover their greenhouses. The flexible, thin wall sheeting is a strong insulator and can easily last more than 20 years. Polycarbonate is cheaper than glass to install and allows almost as much light transmission as glass.
c. Polyethylene plastic film is the best choice to cover their greenhouses. Polyethylene is extremely affordable and resilient, lasting several years before being replaced. Polyethylene is flexible enough to easily cover the contour of the hoop house structure.
d. Acrylic panels are the best choice for the greenhouse. The acrylic panels are inexpensive and provide similar light transmission as glass. The acrylic panels are also more resilient than glass.

45. When propagating softwood and semi-hardwood cuttings, it is important to ensure that all steps of the propagation process are followed. Explain how softwood and semi-hardwood cutting propagation is similar to hardwood propagation.

a. Both softwood and hardwood cuttings require light so that the cutting can provide itself food during rooting.
b. Both softwood and hardwood cuttings are commonly taken from ground shoots around the mature parent plant.
c. Both softwood and hardwood cuttings should always be treated with a rooting hormone before being placed in a rooting medium.
d. Both softwood and hardwood cuttings should be covered with a plastic bag to keep the humidity around the plant high.

46. Many plants can reproduce asexually, without gamete fertilization taking place. Asexual reproduction can take place by either vegetative reproduction or apomixis. Which is a correctly paired asexual reproduction type and example?

a. Garlic—corm
b. Ginger—rhizome
c. Potato—corm
d. Strawberry—ground shoots

47. A landscaping company is purchasing fertilizer for their summer business. They typically purchase an 18-8-10 blend of fertilizer that comes in manageable 10 pound bags. They estimate that they will need 80 pounds of phosphorus. How many bags of fertilizer will they need?

a. 80
b. 100
c. 1,000
d. 90

48. A soil's ability to support plant life is perhaps one of its most important contributions to human life. When viewing soil, which horizon is typically the lowest that plant roots will grow?

a. Horizon O
b. Horizon A
c. Horizon B
d. Horizon C

49. An extension agent is called to test the soils of potential crop locations. The crops will vary from year to year. After testing the soils, she determined that there were four main soil types present. Which soil type would be most suited to a crop rotation system?

a. Sandy clay
b. Loamy sand
c. Silty clay
d. Clay loam

50. At a soil judging competition, the soil in one pit is moderately well-drained clay loam with no rock fragments. There is a fragipan at 26". Calculate the available water holding capacity for this pit.

a. 5.20
b. 3.9
c. 1.3
d. 6.4

51. A farmer is using soil amendments to adjust his soil's texture, pH, and aeration. He can use ________ to ____________.

a. lime; lower the soil pH
b. sulfur; raise the soil pH
c. perlite; improve moisture retention
d. gypsum; improve the soil aeration

52. Humans have been responsible for the introduction of plant species in many areas where they would not normally grow. An example of this seen in the southeastern United States is kudzu. According to the US Department of Agriculture, which term cannot be used to describe kudzu in the southeastern United States?

a. Exotic
b. Invasive
c. Translocated
d. Noxious

53. The structures of plants have multiple functions. Explain the less discussed functions of roots, leaves, stems, and reproductive structures.

a. Roots can often store large quantities of plant food and reproduce in some plant species.
b. Fruit functions in seed propagation of the plant and attracts pollinators.
c. The stem anchors the plant and aids in food and water movement and storage.
d. The leaves, the main body of the plant, function in transpiration and water absorption.

54. An apple orchard would fall under which plant science classification?

a. Olericulture
b. Pomology
c. Horticulture
d. Floriculture

55. There are multiple types of intercropping. Intercropping can reduce pest populations, increase land productivity, and prevent erosion. Chili peppers are often intercropped with coffee in Colombia. The coffee plant grows to 3 meters in height and requires full sun. The chili pepper plant is smaller and can grow in shaded areas. Which intercropping system would be best suited to growing coffee and chili peppers in the same field?

a. Relay cropping
b. Row intercropping
c. Contour strip cropping
d. Field strip cropping

56. Why do large particles of food usually not make it into the ruminant intestinal tract?

a. The rumen has many folds of microvilli that trap larger particles of food.
b. The reticulum holds large amounts of bacteria that prevent large particles from passing.
c. Large particles get trapped in the leaves of the omasum, trapping them in the stomach.
d. The abomasum, the largest stomach compartment, holds strong acid that breaks all food particles down.

57. Calculate a balanced ration for a total 15 percent crude protein using soybean meal (45% CP) and corn (10% CP).

a. 10 parts corn, 45 parts soybean meal
b. 45 parts corn, 10 parts soybean meal
c. 5 parts corn, 30 parts soybean meal
d. 30 parts corn, 5 parts soybean meal

58. A cattle producer notices multiple calves that lay around and do not attempt to get up. This is most likely ___________, caused by ___________.

a. white muscle disease, selenium deficiency
b. pica, phosphorus deficiency
c. bloat, excess gas buildup
d. grass tetany, pastures with high nitrogen or potassium content

59. A cattle producer is choosing a new bull to use with first calf heifers in her Angus breeding operation. She is given the following expected progeny differences (EPD) information:

Bull	BW	WW	YW	Milk
1	6.6	31.3	39.5	–5.6
2	0.1	14.6	24.6	6.0
3	0.0	0.3	11.1	18.9
4	–5.9	–3.8	–14.4	10.3

Based on the information in the EPD table, which is the most productive bull for the operation?

a. Bull 1
b. Bull 2
c. Bull 3
d. Bull 4

60. Using the chart, at which point would the mare be most fertile for breeding?

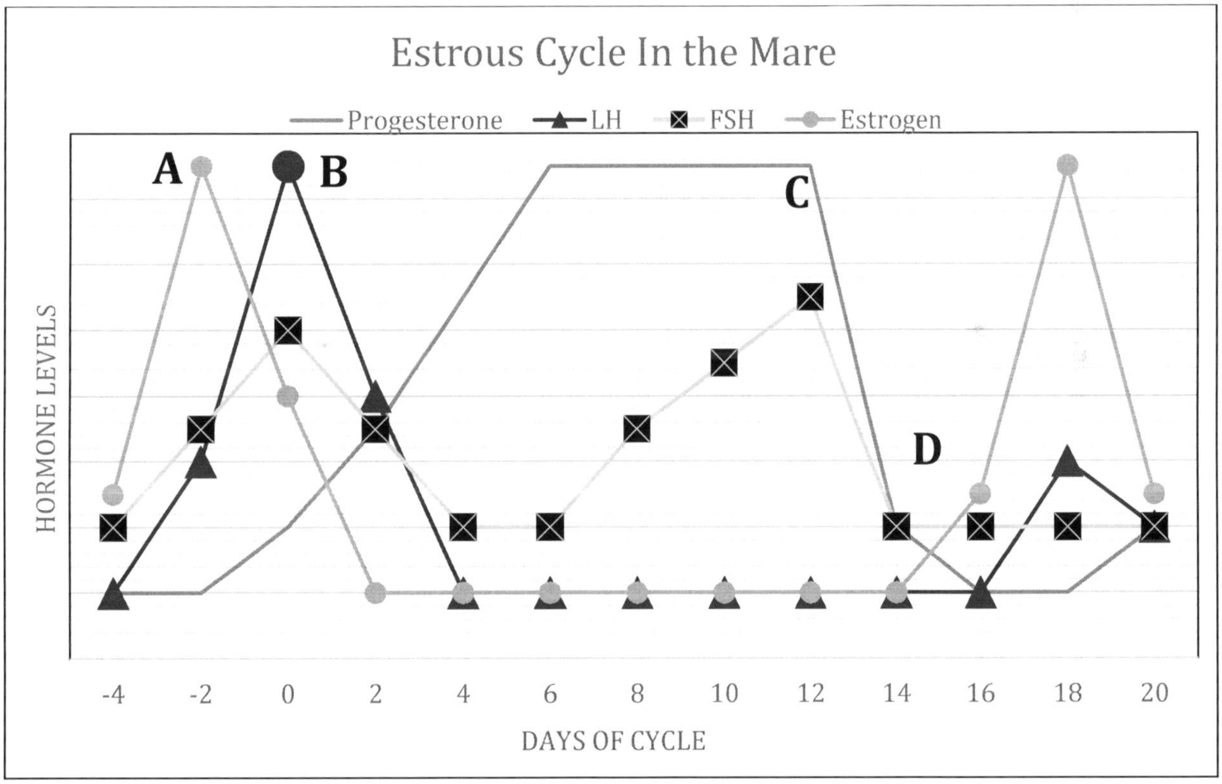

a. Point A
b. Point B
c. Point C
d. Point D

61. A goat owner purchases a new doe to use in his dairy herd. His veterinarian determines that she is approximately 10 months old. What clue did he use to determine her age?

a. Her horns only had two rings on them, and each ring indicates approximately six months of age.
b. Her top teeth were all in but did not have the characteristic groove seen in goats older than two years.
c. Her bottom teeth were all still small and fairly equal in size.
d. Her mutton joint wasn't completely fused, which occurs around one year of age.

62. Parasite control is imperative for livestock producers. The following are parasite control routines that are commonly seen in the livestock industry. Which parasite control routine has been proven both ineffective and harmful?

a. A race horse farm performs fecal samples on their horses. The horses are wormed only when the fecal samples have high counts of parasites.
b. A goat farmer routinely worms the goats in her dairy breeding herd every eight weeks due to the large amount of barber pole worms in the area.
c. A cattle farmer uses rotational grazing methods with his cattle. The cattle rotate pastures so that the grass does not get shorter than four to six inches.
d. A producer raises both sheep and cattle on the same pastures in a co-grazing system to help control parasites.

63. A swine producer has four boars that he is considering using as replacement boars in his breeding program. He is paid incentives to produce lean carcasses. Based on the performance data, which of the boars is most likely to sire the most productive offspring for his operation?

Boar	Days to 250	BF	LEA	Stress
1	135	0.75	7.00	Pos
2	138	0.61	7.50	Neg
3	148	0.78	7.20	Neg
4	152	0.60	8.10	Neg

a. Boar 1
b. Boar 2
c. Boar 3
d. Boar 4

64. Livestock producers can implement breeding systems to improve the quality of their livestock herds. Which breeding system is incorrectly described?

a. A rancher uses Quarter Horses to cut and sort his cattle. Many of his horses come from the same sire, several generations back. This sire can be found in many cutting horse lineages. This is an example of incross breeding.
b. A pork producer gets paid incentives for highly marbled meat products. To achieve this, he only raises Berkshire pigs. The Berkshire sows are bred to registered Berkshire boars. This is an example of a purebred breeding system.
c. A cattle farmer in South Mississippi wants to raise cattle that have a high level of heat and pest resistance as well as high-quality meat. She has a herd of purebred Brahman cows that she breeds to purebred Angus bulls. This is an example of a crossbreeding system.
d. A sheep producer wants to increase the staple length of her herd's wool. She breeds her ewes to rams using artificial insemination so that she can select rams with higher staple length EPDs to increase her herd's staple length in each generation. This is an example of grading up.

65. In cattle, black coat color and horns are dominant traits, whereas red coat color and being polled are recessive traits. If a bull that is heterozygous for both horns and coat color is crossed with a polled cow that is heterozygous black, what are the odds that the resulting calf will be both polled and red in color?

a. Out of 16 possible gene combinations, 6 calves would be both polled and red.
b. Out of 16 possible gene combinations, 4 calves would be both polled and red.
c. Out of 16 possible gene combinations, 12 calves would be both polled and red.
d. Out of 16 possible gene combinations, 2 calves would be both polled and red.

66. A boar stud farm is implementing a new biosecurity plan to protect its boar herd from contracting disease and minimizing the spread of pathogens. The following items are being proposed to implement in the biosecurity plan. Identify the item that does NOT fall under biosecurity planning.

a. People handling the animals must step through a foot bath both before entering and after leaving barns where pigs are.
b. After a group of pigs leaves a barn, the barn is cleaned and sanitized prior to a new group of animals moving in.
c. When pigs leave the farm, they are moved onto the trailer at night and transported in cool weather to minimize pathogen growth.
d. Animals that are brought into the farm must come with a clean bill of health and remain in isolation for 90 days.

67. A horse breeder is giving annual vaccinations to a breeding herd. One of the vaccinations is to be given IM, whereas two others are to be given SQ. Which of the following statements is correct?

a. SQ stands for subcutaneous and should be given into the muscle tissue directly under the skin of the neck.
b. IM stands for intermuscular and should be given into the muscle tissue directly into the muscle of the neck or the hindquarter.
c. SQ stands for skin quarters and should be divided into fourths and given in four different areas of skin on either side of the neck.
d. IM stands for intramuscular and should be given into muscle tissue along the neck or the hindquarter.

68. Scientific names are used to give living organisms names that are universal and can be used in every country by every language. These differ from common names, which can vary greatly from countries and even within countries. Identify the correctly written and identified livestock scientific name.

a. *Capra hircus*—sheep
b. *Bos indicus*—cattle
c. *Sus scrofas*—swine
d. *Gallus gallus domesticus*—chickens

69. Explain why a cattle producer would be interested in performing embryo transfer.

a. Embryo transfer allows producers to maximize the production of one high-quality cow.
b. Embryo transfer allows producers to sell semen at a more reasonable price than the donating animal can be purchased for.
c. Embryo transfer gives producers the opportunity to delete unwanted genes from a potential offspring.
d. Embryo transfer gives producers a way to market their bull herd more effectively.

70. An agriculture teacher is coaching his livestock judging team about the importance of visual assessment of livestock. A student asks the following question: "When we are looking at breeding gilts to breed for a terminal system, what is the most important trait to assess?"

a. A terminal system is used to produce breeding offspring, so the most important trait to look at is overall muscle quality and balance.
b. A terminal system is used to produce animals for meat, so the most important trait to look at is overall muscle mass.
c. When looking at gilts that will be used for breeding, the most important trait to look at is foot and leg structure.
d. When looking at gilts, or any animals, that will be used for meat production, the most important trait to look for is the muscle leanness and shape.

71. A cattle producer is working cattle and brings an emasculator with him. Identify the situation that requires an emasculator.

a. Castration
b. Gestation
c. Lactation
d. Parturition

72. A cattle farm is purchasing new heifers for their breeding herd. The owner contacts a farm about a potential heifer to get more information about her. The heifer's owner tells the farm owner that she is up to date on all vaccines, open, and an M1. Which of the following statements are true?

a. M1 means that the heifer is a hybrid cross created by crossing two purebred animals.
b. M1 means that the heifer has a moderate frame size and is well-muscled and of good beef quality.
c. M1 describes the amount of marbling in the heifer's muscle tissue, which can indicate a high quality score.
d. M1 describes the approximate size of the loin eye area, estimated by ultrasound at the 13th rib.

73. A research scientist is studying the crop of an organism's digestive system. Which group of animals does this scientist study?

a. Avian
b. Bovine
c. Porcine
d. Equine

74. A veterinarian is checking an animal that is overdue for parturition by a couple of days. The animal's length of gestation is 283 days when the veterinarian checks her. What type of animal is the veterinarian checking?

a. Horse
b. Sheep
c. Pig
d. Dairy cow

75. A car that is currently driven in Miami, Florida, uses 10W-40 oil. The owner is moving to Alaska with the car. Which oil would a mechanic most likely recommend for the car in Alaska?

a. 10W-40 with added graphite
b. 5W-40 with added graphite
c. 5W-30
d. 10W-30

76. A student welded two metals together during an agricultural mechanics shop class and showed his instructor. The instructor notices the weld is full of brittle, intermetallic compounds and is a weak weld joint. What two metals did the student most likely weld together?

a. Stainless steel and cold-rolled steel
b. Cast iron and nickel
c. Low carbon steel and high carbon steel
d. Aluminum and cold-rolled steel

77. In an electrical circuit, 3 volts are applied across a 6Ω resistor. Calculate the current.

a. 0.75 A
b. 0.5 A
c. 2 A
d. 6 A

78. Gear reduction can be used to either reduce speed and increase torque or increase speed and decrease the torque. An electric motor drives a 13-tooth pinion gear that meshes with a 65-tooth gear. If the electric motor speed is 3,450 rpm with 10 lb-in torque, what is the speed and torque after reduction?

a. Speed = 690 rpm; torque = 50 lb-in
b. Speed = 50 rpm; torque = 690 lb-in
c. Speed = 17,250 rpm; torque = 50 lb-in
d. Speed = 1,323 rpm; torque = 4.0 lb-in

79. An agricultural mechanics shop is labeling the safety hazards to meet Occupational Safety and Health Administration (OSHA) standards. They learn that one area is incorrectly labeled. Identify the mislabeled hazard.

a. The fire extinguisher near the exit door is red and held in a red, wall-mounted extinguisher box.
b. The storage cabinet that is used to hold flammable materials and liquids is painted yellow.
c. The machines in the shop have dangerous parts painted orange.
d. The lockout-tagout cards are purple in color.

80. A new hire for a construction framing company is packing a tool belt. Which three items are most important for him to have in a tool belt?

a. Tape measure, speed square, and compass
b. Chisel, chalk line, and framing hammer
c. Tape measure, framing hammer, and speed square
d. Chisel, nail gun, and contour guide

81. A field is 0.5 km long. The starting end of the field is determined to be 340 meters above sea level. The elevation at the ending side of the field is 420 meters above sea level. Calculate the percent slope of the field.

a. 1.6 percent
b. 25 percent
c. 16 percent
d. 84 percent

82. The two most common types of internal combustion engines are diesel engines and gasoline engines. Which of the following statements is NOT true?

a. Both diesel and gasoline engines are designed to convert thermal energy into mechanical energy.
b. In a gasoline engine, fuel is mixed with air and ignited with a spark from a spark plug.
c. In a diesel engine, fuel is injected into compressed air, which causes the fuel ignition.
d. Gasoline engines use a carburetor to mix fuel and air together and then inject the mixture, whereas diesel engines use injectors to inject a fine mist of fuel into the compressed air.

83. Many engineers who desire a high degree of precision often request a nonconsumable electrode welding technique. Which of the following is a nonconsumable electrode form of welding?

a. MIG
b. TIG
c. SMAW
d. FCAW

84. Welding stick rods are classified by a system created by the American Welding Society (AWS). The AWS created a standardized coding system to indicate specific electrode properties with a combination of numbers and letters located on the sides of individual welding rods. Which welding rod would be the most versatile rod to use?

a. E6010
b. E6024
c. E6022
d. E6013

85. Copper pipe has been used in the United States for plumbing for more than 70 years. CPVC, a newer alternative to copper, is a commonly used plumbing option in the United States today. Which of the following statements is not true regarding copper and CPV materials for plumbing?

a. CPVC is a more financially stable option and is accepted by all major building codes.
b. Copper is more durable and is much less prone to break or crack on the job site if it is dropped or stepped on.
c. Copper is acceptable for potable water, drains, vents, natural gas supplies, and pressure steam.
d. CPVC has remained fairly stable in terms of price, whereas the cost of copper has risen slightly and is more likely to be stolen.

86. Global positioning systems (GPS) and geographic information systems (GIS) are two relatively new pieces of technology. GPS is more commonly known, whereas GIS is not as well-known. Which is NOT a function of GIS?

a. Location analysis
b. Data mapping
c. Proximity analysis
d. Locating positions

87. A machinist is creating replacement parts for industrial equipment. The metals she is using are sensitive to heat and must be precise. Which cutting method is most suitable for the current task?

a. Water jet
b. Lathe
c. Punch
d. Plasma cutter

88. A new homeowner in Texas realizes that his electric bill seems higher than it should be. He wants to check his kilowatt hour usage. He starts with an appliance that uses 12 amps and is used 20 hours per day. Calculate the number of daily kilowatt hours used.

a. 52.8 kwh
b. 28.8 kwh
c. 14.4 kwh
d. 12.0 kwh

89. Circuit breakers are the load center for the electrical circuits in homes and buildings. They are often called breaker boxes. Which statement is NOT true about breaker boxes?

a. The main circuit breaker is a double-pole service disconnect and controls the live power energizing the circuits in the electrical panel.
b. The main circuit breaker identifies the total amperage capacity of the service panel and is usually indicated with a number (i.e., 150, 100, or 200).
c. Single-pole breakers provide 120 volts and have a typical rating of 15 to 20 amps.
d. Arc-fault circuit interrupter (AFCI) breakers protect an entire circuit from ground faults.

90. Wiring is often labeled to help identify the wire material, size of wire, and the type of insulation. Which wire is coated in a synthetic, flame-retardant insulation?

a. XHHN
b. THWN
c. THW
d. THHN

91. Conduction, convection, and radiation describe the ways that heat energy is transferred. Which description is an incorrect example of heat transfer?

a. The inside of a greenhouse is heated with convection.
b. Putting wet shoes on the floor vent to dry uses conduction.
c. Touching a metal spoon that is in a pot of boiling water is conduction.
d. Warming your hands over a warm fire uses radiation.

92. Copper pipes must be soldered properly to seal. Which statement is incorrect regarding soldering copper pipe?

a. A wire brush is needed to remove burrs from inside of the pipe.
b. A flux dip is used to clean the pipe surface and prepare for the solder.
c. A torch is used to melt the wire that solders the copper pipes together.
d. The joint should be filled with solder until it drips out, then the excess can be wiped away.

93. Insulation is used to prevent heat flow through materials and is commonly used in homes and businesses. What does the R-factor measure?

a. Conduction
b. Radiation
c. Convection
d. Infiltration

94. Conductors are objects that allow the flow of electricity and insulators prevent it. An example of a conductor is ________, and an example of an insulator would be _________.

a. concrete; ceramic
b. asphalt; steel
c. pure water; oil
d. salt water; graphite

95. Young plants absorb nitrogen in the form of ammonium more readily than they do nitrate. However, older plants absorb nitrate faster than ammonium. A farmer tests the soil to see which type of nitrogen needs to be added to the field and finds a large amount of ammonium and little nitrate. Explain why there could be less nitrate in the field.

a. There is an abundance of nitrifying bacteria present in the soil that is creating large amounts of volatile nitrogen.
b. Frequent storms are fixing too much atmospheric nitrogen, creating an abundance of nitrite.
c. Ammonia is not being nitrified by bacteria, possibly due to antibiotics coming into contact with the soil and killing the nitrifying bacteria.
d. Nitrogen-fixing bacteria are converting nitrate into nitrite too rapidly.

96. One of the most common ways to classify molecules is by sorting them as either organic or inorganic molecules. Identify which of the following molecules is NOT an organic compound.

a. $C_6H_{12}O_6$
b. C_6H_6
c. $NH_2CH(C_4H_5N_2)COOH$
d. $CaCO_3$

97. DDT was commonly used in the past to control mosquito populations. This pesticide was found to have a pronounced impact on bird populations. Explain how DDT affected the bird populations.

a. The toxin DDT accumulated in both the mosquito and bird populations due to bioaccumulation. The birds came into contact with DDT in the environment, like the mosquitoes, and died.
b. DDT was absorbed readily by mosquitos, which are lower on the food chain than birds. Each trophic level above the mosquito received increased concentrations of the DDT due to biomagnification.
c. Many birds are consumers of insects, including mosquitoes. When the birds ate the mosquitoes treated with DDT, the amount of DDT in the birds did not increase but had enough of an effect to kill many birds due to toxic nature of DDT.
d. The birds consumed the mosquitoes that were treated with DDT. All animals in trophic levels below the mosquitoes experienced increased concentrations of DDT in their bodies due to bioaccumulation.

98. The graph illustrates a population growth chart for a population of white-tailed deer in a given area. A pack of wolves is released into the same area. Where on the graph is the carrying capacity reached?

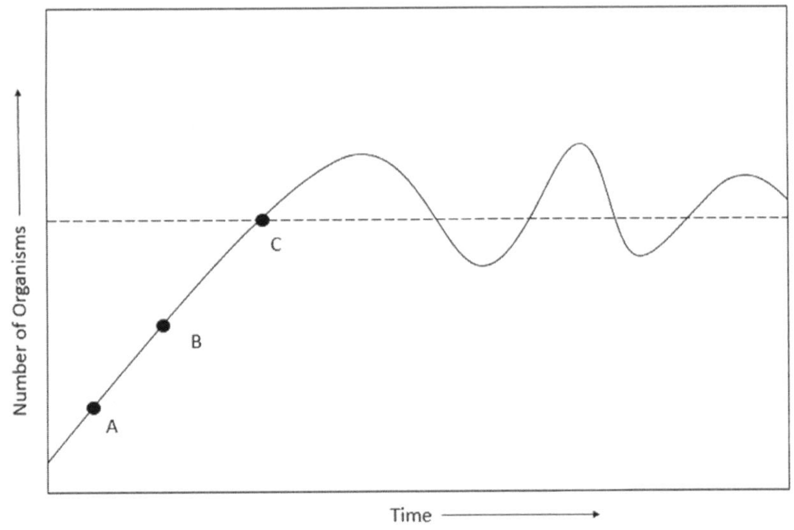

a. Point A
b. Point B
c. Point C
d. Along the dotted line

99. A mature forest was completely destroyed after a wildfire removed all of the vegetation. The area is starting to see regrowth—what is happening?

a. Primary succession
b. Secondary succession
c. Forest succession
d. Autogenic succession

100. A large feeder swine operation is classified as a large concentrated animal feeding operation (CAFO). Which legislative act should the operation be most concerned with?

a. Clean Air Act
b. Endangered Species Conservation Act
c. Noise Control Act
d. Clean Water Act

101. The increase in the threat of global warming has led to the proposed decreased use of fossil fuels as an energy source. These energy sources are being used less, with renewable energy use becoming more popular. Which statement about alternate energy sources is NOT correct?

a. Photovoltaic cells transform sunlight into useable energy. These are not commonly used on a large scale due to the higher cost and land requirements.
b. Turbines have become popular in states like Texas, Oklahoma, and Kansas, where winds are frequent. The turbines provide a cheap energy source and do not require much land space.
c. Hydropower is a small energy source for electricity in the United States. Hydropower relies on rapidly moving water to spin turbines and converts the motion into power.
d. Tidal and wave energy is being explored as an alternate energy option. Harnessing wave and tidal power relies on dam-like structures or ocean-floor-anchored devices that interfere with local ecosystems.

102. Environmental researchers can use indicator species to identify when toxins or pollutants are disrupting the habitat. A team of researchers is studying the effects of pollutants near a recreational lake used for fishing. Which would be best suited as an indicator species?

a. White-tailed deer
b. Largemouth bass
c. White oak tree
d. American bullfrog

103. Renewable resources are resources that can be harvested and replenished when used sustainably. Nonrenewable resources are natural resources that cannot be replenished within 100 years. Choose the statement that does NOT correctly explain the natural resource.

a. Trees are a common renewable resource when managed sustainably. Many forested areas that are harvested can be replanted and harvest again within 50 years or less, making trees a renewable resource.
b. Mega-dams are often considered a form of nonrenewable energy. These giant hydroelectric dams require intense changing of the environment, causing so much damage to the water cycle that they are classified as nonrenewable sources of energy.
c. Soil is considered a renewable resource. Soil that is eroded away is simply relocated to another location and is not truly consumed. Soil can be replenished by relocating it, making it a renewable resource.
d. Fossil fuels are a nonrenewable resource despite the fact that the Earth's crust continues to make fossil fuels. The fuels are consumed so rapidly by humans that the fossil fuels being produced cannot keep up with the current demand.

104. Intensive agriculture can have negative impacts on the environment. Soil erosion and fertilizer runoff are common issues that can have detrimental effects on ecosystems thousands of miles away. Which choice best explains how fertilizer runoff in the northern Midwest can most impact the ecosystems in the Gulf of Mexico.

a. Fertilizer runoff is created when excess fertilizer leaches down into the soil and the water table. Excess potassium from the runoff gets into the water that humans consume and then into the water waste systems, which make its way down to the Gulf of Mexico.
b. Fertilizer runoff is created when farmers use excessive fertilizer that the plants cannot use. Excess nitrogen and phosphorus run off of the fields during rain events and get into the river ways and eventually the Mississippi River, where they are poured into the Gulf of Mexico.
c. Fertilizer runoff contains high levels of nitrogen, which feeds algae blooms in the Gulf of Mexico. The algae blooms grow rapidly, and when they decompose, they use up the available oxygen in the water, causing massive dead zones where organisms cannot live.
d. Dead zones caused by fertilizer runoff in the Gulf of Mexico can be linked to agriculture in at least 12 states in the United States, including Minnesota. The dead zones impact the fishing and shrimping industries in the Gulf of Mexico.

105. Abiotic and biotic factors both contribute to an ecosystem. To survive, biotic factors require abiotic factors. Biotic factors can also limit other biotic factors in an ecosystem. An example of a(n) ___________ factor would be a(n) ___________.

a. abiotic; detritivore
b. biotic; climate
c. abiotic; edaphic factor
d. biotic; social factor

106. The Environmental Protection Agency (EPA) and the Clean Water Act define point and nonpoint pollution. Both pollution types are controlled and monitored by the EPA. An example of a point solution would be ___________, whereas an example of a nonpoint solution would be ______________.

a. nutrients and bacteria released from a sewage treatment facility; nutrients and bacteria from livestock operations
b. pharmaceuticals released into water from faulty treatment facility pipes; salt from irrigation
c. stormwater discharge; acid drainage from abandoned mines
d. thermal pollution from factory smokestacks; atmospheric deposition

107. Soil is a major resource required by agriculture and the environment. The productivity and health of soil is used to determine the productivity of an area. Which method of preventing soil erosion is correctly defined?

a. The no-till method disturbs the soil very little, if at all, to reduce erosion by using a machine to insert the seed into the soil.
b. Contour planting is used when farming on sloped land. Steps are cut into the soil or crops are planted on the slope of land to reduce the rate of water runoff.
c. Terracing plants crops in rows that are perpendicular to hills to form water breaks that prevent soil erosion.
d. Strip cropping uses a row of trees planted as a windbreak to prevent soil erosion due to wind.

108. A consumer has been recently diagnosed with celiac disease. He is shopping for baking items to replace old items in his pantry that will irritate his newly diagnosed disease. Which of the following items is he most likely shopping for?

a. Organic
b. Gluten free
c. Low fat
d. Sugar free

109. Nutrition labels can provide consumers with valuable information regarding food composition. Which of the following is NOT true?

a. All ingredients in a food item must be listed on the label, in order, from largest amount to smallest amount.
b. Fat, protein, and carbohydrates can be used to calculate the calories in a food.
c. All calorie listings are based on a 100-gram serving.
d. Sodium amounts should be listed on the label, measured in milligrams.

110. The US Department of Agriculture requires a country of origin label (COOL) in many instances for many food items. Which statement is true regarding the COOL law?

a. Fruit and vegetables must be correctly and individually labeled with the country of origin, requiring the use of food-safe ink.
b. COOLs are required internationally and must be marked on both US imports and exports.
c. The COOL law is required in full-line grocery stores, supermarkets, and club warehouse stores.
d. The COOL law includes beef, pork, lamb, goat, chicken, fish, and shellfish.

111. The US Department of Agriculture uses quality grades to evaluate meat products. Which grade would be served in a five-star restaurant?

a. Select beef
b. Prime beef
c. Choice beef
d. Utility beef

112. Pasteurization is a food-processing procedure that involves rapidly heating and then cooling a food product to kill potential pathogens. Many food items are frequently pasteurized. Which of the following is not frequently pasteurized?

a. Butter
b. Fruit juice
c. Vinegar
d. Honey

113. A strawberry farmer wants to increase her customer reach by offering more products. Which of the following would NOT be a value-added product that she could sell?

a. Strawberry jam
b. Bulk boxes of strawberries
c. Organically produced strawberries
d. U-pick strawberries

114. A common processing method used in the dairy industry is __________, which ______________.

a. pasteurization; separates fat globules
b. homogenization; forces fat globules through a sieve to mix them
c. homogenization; rapidly heats and cools products to kill potential pathogens
d. fermentation; allows aerobic bacteria to create chemical changes in the product

115. There are many methods of increasing the shelf life of foods. Which is the best method to increase the shelf life of processed meat products?

a. Wrapping them in one-sided waxed freezer paper
b. Vacuum sealing the products, ensuring a complete seal before freezing
c. Freezing in meat trays and cellophane wrap
d. Using an irradiation method and then freezing in meat trays and covering in cellophane wrap

116. The US Department of Agriculture (USDA)requires inspections of live animals that are slaughtered and intended for resale meat product production. Which description is NOT true regarding the inspection process?

a. The USDA contracts individually licensed livestock veterinarians to inspect livestock before the animals are slaughtered to ensure the animal is apparently free from disease and is in good health.
b. USDA officials must be present for all slaughters that result in meat products that can be sold to consumers in butcher shops, meat markets, and grocery stores.
c. USDA inspectors are individuals trained by the USDA and must attend training through the Food Safety and Inspection Service (FSIS) prior to working as inspectors.
d. Inspectors oversee the slaughter of the animals to ensure humane treatment and perform postmortem inspections that include detailed lymph node inspections.

117. There are many trends in food production that can be misleading. Which statement regarding poultry and egg food labeling is true?

a. The Humane Farm Animal Care (HFAC) Free Range label designates that animals are raised outdoors on pasture, providing at least two square feet per bird.
b. The HFAC Pasture Raised label designates that birds are raised entirely on pasture and provide at least 108 square feet of space per bird on rotated fields.
c. The USDA Cage Free label is used to claim that birds are raised free of forced caging or housing. Birds can be kept in poultry fenced acreage with voluntary housing provided.
d. Naturally Raised labels indicate poultry meat products that are raised without growth promotants, antibiotics, or animal by-products in the feed.

118. With the rapidly growing human population, it is no surprise that increasing the food supply has become a major topic of concern. Many biotechnological advances have been developed to increase food supply. A greenhouse farmer in the Southeast who grows tomatoes is shipping the majority of his crop to European countries. What biotechnology would he most likely be interested in?

a. Genetically modified organisms (GMOs) with increased yields
b. GMOs with longer shelf life
c. GMOs with herbicide resistance
d. GMOs with drought resistance

119. Hazard analysis and critical control points are commonly used to maintain food processing safety standards. Which of the following statements is NOT true regarding Hazard Analysis Critical Control Points (HACCP)?

a. A control point is any step at which biological, chemical, or physical factors can be controlled.
b. A hazard is a biological, chemical, or physical agent that is reasonably likely to cause illness or injury in the absence of its control.
c. A step is a point, procedure, operation, or stage in the food system from primary production to final consumption.
d. A critical control point is failure to meet a critical limit.

120. Both the US Department of Agriculture (USDA) and Food and Drug Administration (FDA) are responsible for inspection of food and food processing. There is often confusion as to which federal agency inspects which products. Which is an item inspected by the FDA and not the USDA?

a. Ground beef
b. Cage-free eggs
c. Gulf-caught shrimp
d. Farm-raised catfish

Answer Key and Explanations

1. A: Choice B is similar to the correct mission statement but uses incorrect terms (academics, development, and lifetime) toward the end of the mission statement. Choice C is the National FFA motto. Choice D provides two ways that the National FFA Organization strives to implement the mission statement, but this is not the mission statement itself.

2. C: To calculate this, first you must complete a Punnett square cross for the potential offspring. To create a Punnett square cross, you must determine the genotypes of the cow and the bull. The cow is polled; therefore, her genotype must be hh (polled is recessive). The bull is horned but has produced both horned and polled offspring; therefore, his genotype must be Hh as he can pass both genotypes to his offspring. After filling out the Punnett square, it's easily determined that two out of four potential offspring will be horned, and two out of four potential offspring will be polled.

3. A: The only student eligible to receive an American degree is the graduated National FFA member. Students can receive American degrees after they have been graduated from high school for at least a year and meet all other requirements. Students must be members of FFA for at least three years and must have received a Greenhand degree, Chapter degree, and a State degree before becoming eligible to receive the American degree. The National Proficiency Award is an award separate from the American degree.

4. D: According to the Agricultural Marketing Service vegetable grading standards, tomatoes can be sorted into US No. 1, US No. 2, US No. 3, and US Combination grades. US No. 2 tomatoes must meet certain quality requirements, including being free from sunscald. US No. 3 tomatoes, however, need only be free from serious damage caused by sunscald. Because the tomato described has sunscald but is not seriously damaged by it and is misshapen while still being mature and free from decay and freezing injury, it would most likely be classified as US No. 3.

5. B: Alumni memberships are available to former active or collegiate National FFA members. Citizen memberships are not a type of membership within the National FFA Organization. Active membership is available to students at a secondary school with an active FFA chapter. Alumni memberships are reserved for former active or collegiate members. Collegiate memberships are for students at postsecondary schools with active FFA chapters. Honorary FFA memberships can be presented to individuals who have served the National FFA Organization or agricultural education.

6. B: If the landscaping company would have started the job in the winter, they could have applied a pre-emergence herbicide that would prevent any seeds from developing. Because they are starting in the spring, they will need to use a nonselective herbicide to remove all plant growth. This will kill all existing plant growth to eliminate any competition that the Bermuda grass would have. Selective herbicides are used in lawn care to kill weeds but will not kill grasses that would compete with the Bermuda. A postemergence herbicide that is specific to broadleaf weeds would kill only the weeds in the lawns and not the other grass types. The remaining grass types would still be competition for the Bermuda grass.

7. B: The term *supplemental* is used to describe a type of supervised agricultural experience (SAE). Supplemental SAEs are performed in addition to other SAE projects. Agriscience is the basic course that agricultural education students begin an agricultural education program with. Experiment is also not used in the acronym.

8. C: Red, white, and blue are American flag colors, not the colors of the National FFA Organization, even though the FFA is a national organization. Although the FFA jackets are made with blue corduroy, corduroy blue is not the official shade of blue. The FFA jackets are colored national blue, the official blue of FFA. Harvest yellow and bumblebee yellow are also not the official shade of yellow. The National FFA Organization adopted national blue and corn gold as the official colors of FFA in 1929. National blue is the same blue as that on the American flag, and corn gold is the color of golden fields of ripened corn. Corn is grown in every state, so national blue and corn gold represent that FFA is a national organization.

9. C: Natural resources will cover the concepts of forestry and sustainable forestry management. The student will learn the economics of how agricultural businesses affect one another in agribusiness and agricultural economics. Choice A mentions plant and soil science, which could give some input into forestry. Agribusiness focuses on business types and business management, but this course alone doesn't have a strong focus on economics. Choice B lists natural resources and environmental science, which would give understanding into forestry, but they would not cover the economics needed to understand the relationships among forestry and other businesses. Choice D is completely unrelated to economics or forestry.

10. A: The National FFA's motto is "learning to do, doing to learn, earning to live, and living to serve." Choice B is a statement made by attending National FFA members during the opening ceremony of FFA meetings. The FFA salute, also the Pledge of Allegiance, is given in Choice C. Choice D is one of the 11 points in the Code of Ethics for FFA members.

11. D: According to Maslow's theories, a person's physiological needs must be met first. This includes food, water, warmth, and rest. Once physiological needs are met, safety needs such as the feelings of safety and security can be met. Next, the needs of love and belonging can be met. This includes the need for friendships and intimate relationships. Esteem needs are met next and involve meeting the need for prestige and accomplishment. Last, self-actualization needs can be met. These include creative activities and meeting one's potential. The theory states that higher needs cannot be met unless the levels of needs below them have been fulfilled.

12. C: There are five symbols included on the National FFA emblem: the rising sun, the plow, the owl, the eagle, and the cross section of an ear of corn. Owls have traditionally been associated with wisdom and represent that knowledge is required in agriculture. Agriculture requires labor and soil cultivation; therefore, it is represented with the plow. The rising sun signifies progress and holds a promise that tomorrow will bring a new day filled with opportunity. The eagle is a national symbol that serves as a reminder of our freedom and ability to explore new horizons for the future of agriculture. The cross section of the ear of corn not only represents the foundation of agriculture, but it is also a symbol of unity, as corn is grown in every state of the nation.

13. D: Although lesson plans can be used by teachers, students, and administration, the key purpose of lesson plans is to give the teacher a guide or reference during a time of instruction. Lesson plans can also be a useful tool when reviewing material or lessons for effectiveness at the end of the year.

14. D: During the opening ceremony, each officer is responsible for reciting statements. The president opens the ceremony and turns the ceremony over to the vice president to call the roll of officers. Each officer position recites a statement explaining the officer's role. The ceremony is then turned back over to the president, who then makes the statement, "Thank you. FFA members, why are we here?"

15. A: Motions must be seconded. Seconding a motion does not mean approval of a motion but that it should be discussed. After a motion is seconded, the chair states the motion, which opens the floor for discussion. Members then can debate the discussion. After debate has taken place, the chair presents the question, and the members vote on the motion. The chair then states the results of the vote.

16. C: The student development section covers activities that are related to individual student growth: supervised agricultural experience (SAEs), convention attendance, and so on. The chapter development section covers activities that help grow the Future Farmers of America (FFA) chapter: membership percentage, fund-raisers, and so on. The community development section outlines activities that will get students involved with the community: food drives, volunteer work, and so on. Activities added to the program of activities should be added to the proper section, not the amendments section.

17. A: The bronze emblem pin is awarded to Greenhand degree recipients, which can be given only to first-year National FFA members members. Students receiving a Chapter degree receive a silver emblem pin. Students receiving a State degree will receive a gold emblem pin. The gold key and chain pin are presented to American degree recipients.

18. B: The first step in establishing a new National FFA chapter is to contact the state supervisor of agricultural education to make him or her aware of the founding chapter. The advisor will complete an application packet with the supervisor to begin the chapter founding. The local school board administration should approve of the new chapter and create any necessary funding or accounts for the chapter. The advisor shall draw up a chapter constitution and program of activities and help members elect officers for the new chapter. The only time contact with the National FFA Center is required is if the new chapter is located in a US territory, such as the Virgin Islands.

19. C: National FFA chapters are encouraged to have chapter officer leadership training (COLT) sessions. These sessions are used to prepare officers for their official duties and can be used to brainstorm ideas. COLT sessions can occur over small time increments, for example, lunchtime on Wednesdays, or over extended periods of time, such as an officer retreat weekend.

20. D: A course syllabus should be flexible and should not give "hard" dates for tests and assignments in case they should be changed later. An estimate of sections covered and due dates will suffice. Although a course syllabus should introduce the material covered in the course, a paragraph outlining the course objective or main ideas is enough. The syllabus should include materials required for the classroom and describe what any fees or dues cover. The syllabus should list rules or expectations for the classroom but does not have to list school or district-wide rules. These should be found in the school or district student handbook. A course syllabus should be intended to give students a brief overview of the course, what the teacher expects, and what the students can expect. Contact information for the teacher should be listed on the syllabus.

21. C: Whole child learning includes transformational leadership, global engagement, poverty and equity, redefining student success, as well as teaching and learning. Flipped learning introduces students to new lessons at home so that they can dig deeper into the content in the classroom. Project-based learning allows students to apply knowledge and skills in real-world project applications. Differentiated instruction allows teachers to divide their teaching time to meet the needs of all students in the classroom.

22. C: The seven intelligences are linguistic, logical-mathematical, visual-spatial, body-kinesthetic, musical-rhythmic, interpersonal, and intrapersonal. Visual-spatial learning is the ability to mentally visualize objects and spatial dimensions. Audial learning is a learning method and not one of the seven intelligences in Gardener's theory. Intrapersonal is the ability to understand one's own emotions, motivations, inner states of being, and self-reflection. Interpersonal is the ability to understand and communicate with others. Linguistic students have a strong ability for the written and spoken word.

23. A: The stages of development in the Model of Hierarchical Complexity are: calculatory, automatic, sensory or motor, circular sensory-motor, sensory-motor, nominal, sentential, preoperational, primary, concrete, abstract, formal, systematic, metasystematic, paradigmatic, cross-paradigmatic, and meta-cross-paradigmatic (or performative-recursive). The nominal stage is defined as being able to use names for objects or simple commands. The primary stage is defined as being able to add, subtract, multiply, divide, count, prove, or perform a series of tasks alone. The sensory stage is when children can move limbs or their heads to view an object. The formal stage is the 11th stage of development and is reached when students can use algebraic, empirical evidence or logic to argue.

24. C: Bloom's Taxonomy breaks question or activity types into levels of understanding: remember, understand, apply, analyze, evaluate, and create. Webb's Depth of Knowledge breaks questions into four levels: recall, skill/concept, strategic thinking, and extended thinking. Asking higher-order questions allows the student to show a deeper knowledge about the content. Choice A would fall into the Bloom's apply level. Students are taking a concept (energy conservation) and explaining why it is important to study. Choice B falls into the create category. The student is familiar enough with a concept that he or she should be able to design an experiment to test concepts. Choice D is a simple remember, or recall, question. The student can memorize the steps of the scientific method and repeat them. Choice C is the only option that falls into the evaluate category. Students must understand an experiment and concepts well enough that they can explain potential points of error in an experimental design.

25. B: Authoritarian leaders take control of a classroom and lay down rules and regulations to be followed. This is most likely the type of leader that the mentor teacher is. Democratic leaders take votes or the opinions of those they are leading into consideration. Laissez-faire literally means "let go" and is a highly ineffective way of maintaining order in a classroom. Laissez-faire leaders are successful only when managing people who are highly self-motivated. This is likely the leadership style of the teacher next door. Servant leaders work to encourage, support, and enable others to reach a goal. Charismatic leaders are enthusiastic and create a sense of purpose in people. It's important to note that teachers are not usually completely one leadership type or another. Good educators can skillfully combine leadership types to encourage students, promote independence, and maintain order.

26. A: A corporation would allow the brothers to protect their personal assets, and they can serve as the directors of the corporation to make business decisions. A partnership would allow the brothers to share management, but it would not help protect their personal assets. A cooperative is owned and controlled by the people who purchase and use the goods the cooperative produces. A sole proprietorship is a business that is owned and operated by one individual, and the individual's assets are linked to the business.

27. D: Diversification involves adding more products to the products that a company currently sells. Specialization involves creating one product or multiple products from one particular commodity. Choice A is an example of diversification, whereas choice C is an example of specialization. Choice B would neither diversify the products nor specialize products. Because the orchard currently grows only Fuji apples, the specialization should be on Fuji apple products. The owner can diversify the product line by adding additional products created using Fuji apples.

28. B: This graph represents the law of diminishing returns. The law of diminishing returns states that that if one factor of production (e.g., number of workers) is increased, while other factors (e.g., machines and workspace) are held constant, the output per unit of the variable factor will eventually diminish. Although the productivity of the workforce decreases as output increases, diminishing returns do not mean negative returns until (in this example) the number of workers exceeds the available machines or workspace. In this graph, point A represents the point of increasing product output, whereas point C represents the amount of decreasing output. The point just before the dramatic decrease is the point of diminishing returns, shown as point B.

29. A: The equation to calculate owner's equity is: owner's equity = assets – liabilities. In this example, the assets would be the warehouse premises, the factory equipment, the inventory, and debt owed to the mill. Total these amounts to calculate $3.2 million in assets. The liabilities include money owed to the bank and creditors as well as wages and salaries. Total these amounts to calculate $2.1 million in liabilities. To find owner's equity, plug the numbers into the equation: $3.2 million – $2.1 million = $1.1 million. This means the cotton mill business is currently worth $1.1 million.

30. C: As each market for the same stock moves, market inefficiencies, pricing mismatches, and even exchange rates can affect the prices of commodities temporarily. Hedging is used to minimize or eliminate the probability of profit loss by minimizing the risk. Speculators use risk to try to make larger profits. Arbitrage is used to both increase profits and reduce risk. Arbitrageurs will often purchase stock from one location (e.g., the New York Stock Exchange) and simultaneously sell it at another location (e.g., the London Stock Exchange) to increase profits.

31. B: Free cash flow calculates how much cash a business generates after accounting for capital expenditures such as buildings or equipment. This cash can be used for expansion, dividends, reducing debt, or other purposes. To calculate free cash flow, the following equation is used: free cash flow = net income + non-cash expenses - increase in working capital - capital expenditures. Calculating free cash flow requires multiple steps but is one of the most useful calculations that a business owner can make to determine the financial health of a business. An enterprise budget is an estimate of the costs and returns to produce a product. Although this would be helpful to her, she needs to determine if the business can afford to expand first. Net income measures a business's profit (revenues minus expenses, including interest on debt), but because it is based on accrual accounting and excludes capital expenditures and principal debt repayments, it may not reflect the actual cash available for expansion.

32. D: There are many risks that affect agribusinesses. These risks can be categorized into five general areas: production, marketing, financial, legal, and human resources. One of the best ways to reduce risk is to become more flexible as a producer. A row cropper may be interested in multicropping practices to offer more commodities. Crop insurance is a way to manage risk that is created by weather conditions. New technology is also a way to decrease risk (e.g., a chemical pesticide that can kill crop-destroying pests). Contract production is a way to decrease risk as well. Contracts provide producers with a set price and a guarantee to purchase. Eliminating contracts can increase risk. Producers may not sell for as high of a price and may not sell all of the produced good.

33. C: An enterprise budget is broken down into production, operating costs, and fixed costs. To calculate the return above total costs, the following equation can be used: return above total costs =

production – total costs. The total costs can be calculated by adding the operating costs with the fixed costs. In this example, the operating costs include the feed, pasture management, veterinary services, and machinery repair. Fixed costs include the farm loan, machinery and land loans, insurance, and depreciation. These values can then be plugged into the equation: returns above total costs = $60,000 – ($35,000 + $60,000).

34. B: In this example, the computer purchase should be entered as a $1,000 debit to increase the income statement "technology" expense account and a $1,000 credit to decrease the "cash" account. The double-entry accounting method requires a chart of accounts, which consists of all of the balance sheet and income statement accounts in which accountants make entries. As a company's business grows, the likelihood of clerical errors increases. Although double-entry accounting does not prevent errors entirely, it limits the effect any errors have on the overall accounts. The double-entry accounting method is a way to double-check that accounting entries are accurate.

35. A: The balance sheet equation is: assets = liabilities + equity. The equation net income = revenues – expenses is the equation used to calculate net income. The balance sheet equation is also often called the accounting equation. The balance sheet displays the company's total assets and how these assets are financed, through either debt or equity. It can also be referred to as a statement of net worth or a statement of financial position.

36. C: A resource is wealth or an asset. Regulatory items are items that control or direct a business operation. An agribusiness manager must be familiar with the options that are available to managing wealth and assets of a company. Agribusiness managers must also be aware of the different types of business management and how resources, stocks, and shareholders affect the management. Businesses can be sole proprietorships, individuals, joint ventures, or corporations. Each business types has different involvement and liabilities associated with it.

37. D: Sales commissions are dependent on sales being made, making it a straightforward example of a variable cost. Fixed costs are costs that are independent of output and are fairly constant. Examples of fixed costs include rent, advertising, depreciation, insurances, taxes, and so on. Variable costs are dependent on production output and can change considerably over time. Examples of variable costs include raw materials, labor wages, shipping costs, and sales commissions.

38. D: Commodities futures create a contract to sell a good at a set amount. Commodity buyers use futures contracts to fix the price of the commodity they are purchasing. That reduces their risk that prices will go up. Sellers of these commodities use futures to guarantee they will receive the agreed-upon price, removing the risk of a price drop on their end of the agreement. Commodity traders can fulfill the contract by delivering proof that the product is in the warehouse. They can also pay the cash difference or provide another contract at the market price.

39. B: The allocation problem asks the question: what do you do with resources that cannot be priced, such as air or water? This question is becoming increasingly pressing for agriculture economists as the growing population rapidly depletes resources, including air and water. Extensification and intensification are two methods that are being used to supply the increasing demand for food and other agricultural commodities. The philosophy of scarcity explains partially how the demand for commodities has superseded the supply.

40. B: The root system of monocots is fibrous, and the root system of dicots is a taproot system. Another distinct difference between the two plant types can be seen in the leaf veins. Monocots usually have parallel leaf veins, whereas dicots have netlike leaf vein patterns. The differences between cotyledons, vascular bundles, and floral parts can help determine whether a plant is a monocot or dicot. An example of a monocot would be a corn plant. An example of a dicot would be a maple tree.

41. A: Plants use photosynthesis to combine carbon dioxide, water, and sunlight to create glucose and oxygen. The equation of photosynthesis must be balanced correctly. During the process, plants will use six molecules of carbon dioxide and six molecules of water to create one molecule of glucose and six molecules of oxygen. Choice B is the same general equation but does not have the appropriate number of molecules. Choice C gives a related equation, that of cellular respiration. The last equation given in choice D is a chemosynthesis equation illustrating how chemosynthetic bacteria can oxidize hydrogen sulfide and add carbon dioxide and oxygen to produce sugar, sulfur, and water.

42. C: Photosynthesis stores glucose as a form of energy. Cellular respiration is the process of breaking down the glucose into a usable form of energy: adenosine tri phosphate (ATP). The ATP is created through either aerobic or anaerobic respiration. Respiration does create carbon dioxide as a by-product, but it is not required to take place before photosynthesis begins to take place.

43. D: Greenhouse growers often use supplemental lighting to increase the production of greenhouse-grown plants. Knowing how many supplemental lighting fixtures to use is important to decrease unnecessary costs and increase production. To calculate the number of lights required, use the equation N = (light level x surface area)/effective flux. N is the number of fixtures. This equation would be [(800 x 9 x 128)/38,400] = 24.

44. C: The structure of a hoop house is semicircular; therefore, a flexible covering is required. Glass and acrylic panels, although they last a long time, are both some of the most expensive options for covering a greenhouse. Polycarbonate panels are also expensive and do not have the flexibility needed to cover a hoop house. For this reason, most hoop house structures are covered in polyethylene plastic film.

45. B: Softwood and semi-hardwood plants are typically harder to propagate than hardwood plants are and require more care. To propagate cuttings from softwood plants, the cuttings can be taken from either the tip of a branch or a ground shoot. The cutting is treated with rooting hormone and inserted into moist rooting medium. The atmosphere around the cutting must be controlled using plastic bags or mist systems to keep humidity and moisture high. Softwoods are propagated while they have leaves, so they need access to sunlight to create food. Hardwoods are propagated during dormancy and have no leaves. This lowers the amount of maintenance that the cutting needs as it is not actively performing photosynthesis. Hardwoods do not need to always be treated with rooting hormones and can expect a 60 percent to 80 percent rooting percentage. Hardwoods are also commonly taken from ground roots around the mature parent plant.

46. B: Garlic is a bulb, not a corm. A bulb is an underground bud that forms around a central stem. A corm is solid, whereas a bulb includes layers of immature leaf tissue. A potato is an example of a tuber, which is a modified root formation used to both reproduce and store starch. A strawberry sends out immature plants that are stolons. When these stolons touch the ground, they develop roots and eventually become a separate plant from the parent plant. Ginger is a rhizome, which is a mass of stems that can create multiple plants.

47. B: Fertilizer blends are often described and usually labelled with three numbers. These three numbers describe the amount of nitrogen, phosphorus, and potassium, respectively. In this example, the fertilizer bag contains 18 percent nitrogen, 8 percent phosphorus, and 10 percent potassium. In a 10-pound bag of 18-8-10, there is 0.8 pounds of phosphorous. To get 80 pounds of phosphorus, they will need 1,000 pounds of the fertilizer. The fertilizer comes in 10-pound bags, so they will need to order 100 bags of the fertilizer.

48. C: Horizon O is the rich organic layer of soil often present as a dark, black line at the top of the soil. Horizon A is the surface or topsoil layer, which is rich and generally darker in color. Directly under this is Horizon B, the subsoil. Subsoil is generally lighter in color than the topsoil layer but still has enough water and nutrients to support plant root growth. The texture of the subsoil is usually light enough that roots can develop. Horizon C is the parent material. Parent material has a dense texture that prevents root growth. Parent material often lacks the color and structure of the other soil horizons.

49. D: Loamy soil is the best suited for many crops and can easily support growth with its almost equal combination of sand, silt, and clay particles. Loamy soil is well drained and has a high water holding capacity. Sandy clay has very little silt present and is mostly clay with some sand. Loamy sand is between 70 percent and 90 percent sand with a small amount of clay and very little silt present. Silty clay is mainly clay with a small amount of silt present. Silty clay is suitable for growing crops but can have frequent water drainage issues due to the lack of sand. Clay loam is mostly clay with nearly equal amounts of silt and sand, allowing for moderate drainage. Therefore, of the options given, clay loam would be most suited to the crop rotation system due to its superior water holding capacity and drainage ability.

50. A: To calculate available water holding capacity (AWHC), determine the texture of the soil and the rooting depth. The texture of the soil will determine how much water can be held in the soil. A coarse soil will hold 0.05 inches of water per inch of soil, a medium soil holds 0.20 inches of water, and a fine-textured soil holds 0.15 inches of water. The rooting depth of most crops is generally stopped at 36 inches. Rock fragments of 15 percent or more will reduce the AWHC by the percentage equal to the percentage of rock fragments. Do not calculate the effect of rock if there is less than 15 percent. If there are two separate textures in the topsoil and subsoil, calculate them separately, and then add the two to get the AWHC. A fragipan is a hard, dense layer of soil that will prevent root growth. If a fragipan is present, do not calculate AWHC below the fragipan. For this example. 26 inches x 0.20 inches/inch = 5.20 inches available water capacity.

51. D: Lime can be used to raise the soil pH, reducing acidity. Sulfur can be used to lower the soil pH, reducing the alkalinity of soil. Perlite is often used to improve soil aeration and drainage. Vermiculite can be used to improve moisture retention and aeration. Gypsum is used to improve aeration and drainage of compacted soil.

52. C: A translocated plant is a plant that is moved to a new location on the same continent that it is native to. Kudzu is originally from Japan, so it is not native to the North American continent. Exotic plants are plants not native to the continent on which it is now found. Invasive plants are plants that are both non-native and, due to the lack of competition, are able to spread rapidly and disrupt plant communities or ecosystems. Noxious plants are defined as troublesome and can directly or indirectly cause damage to crops, livestock, agriculture, irrigation, navigation, or natural resources.

53. A: Roots are commonly discussed as being the anchor for the plant and absorbing nutrients. They also store large amounts of food and can reproduce in many plant species. The fruit is the structure that carries the plant. It is often used as the mode of transporting the seed. It can also protect the seed and nourish a young seedling. The stem, the main body of the plant, supports it and contains passages (xylem and phloem) that transport food, water, and nutrients between the leaves and root system. The leaves are mostly known for being the site of photosynthesis. Leaves also protect the plant from losing too much moisture through guard cells and transpire through stoma.

54. B: Pomology is the agricultural science of growing fruit. Olericulture is the science of growing vegetables. Horticulture is the science of garden cultivation and management. Floriculture is the cultivation of flowers from ornamental plants for gardens and floristry.

55. B: To maximize the shade provided by the coffee plant, chili peppers should be grown between each row of coffee plants in a row intercropping system. Relay cropping involves another crop on top of an existing mature crop before it is harvested. This is commonly seen with wheat being planted after other crops have been harvested. Strip cropping is an intercropping system in which two types of crops are planted in strips. The strips may be several rows wide before the strip ends. There are two types of strip cropping: field and contour. Contour strip cropping uses strips that follow the contour of the land and are common in areas that have uneven topography. Field strip cropping uses straight strips of crops across the field.

56. C: The ruminant stomach is composed of four compartments: the rumen, reticulum, omasum, and abomasum. The rumen is the largest compartment that holds fermentation bacteria. The reticulum is the second compartment where food is further fermented and passed into the omasum. The omasum, often referred to as the "leaves of the Bible," is full of folds of tissue that both absorb water and trap larger particles, preventing them from passing into the abomasum. The abomasum, or the true stomach, contains strong acid that breaks down digested matter.

57. D: This is calculated using the Pearson's square method. The total crude protein goes into the center of the square. The protein amounts for corn and soybean meal go on the upper left corner and lower left corner. The amounts are subtracted on the diagonal. To calculate parts soybean meal, subtract 15 – 10 to get 5 parts soybean meal. To calculate parts corn, subtract 45 – 15 to get 30 parts corn, then 5 parts soybean meal + 30 parts corn = 35 parts total.

58. A: White muscle disease is a common nutrient deficiency in cattle and results in weak calves that lay on the ground. Pica, a result of phosphorus deficiency, causes calves to chew and nibble on non-food items. Bloat is characterized by cows laying on their sides with largely bloated rumens due to excess gas buildup from bacteria in the rumen. Grass tetany is typically seen in lactating cows and older cattle. Grass tetany results in muscle spasms and convulsions due to low magnesium or high nitrogen or potassium.

59. B: When interpreting EPD data, it is important to remember that these values represent expected progeny differences. The EPD table gives us values for birth weight (BW), weaning weight (WW), yearling weight (YW), and milk. Because the bull will be used on first-calf heifers, a bull with moderate birth weights should be chosen. However, an ideal bull would have calves with moderate BW along with larger weaning and yearling weights. Bull 4 can be eliminated quickly as it will produce calves that are consistently small. Bull 1 can also be eliminated quickly, as BW is too large for first-calf heifers. When comparing Bulls 2 and 3, they have comparable BW. However, Bull 2 calves will out produce Bull 3's calves in both WW and YW. Bull 2 is the best choice for the scenario.

60. B: Estrogen, progesterone, luteinizing hormone, and the follicle-stimulating hormone all work together to grow a follicle to maturity, release the egg, and prepare the female reproductive tract for pregnancy. Estrogen will cause the mare to exhibit signs of heat slightly before an egg is released. The mare is considered most fertile right before the egg is released. The egg is released with the peak of the luteinizing hormone. Progesterone, the pregnancy hormone, peaks and remains high after the release of the egg to prepare for pregnancy. Follicle-stimulating hormone also peaks a few days after the release of an egg to prepare another egg if fertilization does not occur.

61. C: Goats cannot be aged by rings on their horns; only sheep can. Goats, like all other ruminants, do not have top teeth. Horses can be aged by viewing indicators on the top teeth. Mutton joints are used to age and classify sheep carcasses as either lamb carcasses (less than one year and unfused mutton joint) or mutton (greater than one year and fused mutton joint). Goats can be approximately aged by viewing their bottom teeth. The bottom teeth are all fairly equal in size until one year of age. The center two teeth grow larger, followed by the teeth beside them, until all bottom teeth are fairly long.

62. B: In the past, animals were dewormed frequently and routinely, usually every six to eight weeks. However, this led to internal parasite populations that were resistant to antiparasitic drugs. These resistant populations were extremely difficult and expensive to treat. Today it is recommended that these drugs are used only as needed to prevent resistant parasite populations. Co-grazing animals is an effective way to prevent parasites, as most parasites are species specific. Rotational grazing also helps control parasite populations, as the animals don't consume the lower portions of the grasses where parasite eggs are. Fecal samples are an effective way to determine the parasite load of an animal and determine if parasite treatment is necessary.

63. B: This producer wants pigs that will create lean cuts of meat quickly. Days to 250 indicates how many days it took these boars to reach 250 pounds. The lower this number is, the better. Backfat (BF) numbers should also be low because this producer wants lean meat. Loin eye area (LEA) should be high as this is the measurement of the LEA in inches squared. Breeding animals should always test negative for the stress gene. Using this information, Boar 1 can quickly be eliminated due to the positive stress gene he carries. Boar 4 can also be eliminated because of the longer time it took him to reach 250 pounds. With Boars 2 and 3 left, it's easy to choose Boar 2 due to his shorter days to 250 and lower BF amount.

64. A: Linebreeding, crossbreeding, purebred breeding, and grading up are a few of the breeding systems that can be used. Purebred breeding creates animals that are one breed and eligible for registration with a breed organization. A linebreeding system is a breeding system that continues to breed back to one individual. This form of inbreeding can increase the homozygosity for desired genes, as seen in the Quarter Horse cutting industry. Crossbreeding crosses two separate lines of animal breeds. Grading up is a breeding system commonly used by producers to continuously improve the productivity of their herds. A crossbreeding system is used to increase the heterozygosity of animals and combine two different breeds of animals to get potentially "the best of both worlds."

65. D: To calculate the gene combinations, you must first determine the parent genotypes. The bull is heterozygous for both horns (Hh) and black coat (Bb), whereas the cow is polled (hh) and heterozygous for black coat (Bb). The bull's genotype is HhBb, and the cow's genotype is hhBb. These genotypes can be split into alleles and combined to create the possible genotype combinations. For the bull, the possible combinations are HB, Hb, hB, and hb. For the cow, the possible combinations are hB, hb, hB, and hb. After completing a two-factor Punnett square, you will notice that six should be black with horns, six should be black and polled, two should be red with horns, and two should be red and polled.

66. C: The purpose of a biosecurity plan is to minimize the growth and transporting of pathogens, that is, disease-causing organisms. A biosecurity plan aims to reduce illness on a farm. Many illnesses can be transmitted accidentally on the feet of animal handlers; therefore, footbaths are a common measure seen on operations with biosecurity. The footbaths can reduce contamination from barn to barn. When a group of animals is removed from an area, the area is cleaned, sanitized, and given a resting period before a new group is moved in. This removes pathogens from the barn and prevents the new animals from coming into contact with possible pathogens carried by the previous group. Any time that animals are brought onto a farm for replacement from another farm, they must come with a clean bill of health from a veterinarian. This includes being up to date on vaccinations and not showing outward signs of illness or disease. Many biosecurity plans require that animals remain in isolation in case there is an underlying illness. Swine infections can take longer to manifest, so the isolation period suggested for pigs is 90 days. Transporting pigs at night can help reduce heat stress but has no effect on preventing pathogen growth.

67. D: IM stands for intramuscular (not intermuscular) and should be given into large areas of muscle tissue. In horses, IM injections are typically given into neck muscle or hindquarter muscle. SQ stands for subcutaneous and is given into the skin tissue only, not into the muscle. For SQ injections, the skin is pulled up and tented to give the needle room for injection.

68. D: When writing scientific names, the genus and species are both written in italics. The genus is capitalized, whereas the species is not. When there is a variety or subspecies, that name is written in lowercase after the species name. Answer choice A is incorrect because the scientific name for sheep is *Ovis aries*. *Capra hircus* are goats. Cattle have two scientific names depending on the type of cattle. Answer choice B is incorrect because domesticated bovine are *Bos taurus* while humped cattle (zebu) are *Bos indicus*. Answer choice C is also incorrect because *Sus scrofa* are wild boar while *Sus domesticus* are domesticated swine. Answer choice D, *Gallus gallus domesticus*, is the correct scientific name for chickens as they are considered a subspecies of the red jungle fowl, or *Gallus*.

69. A: Embryo transfer is a process that allows producers to get the most out of a high-quality breeding female. For example, a breeder may have a purebred Angus heifer with outstanding performance data, genetics, and overall style. The breeder would want to breed her as much as possible to maximize the offspring that she would have. However, she will have only one calf per year. He can cause her to superovulate and flush the embryos. These embryos can be fertilized and transferred to other cows to grow and raise. This can allow that top-quality cow to have multiple offspring with her genetic makeup each year. Embryo transfer itself does not provide gene manipulation, insertion, or deletion. It also does not affect semen prices or bull prices because the process revolves around the mother.

70. C: Breeding animals and market animals are viewed differently when judging and comparing livestock. A market animal is viewed best by asking the question: "Which animal will I get the most pounds of high-quality meat from when on the rail?" In market animals, overall leg structure isn't as much of an issue because the animals will not live long enough to see ill effects of poor structure. However, breeding animals must have sound structure and good framework. Animals that have good structure will live longer and be more productive than ones with poor structure. Although meat quality, muscling, and overall appearance are important for livestock breeding animals, in breeding gilts, feet and legs must be structurally correct. Pigs are well-known for having lameness issues from feet and leg structure and will break down quickly, resulting in sows that are not productive.

71. A: An emasculator is a tool used to crush the spermatic cords of male livestock to sterilize them. Castration is the term used to describe a process used to sterilize a male. This can be done by removing the testicles surgically or through banding. Emasculators and emasculatomes can also sterilize livestock. Gestation is the term used to describe the length of time an animal is pregnant.

Lactation is the term used to describe the time period that an animal is nursing young. Parturition is the term used to describe giving birth.

72. B: M1 is a frame score. Frame scores indicate the overall predicted frame size of the animal as small, moderate, or large (S, M, or L) and are scored 1 to 4 based on the muscling and fat cover present. Heifers with a score of 1 are well-muscled, whereas 4 indicates thin and almost no muscling. An M1 would indicate a moderately framed heifer with good muscling and fat cover. An F1 is a term used in genetics to indicate a cross between two parental pure animals. Quality and yield grade scores are not given until after slaughter so that muscle tissue can be measured and analyzed. Quality and yield grade are often used to determine if incentive payments will be given.

73. A: The crop is a digestive organ found in bird species. Avian refers to livestock species of birds (i.e., turkey and chickens). Bovine refers to beef and dairy cattle. Porcine is a term used to describe pigs. Equine is used to describe horses. Ovine is a term that is used to describe sheep. Caprine is used to describe goats. Avian digestive systems are unique in that they contain a crop and a gizzard. These organs provide similar functions to the stomach of other livestock animals but are found only in birds.

74. D: Gestation is the length of time that an animal is pregnant. The average length of gestation for both beef and dairy cattle is 281 days. Because the animal in the question is a couple of days overdue, it is safe to assume that the animal is a cow. Parturition is a term used to describe the act of giving birth. The gestation length of sheep is 147 days. The gestation length of pigs is 114 days. The gestation length for horses is 340 days.

75. C: When reading the label on oil, the numbers indicate the viscosity of the oil. The first number tells the viscosity in low temperatures. The second number tells the viscosity when the engine is running and warm. Thicker oil is indicated by a larger number. In colder climates or during the winter, 5W oils are better because they resist thickening when cold. In hotter climates, a thicker oil is better for the car, so a 40 would be best. That's why the car was using a thicker oil. When the car is in Alaska, a thinner oil will help the engine run when it is cold. Many oils have additives in them. Graphite is typically used as a dry lubricant and is not useful in determining the viscosity of oil in various temperatures.

76. D: Welding the same types of metals together is fairly simple. Steel can be welded to types of steel with little complication. When welding together two different types of metals, it's important to know the methods used to weld the metals and how to combine them. Cast iron is usually stick welded with nickel rods; therefore, cast iron and nickel can be welded together. Aluminum cannot be welded to most other metals without either hot dip aluminizing the second metal or using a bimetallic transition insert that contains the two different metals. If aluminum is not welded properly to another metal, it creates a weak, brittle weld joint.

77. B: Ohm's law is used to calculate voltage, current, or resistance in Ohms if two of the three items are given. Ohm's law describes the relationship between V (voltage in volts), I (current in amps), and R (resistance in Ohms, Ω). Ohm's law can be written in three ways: $V = I \times R$; $I = (V/R)$; or $R = (V/I)$. To calculate the answer to this problem, use the equation $I = (V/R)$. $I = (3/6)$. $I = 0.5$ A (amps).

78. A: The first step in this problem should be to calculate the gear reduction. This gear reduction is an example of a 5:1 reduction. This is found by using the second gear (65) and dividing it by the original (13): 65/13 = 5. The speed will be decreased, and the torque will be increased. If it was a 1:5, the opposite effect would occur. To find the new speed, divide 3,450/5 to get 690. This is the new speed of the motor. The torque is increased by 5: 10 x 5 = 50 lb-in.

79. D: Occupational Safety and Health Administration (OSHA) uses colors to indicate safety hazards. The lockout-tagout cards should be colored blue to warn against the operation of equipment that is undergoing repair. Purple is used to indicate a radiation hazard, such as an X-ray room. Green is used to indicate safety and could be used to highlight an eye wash station or an emergency shower. Black and white together are used to outline traffic areas.

80. C: A tool belt is a lightweight belt that is worn in construction to hold hand tools. Tool belts are used to hold items such as nails and screws, hammers, a tape measure, and other hand tools. Framing work would frequently require the use of tape measures to measure and cut studs, framing hammers to set studs and adjust them, and speed squares to mark straight lines and quickly check angles. A compass can be used in framing but is uncommon and is generally used to quickly get an idea of direction. A chisel and chalk lines are rarely used in framing work. A nail gun is used frequently to secure studs in framing but is not carried in a tool belt. Contour guides are used to draw the shape of a curve or irregular edge but are not used in framing work.

81. C: First, the units of the measurements must be the same. Quickly convert 0.5 km into 500 meters. When calculating slope use the equation: (rise/run) = slope. The run is the distance between the two elevation measurements. Therefore, the run for this equation is 500 m. To find the rise, subtract the starting elevation from the ending elevation: 420 – 340 = 80 m. To calculate the slope: (80/500) = 0.16. To make this a percentage, multiply 0.16 by 100. The slope is 16 percent.

82. A: Diesel and gasoline engines both create mechanical energy from the chemical energy that is stored in fuel. They do this by going through a four-stroke combustion cycle. This includes the intake, compression, combustion, and exhaust stroke. The major difference between the two is that diesel engines are compression engines. There are no spark plugs to create an ignition. Air is compressed, which becomes hot and causes the injected fuel to ignite upon contact. Gasoline engines are spark-ignition engines and require a spark for the fuel to ignite because the compression is not great enough to create ignition alone.

83. B: TIG welding stands for tungsten inert gas. In TIG welding, a tungsten electrode along with an inert gas such as argon are used to create an electrode that will melt a metal wire to create a weld pool. A consumable electrode uses up the electrode itself in the weld pool. In TIG welding, the electrode is not melted; a metal wire is instead. MIG welding stands for metal inert gas welding. In MIG welding, metal wire that is passed through an electrode is used to create the weld pool. SMAW welding stands for shielded metal arc welding. This process is also often referred to as stick welding. A consumable electrode coated in flux is used to lay the weld. This process is called stick welding because it uses welding sticks or rods that are made up of filler material and flux. FCAW welding stands for flux-cored arc welding. FCAW is similar to MIG welding except for the fact that it uses a special tubular wire filled with flux, and the shielding gas is not always needed, depending on the filler type.

84. D: The American Welding Society (AWS) breaks down the electrode codes into four basic parts. The beginning letter, E, indicates it is an electrode. The first two numbers indicate the tensile strength in ksi. All of these rods would have a tensile strength of 60,000+ ksi. An E7010 rod would have a tensile strength of at least 70,000 ksi. The third number indicates the welding positions that the rod can be used for. This number can either be a 1 or 2. A 1 can be used for all positions, and a 2 can be used only for flat and horizontal welds. The last number indicates the type of welding current that can be used. Alternating current (AC), direct current electrode positive (DCEP), and direct current electrode negative (DCEN) can be indicated by these numbers: 1 indicates AC or DCEP, 2 indicates AC or DCEN, 3 and 4 can be used by all three, and 8 indicates AC or DCEP. The most versatile welding rod would be one that was used in any welding position using any current type. This makes the E6013 the most versatile rod listed.

85. A: Copper has been used for many applications long before CPVC. Copper is accepted by all major building codes. Some states and cities have restrictions on using CPVC. CPVC is less durable in concrete and does not resist fire or earthquakes as well as copper. Copper prices have risen over the years and, in turn, has become a more commonly stolen item. CPVC is suitable for potable water, corrosive fluid handling, and fire suppression but not all drains, vents, natural gas supplies, or pressurized contents.

86. D: GPS uses satellites to determine location in reference to the Earth. GIS is a computer program that is designed to capture, analyze, interpret, and store data that has been transmitted from navigation systems such as GPS and make the information available for use. GPS can be used to locate positions, get access to emergency support, map and survey, and even prevent automobile theft with the use of GPS trackers. GIS can map and analyze numerous forms of data such as wildlife populations, census data, or even topographical information.

87. B: All metal cutting methods have ideal uses. Lathes are used to create precise cuts and are most commonly used by machinists. A punch uses sharpened blades and an extreme amount of force to punch out metal. Punches can be extremely productive, with some punches exceeding 1,000 punches per minute. A plasma cutter uses an intense, hot flame to melt through metal. Plasma cutters are precise but cannot be used with metals sensitive to heat. A water jet works similar to a plasma cutter but uses water as an abrasive compound in a concentrated jet to cut through metal. A water jet is not as precise as a lathe but is a good option for metals that are too heat sensitive for plasma cutting.

88. B: The first step is to calculate the watts. This can be done if the amps and volts are known. The appliance uses 12 amps and would use the 120 voltage that is used in the United States (other countries used 220–240). Multiply amps by volts to find watts: 12 amps x 120 volts = 1,440 watts. Divide this by 1,000 to get kilowatts: 1,440/1,000= 1.44 kilowatts. Multiply the kilowatts by the number of hours used to calculate the daily kilowatt hours used: 1.44 x 20= 28.8 kwh.

89. D: Arc-fault circuit interrupter (AFCI) breakers protect the entire circuit from an arc-fault. Ground-fault circuit interrupter (GFCI) breakers protect the circuit from ground-faults. There are dual-function breakers that can protect the circuit from both. A double-pole breaker can provide 240 volts with 15 to 50 amp ratings to protect large appliances. Breakers have been used since the 1960s. Homes and buildings constructed prior to this used fuses instead of circuit breakers.

90. A: The different letters are used to indicate the type and characteristics of insulation. The T is used to indicate a thermoplastic insulation that is a fire-resistant material. A single H indicates that the wire is heat resistant up to 167 degrees Fahrenheit. HH indicates a highly heat-resistant wire that is resistant up to 194 degrees. W stands for wet and indicates the wire is approved for use in wet and damp areas. W wire can also be used in dry areas. X wire is coated with a synthetic, flame-retardant insulation. N wire is nylon coated for both oil and gas resistance. The only option that is coated in a synthetic, flame-retardant insulation is the wire XHHN.

91. B: Conduction is the transfer of heat energy by direct contact. Convection is the movement of heat energy through the motion of matter such as steam or hot air. Radiation is the transfer of energy with the help of electromagnetic waves. When boiling water in a pot over a fire, all three types of heat transfer can be seen. The fire gives off radiation, which heats the pot. The boiling water creates steam, which is a form of convection. When you grab the hot handle, the heat of the pot is transferred to your hand through conduction.

92. D: When cleaning copper pipe in preparation for soldering, sandpaper or steel wool is used to scrub the surface until it shines. Then flux can be applied. Propane or methylacetylene-propadiene propane (MAPP) gas torches are used to melt the wire to seal the pipes together. When copper pipes are cut, burrs are created. Burrs are small shards of copper that can interfere with the soldering process and lead to a leaky joint. The insides of fittings and the outsides of pipe that will go into the fitting must be cleaned prior to soldering.

93. A: Heat moves in and out of a home through all four of the listed methods. The R-value measures the insulation's resistance to heat flow, or conduction. The higher the R-factor, the better it insulates per inch of thickness. For example, an R-25 insulation is more resistant to heat loss than an R-11 insulation. If you lived in a cold climate, you would want an R-25 insulation in your home to prevent heat loss.

94. A: It is important to be familiar with conductors and insulators any time you are working with electricity. Many people are familiar with the fact that many metals are conductors, and plastic is a commonly used insulator. It's also important to understand other common objects that act as conductors and insulators. Some materials are insulators in pure form but can become conductors when other molecules are added. An example of this is seen with water. Pure water is an insulator, but salt water or dirty water become strong conductors. Many organic molecules are insulators because they are held by strong covalent bonds and prevent the movement of electricity. Some examples of conductors are silver, steel, iron, concrete, and lemon juice. Some examples of insulators are rubber, glass, air, dry wood, plastic, asphalt, and ceramic.

95. C: There are many processes involved with the nitrogen cycle. Generally atmospheric nitrogen is converted into ammonium through the process of nitrogen fixing by certain bacteria. Ammonium can then be nitrified by nitrifying bacteria that convert the ammonium into nitrites. Nitrite is then converted into nitrate by more nitrifying bacteria. Denitrifying bacteria convert nitrates that are not absorbed by plants and convert it into atmospheric nitrogen. This starts the cycle over. Storms with lightning can fix nitrogen in the atmosphere and create nitrates in soil. Soil bacteria are sensitive to antibiotics just like other bacteria. If antibiotics are spilled or poured onto the soil, this could kill the nitrifying bacteria that convert ammonium into nitrate.

96. D: Organic compounds are those that contain carbon, typically bonded to hydrogen, and are associated with living organisms. A few organic compounds do not contain carbon, although they are rare. While some carbon-containing substances are still considered inorganic, an easy way to differentiate between organic and inorganic molecules that contain carbon is to look for the presence of a carbon-hydrogen bond. Choice A, glucose; Choice B, benzene; and Choice C, histidine all contain carbon-hydrogen bonds, making them easily identified as organic compounds. Choice D, calcium carbonate, lacks the carbon-hydrogen bonds that indicates an organic compound.

97. B: Bioaccumulation refers to an increase in the concentration of a pollutant in an organism. For example, fish are known to bioaccumulate mercury. Biomagnification is an increase in concentration of a pollutant, such as DDT, in an entire food chain. This is explained simply by looking at an example. If a mosquito is sprayed with DDT and contains 0.01 mL of DDT when it is consumed by a bird, the amount of DDT does not change. If that bird then consumes 100 mosquitoes with that same DDT level, the bird now contains 1 mL of DDT. As the trophic level increases, so does the concentration of the pollutant.

98. D: Carrying capacity is reached when there is a levelling off or horizontal line on a population growth chart. However, the population of a predator or prey species is rarely a horizontal line and exists as a fluctuation in the graph. The true carrying capacity lies somewhere inside of the fluctuation, which can be represented by the dotted line on the graph. Point A and Point B indicate rapid population growth. Point C indicates the beginning of decelerated growth.

99. B: Primary succession is seen when pioneering organisms start to colonize new habitat. This is the type of succession seen on new volcanic islands that have never experienced plant growth. Secondary succession is succession that follows the disruption of a former community. The existing community is wiped out by natural disasters such as wildfires or tornadoes or agriculture. Forest succession describes the patterns of growth or changes of plant species over time in a wooded area. Autogenic succession is succession that is brought on by a change in the soil. Autogenic succession can also be caused by plants themselves. For example, large, mature trees block most of the sunlight from reaching the forest floor, decreasing the amount of plants on the floor.

100. D: The Clean Water Act prevents the flow or release of sewage into rivers, lakes, and streams. When the act was originally passed, many swine and livestock operations released sewage into river systems. Due to the fact that swine are raised indoors, swine operations were forced to create elaborate sewage management systems that are seen today. The Noise Control Act helps control noise pollution and allows the Environmental Protection Agency (EPA) to set noise limits. The Endangered Species Conservation Act is a predecessor of the Endangered Species Act that was passed to protect wildlife. The Clean Air Act regulates emissions and allows the EPA to set air quality standards.

101. C: Hydropower is among the largest current clean energy source in the United States. The downfall to hydropower is the environmental impact that it causes, especially when mega-dams are used. Smaller plants that are carefully managed have less of an impact on surrounding wildlife. Wind turbines have increased in commonality in the past few decades and are now among the leading clean energy sources in the United States. Wind turbines do not require much land space, allowing agriculture to take place on the same area. Tidal and wave energy is an attractive energy option as tides are created by the pull of the moon. However, the energy source is still in planning phases to reduce the impact on wildlife. Photovoltaic cells, commonly referred to as solar panels, harness energy from the sun and convert it into useable energy. Solar panels require large amounts of space and are expensive, making them a less common option for producing large amounts of energy.

102. D: Indicator species are species that are easily located and studied. The species is also more susceptible to the effects of pollution than other species in the same habitat. Indicator species will exhibit symptoms of pollution before other species in the ecosystem. Many scientists use amphibians as indicator species. The skin of amphibians is porous and allows toxins to readily pass through. This often leads to rapid symptoms from pollutants or toxins. Studying indicator species can tell environmental scientists about the health of the ecosystem. In this example, the best choice for an indicator species would be the American bullfrog.

103. C: Renewable resources are resources that can be replenished within 100 years or one person's lifetime. Trees, plants, and wildlife are commonly thought of as being renewable, along with wind power, hydropower, and sunlight. Hydropower from small dams is considered a renewable source of energy because the environmental impact is small. Mega-dams take up huge amounts of space and significantly alter the habitat and water cycle around them permanently, so environmental scientists consider them a nonrenewable source of energy. Soil is a nonrenewable resource that is usually overlooked. When soil is eroded, it often makes its way into water systems where it is of little use to agriculture. Once soil is lost, it is not renewable. Fossil fuels are continuously created in a process that takes thousands of years. Despite being created continuously, they are consumed rapidly enough that the demand is much higher than the rate at which they are created.

104. C: Fertilizer runoff occurs when fertilizer that is not used by the plants sits on top of the soil. When rain events occur, the fertilizer is swept off of the field and into nearby waterways unless there is an intervention preventing runoff. Many farmers are utilizing buffer strips and grassed waterways to prevent runoff from getting into the water system. Farmers are also becoming more aware of the issue and are utilizing soil testing to avoid overfertilizing to stop the issue of runoff before it can begin. The nitrogen and phosphorus that are present in runoff feed the photosynthetic algae in the Gulf of Mexico. This is referred to as eutrophication. This rapid eutrophication then leads to massive amounts of algae decomposition, a process that requires oxygen from the water. As bacteria decompose the algae, oxygen is depleted, preventing other organisms from surviving there. There are 12 states in the United States that have river systems directly connected to the Mississippi River and therefore can lead to runoff reaching the Gulf of Mexico.

105. C: Biotic factors are living organisms and can include heterotrophs, autotrophs, and detritivores. Abiotic factors include nonliving characteristics of the ecosystem. Some abiotic factors include the climate, geology, the social factor, and the edaphic factor. Edaphic factors include the geography of the land, soil characteristics, and the topography of the land. Social factors include how resources in an area are used (e.g., dam building, mining, agriculture and deforestation).

106. B: Point source pollution is defined by the Environmental Protection Agency (EPA) as pollutants that discharge through a pipe or other conduit from specific discharges (such as an industry or municipal treatment plant) and is defined in Section 502(14) of the Clean Water Act. Nonpoint source pollution is any pollution source that originates over a broader area that is difficult to pinpoint. Examples of nonpoint source pollution include agricultural runoff, urban runoff, sediment, salt from irrigation, acid drainage from mines, bacteria and nutrients from livestock operations, and atmospheric depositions. Examples of point source pollution include discharge that contains heavy metals, pharmaceuticals, oil, thermal pollution, toxic chemicals, nutrients, or bacteria from a single point.

107. A: The no-till method uses a machine that directly sows the seeds into the ground to reduce the impact on the soil and prevent erosion due to tillage. Contour planting plants crops in rows that are perpendicular to hills to form water breaks that prevent soil erosion. Terracing planting is used when farming on sloped land. Steps are cut into the soil or crops are planted on the slope of land to reduce the rate of water runoff. There are many types of multicropping; strip cropping is one of them. Strip cropping is a special type of contour planting that plants alternating rows of crops to reduce erosion. Windbreaks are rows of trees planted on the edge of agricultural fields to reduce soil erosion caused by winds.

108. B: Celiac disease is a disease caused by an intolerance to gluten. The diagnosing of this disease and that of gluten intolerances has led to the movement of many consumers seeking gluten-free items. Gluten is found in many wheat-containing items, such as flour, and is a protein. Organic, low-fat, and sugar-free are other food trends that affect the way consumers shop.

109. C: In the United States, calorie listings are based on a serving size. For example, the calories may be listed for two slices of bread or 15 chips. The United Kingdom differs from this by listing the calories in a 100-gram serving. Nutrition labels must include all ingredients used in the making of the food item. These are listed based on the weight amount of the item, from largest to smallest. Fat, protein, and carbohydrates determine the amount of energy that can be gained from the food (i.e., energy in calories). Sodium content is also listed on a nutrition label, measured in milligrams. Sodium content accounts for various types of salts.

110. C: Labeling is required to inform customers with information regarding the source of food products. Fruit and vegetables are not required to be individually marked. Instead, the entire packaging or container holding the crops can be marked with a COOL. The COOL applies only to certain food items imported into or produced by the United States. The COOL law previously included muscle meat products such as those from beef, pork, lamb, goat, and chicken, but it has since removed beef and pork items from the COOL regulation.

111. B: US Department of Agriculture quality grades are used to explain the tenderness, juiciness, and flavor of a cut of beef. The color and marbling present in the cut are factored into the grade. Prime beef is the highest quality and would be served in a five-star restaurant. These cuts are from young animals and have abundant marbling present. Prime grades are followed by choice, select, standard, and commercial. These grades are lower in marbling and expected quality. These cuts can be sold in grocery stores. Utility, cutter, and canner grades are not typically sold in grocery stores but are used to make ground and processed products.

112. D: Many foods are pasteurized during processing, including many dairy, fruit, and vegetable products. Honey is not typically pasteurized before it is sold.

113. B: Value-added products are a result of a change in the physical state of a commodity or the manner that the commodity is produced or segregated, which adds value to the consumer. A strawberry farmer could take raw strawberries and cook them into jams to sell as a value-added product. She could also grow lines of organic strawberries to sell to consumers who want to purchase organic produce. Selling bulk boxes of strawberries would not be considered a value-added product. She could sell strawberry jam-making kits that have pre-measured bulk amounts of strawberries, jars, and canning supplies in place of the bulk boxes of strawberries, which would count as being a value-added product. A u-pick operation is a popular way to add value to fresh strawberries. Producers do not have to pick, segregate, or grade the strawberries, therefore eliminating those associated costs.

114. B: Dairy products are commonly homogenized and pasteurized. Homogenization is a process that forces a product such as milk through a sieve with tiny holes. The tiny holes break down the fat globules into smaller ones, allowing two substances that would not usually combine to combine easily. Pasteurization is a process that rapidly heats and cools a food product to kill potential pathogens. Fermentation is an anaerobic process, not an aerobic one.

115. B: Vacuum sealing is the best method and can extend the shelf life of meat products to greater than one year. Meat products are commonly sold in grocery stores in either meat trays and cellophane wrap or in vacuum-sealed packages. When purchasing meat from a butcher or having a carcass processed, the meat is typically sold in waxed butcher paper or in vacuum-sealed bags. Meat that is packaged and then frozen in a meat tray and cellophane wrap will start to develop freezer burn after a couple of months. Butcher paper can extend the shelf life and prevent freezer burn up to six months. Meat can be irradiated to kill potential pathogens but is still subject to developing freezer burn.

116. A: The US Department of Agriculture (USDA) will hire licensed veterinarians to work as federal veterinary inspectors. These veterinarians work full time for the USDA as inspectors; this position is not contracted out. Veterinary inspectors must go through training programs through the Food Safety and Inspection Service (FSIS) as new hires. The USDA requires pre- and postmortem inspections of livestock to ensure the animal appears to be in good health and free of disease. All meat that is intended for resale is required to be overseen by inspectors during the slaughtering process. The USDA and FSIS provide training programs to educate individuals with a bachelor's degree or adequate previous work experience to become federal meat inspectors.

117. B: The Humane Farm Animal Care (HFAC) provides regulations for labelling free-range, pasture-raised, and cage-free birds. The free-range requirements do specify that there must be at least two square feet of outdoor area per bird, but the animals do not have to be primarily raised outdoors. The pasture-raised requirements for birds must be space with vegetation available. Birds raised as cage free can be raised indoors as long as it is free of cages. The birds can move around freely within the indoor structure. Naturally raised is a term used only for animals being sold live and cannot be used to describe meat products.

118. B: There are many genetically modified crops that are available to farmers. These genetically modified crops can be modified to withstand drought conditions and survive on minimal amounts of water, produce increased crop yields, withstand heavier pest loads, and resist commonly used herbicides like Roundup (Roundup Ready crops). A greenhouse grower would not need to worry about drought conditions or his crop competing with weeds. Although increased yields are always welcomed, he would likely be most interested in an increased shelf life because he is shipping crops overseas.

119. D: The Hazard Analysis Critical Control Points (HACCP) process includes many steps to ensuring proper food processing safety. A critical control point is a step at which control can be applied and is essential to prevent or eliminate a food safety hazard or reduce it to an acceptable level. A critical limit is a maximum and/or minimum value to which a biological, chemical, or physical parameter must be controlled at a CCP to prevent, eliminate, or reduce to an acceptable level the occurrence of a food safety hazard.

120. C: The US Department of Agriculture (USDA) is responsible for inspecting farm-raised meat products including beef, pork, lamb, poultry, certain egg products, and catfish. The Food and Drug Administration (FDA) is responsible for inspecting all other food products, including seafood and shell eggs. The FDA is therefore responsible for inspecting gulf-caught shrimp. While the FDA inspects shell eggs, like cage-free eggs, for health and safety concerns, the USDA is responsible for the grading program to determine whether or not an egg product can qualify as cage-free.

How to Overcome Test Anxiety

Just the thought of taking a test is enough to make most people a little nervous. A test is an important event that can have a long-term impact on your future, so it's important to take it seriously and it's natural to feel anxious about performing well. But just because anxiety is normal, that doesn't mean that it's helpful in test taking, or that you should simply accept it as part of your life. Anxiety can have a variety of effects. These effects can be mild, like making you feel slightly nervous, or severe, like blocking your ability to focus or remember even a simple detail.

If you experience test anxiety—whether severe or mild—it's important to know how to beat it. To discover this, first you need to understand what causes test anxiety.

Causes of Test Anxiety

While we often think of anxiety as an uncontrollable emotional state, it can actually be caused by simple, practical things. One of the most common causes of test anxiety is that a person does not feel adequately prepared for their test. This feeling can be the result of many different issues such as poor study habits or lack of organization, but the most common culprit is time management. Starting to study too late, failing to organize your study time to cover all of the material, or being distracted while you study will mean that you're not well prepared for the test. This may lead to cramming the night before, which will cause you to be physically and mentally exhausted for the test. Poor time management also contributes to feelings of stress, fear, and hopelessness as you realize you are not well prepared but don't know what to do about it.

Other times, test anxiety is not related to your preparation for the test but comes from unresolved fear. This may be a past failure on a test, or poor performance on tests in general. It may come from comparing yourself to others who seem to be performing better or from the stress of living up to expectations. Anxiety may be driven by fears of the future—how failure on this test would affect your educational and career goals. These fears are often completely irrational, but they can still negatively impact your test performance.

Elements of Test Anxiety

As mentioned earlier, test anxiety is considered to be an emotional state, but it has physical and mental components as well. Sometimes you may not even realize that you are suffering from test anxiety until you notice the physical symptoms. These can include trembling hands, rapid heartbeat, sweating, nausea, and tense muscles. Extreme anxiety may lead to fainting or vomiting. Obviously, any of these symptoms can have a negative impact on testing. It is important to recognize them as soon as they begin to occur so that you can address the problem before it damages your performance.

The mental components of test anxiety include trouble focusing and inability to remember learned information. During a test, your mind is on high alert, which can help you recall information and stay focused for an extended period of time. However, anxiety interferes with your mind's natural processes, causing you to blank out, even on the questions you know well. The strain of testing during anxiety makes it difficult to stay focused, especially on a test that may take several hours. Extreme anxiety can take a huge mental toll, making it difficult not only to recall test information but even to understand the test questions or pull your thoughts together.

Effects of Test Anxiety

Test anxiety is like a disease—if left untreated, it will get progressively worse. Anxiety leads to poor performance, and this reinforces the feelings of fear and failure, which in turn lead to poor performances on subsequent tests. It can grow from a mild nervousness to a crippling condition. If allowed to progress, test anxiety can have a big impact on your schooling, and consequently on your future.

Test anxiety can spread to other parts of your life. Anxiety on tests can become anxiety in any stressful situation, and blanking on a test can turn into panicking in a job situation. But fortunately, you don't have to let anxiety rule your testing and determine your grades. There are a number of relatively simple steps you can take to move past anxiety and function normally on a test and in the rest of life.

Physical Steps for Beating Test Anxiety

While test anxiety is a serious problem, the good news is that it can be overcome. It doesn't have to control your ability to think and remember information. While it may take time, you can begin taking steps today to beat anxiety.

Just as your first hint that you may be struggling with anxiety comes from the physical symptoms, the first step to treating it is also physical. Rest is crucial for having a clear, strong mind. If you are tired, it is much easier to give in to anxiety. But if you establish good sleep habits, your body and mind will be ready to perform optimally, without the strain of exhaustion. Additionally, sleeping well helps you to retain information better, so you're more likely to recall the answers when you see the test questions.

Getting good sleep means more than going to bed on time. It's important to allow your brain time to relax. Take study breaks from time to time so it doesn't get overworked, and don't study right before bed. Take time to rest your mind before trying to rest your body, or you may find it difficult to fall asleep.

Along with sleep, other aspects of physical health are important in preparing for a test. Good nutrition is vital for good brain function. Sugary foods and drinks may give a burst of energy but this burst is followed by a crash, both physically and emotionally. Instead, fuel your body with protein and vitamin-rich foods.

Also, drink plenty of water. Dehydration can lead to headaches and exhaustion, especially if your brain is already under stress from the rigors of the test. Particularly if your test is a long one, drink water during the breaks. And if possible, take an energy-boosting snack to eat between sections.

Along with sleep and diet, a third important part of physical health is exercise. Maintaining a steady workout schedule is helpful, but even taking 5-minute study breaks to walk can help get your blood pumping faster and clear your head. Exercise also releases endorphins, which contribute to a positive feeling and can help combat test anxiety.

When you nurture your physical health, you are also contributing to your mental health. If your body is healthy, your mind is much more likely to be healthy as well. So take time to rest, nourish your body with healthy food and water, and get moving as much as possible. Taking these physical steps will make you stronger and more able to take the mental steps necessary to overcome test anxiety.

Mental Steps for Beating Test Anxiety

Working on the mental side of test anxiety can be more challenging, but as with the physical side, there are clear steps you can take to overcome it. As mentioned earlier, test anxiety often stems from lack of preparation, so the obvious solution is to prepare for the test. Effective studying may be the most important weapon you have for beating test anxiety, but you can and should employ several other mental tools to combat fear.

First, boost your confidence by reminding yourself of past success—tests or projects that you aced. If you're putting as much effort into preparing for this test as you did for those, there's no reason you should expect to fail here. Work hard to prepare; then trust your preparation.

Second, surround yourself with encouraging people. It can be helpful to find a study group, but be sure that the people you're around will encourage a positive attitude. If you spend time with others who are anxious or cynical, this will only contribute to your own anxiety. Look for others who are motivated to study hard from a desire to succeed, not from a fear of failure.

Third, reward yourself. A test is physically and mentally tiring, even without anxiety, and it can be helpful to have something to look forward to. Plan an activity following the test, regardless of the outcome, such as going to a movie or getting ice cream.

When you are taking the test, if you find yourself beginning to feel anxious, remind yourself that you know the material. Visualize successfully completing the test. Then take a few deep, relaxing breaths and return to it. Work through the questions carefully but with confidence, knowing that you are capable of succeeding.

Developing a healthy mental approach to test taking will also aid in other areas of life. Test anxiety affects more than just the actual test—it can be damaging to your mental health and even contribute to depression. It's important to beat test anxiety before it becomes a problem for more than testing.

Study Strategy

Being prepared for the test is necessary to combat anxiety, but what does being prepared look like? You may study for hours on end and still not feel prepared. What you need is a strategy for test prep. The next few pages outline our recommended steps to help you plan out and conquer the challenge of preparation.

Step 1: Scope Out the Test

Learn everything you can about the format (multiple choice, essay, etc.) and what will be on the test. Gather any study materials, course outlines, or sample exams that may be available. Not only will this help you to prepare, but knowing what to expect can help to alleviate test anxiety.

Step 2: Map Out the Material

Look through the textbook or study guide and make note of how many chapters or sections it has. Then divide these over the time you have. For example, if a book has 15 chapters and you have five days to study, you need to cover three chapters each day. Even better, if you have the time, leave an extra day at the end for overall review after you have gone through the material in depth.

If time is limited, you may need to prioritize the material. Look through it and make note of which sections you think you already have a good grasp on, and which need review. While you are studying, skim quickly through the familiar sections and take more time on the challenging parts.

Write out your plan so you don't get lost as you go. Having a written plan also helps you feel more in control of the study, so anxiety is less likely to arise from feeling overwhelmed at the amount to cover.

Step 3: Gather Your Tools

Decide what study method works best for you. Do you prefer to highlight in the book as you study and then go back over the highlighted portions? Or do you type out notes of the important information? Or is it helpful to make flashcards that you can carry with you? Assemble the pens, index cards, highlighters, post-it notes, and any other materials you may need so you won't be distracted by getting up to find things while you study.

If you're having a hard time retaining the information or organizing your notes, experiment with different methods. For example, try color-coding by subject with colored pens, highlighters, or post-it notes. If you learn better by hearing, try recording yourself reading your notes so you can listen while in the car, working out, or simply sitting at your desk. Ask a friend to quiz you from your flashcards, or try teaching someone the material to solidify it in your mind.

Step 4: Create Your Environment

It's important to avoid distractions while you study. This includes both the obvious distractions like visitors and the subtle distractions like an uncomfortable chair (or a too-comfortable couch that makes you want to fall asleep). Set up the best study environment possible: good lighting and a comfortable work area. If background music helps you focus, you may want to turn it on, but otherwise keep the room quiet. If you are using a computer to take notes, be sure you don't have any other windows open, especially applications like social media, games, or anything else that could distract you. Silence your phone and turn off notifications. Be sure to keep water close by so you stay hydrated while you study (but avoid unhealthy drinks and snacks).

Also, take into account the best time of day to study. Are you freshest first thing in the morning? Try to set aside some time then to work through the material. Is your mind clearer in the afternoon or evening? Schedule your study session then. Another method is to study at the same time of day that you will take the test, so that your brain gets used to working on the material at that time and will be ready to focus at test time.

Step 5: Study!

Once you have done all the study preparation, it's time to settle into the actual studying. Sit down, take a few moments to settle your mind so you can focus, and begin to follow your study plan. Don't give in to distractions or let yourself procrastinate. This is your time to prepare so you'll be ready to fearlessly approach the test. Make the most of the time and stay focused.

Of course, you don't want to burn out. If you study too long you may find that you're not retaining the information very well. Take regular study breaks. For example, taking five minutes out of every hour to walk briskly, breathing deeply and swinging your arms, can help your mind stay fresh.

As you get to the end of each chapter or section, it's a good idea to do a quick review. Remind yourself of what you learned and work on any difficult parts. When you feel that you've mastered the material, move on to the next part. At the end of your study session, briefly skim through your notes again.

But while review is helpful, cramming last minute is NOT. If at all possible, work ahead so that you won't need to fit all your study into the last day. Cramming overloads your brain with more information than it can process and retain, and your tired mind may struggle to recall even previously learned information when it is overwhelmed with last-minute study. Also, the urgent nature of cramming and the stress placed on your brain contribute to anxiety. You'll be more likely to go to the test feeling unprepared and having trouble thinking clearly.

So don't cram, and don't stay up late before the test, even just to review your notes at a leisurely pace. Your brain needs rest more than it needs to go over the information again. In fact, plan to finish your studies by noon or early afternoon the day before the test. Give your brain the rest of the day to relax or focus on other things, and get a good night's sleep. Then you will be fresh for the test and better able to recall what you've studied.

Step 6: Take a Practice Test

Many courses offer sample tests, either online or in the study materials. This is an excellent resource to check whether you have mastered the material, as well as to prepare for the test format and environment.

Check the test format ahead of time: the number of questions, the type (multiple choice, free response, etc.), and the time limit. Then create a plan for working through them. For example, if you have 30 minutes to take a 60-question test, your limit is 30 seconds per question. Spend less time on the questions you know well so that you can take more time on the difficult ones.

If you have time to take several practice tests, take the first one open book, with no time limit. Work through the questions at your own pace and make sure you fully understand them. Gradually work up to taking a test under test conditions: sit at a desk with all study materials put away and set a timer. Pace yourself to make sure you finish the test with time to spare and go back to check your answers if you have time.

After each test, check your answers. On the questions you missed, be sure you understand why you missed them. Did you misread the question (tests can use tricky wording)? Did you forget the information? Or was it something you hadn't learned? Go back and study any shaky areas that the practice tests reveal.

Taking these tests not only helps with your grade, but also aids in combating test anxiety. If you're already used to the test conditions, you're less likely to worry about it, and working through tests until you're scoring well gives you a confidence boost. Go through the practice tests until you feel comfortable, and then you can go into the test knowing that you're ready for it.

Test Tips

On test day, you should be confident, knowing that you've prepared well and are ready to answer the questions. But aside from preparation, there are several test day strategies you can employ to maximize your performance.

First, as stated before, get a good night's sleep the night before the test (and for several nights before that, if possible). Go into the test with a fresh, alert mind rather than staying up late to study.

Try not to change too much about your normal routine on the day of the test. It's important to eat a nutritious breakfast, but if you normally don't eat breakfast at all, consider eating just a protein bar. If you're a coffee drinker, go ahead and have your normal coffee. Just make sure you time it so that the caffeine doesn't wear off right in the middle of your test. Avoid sugary beverages, and drink enough water to stay hydrated but not so much that you need a restroom break 10 minutes into the test. If your test isn't first thing in the morning, consider going for a walk or doing a light workout before the test to get your blood flowing.

Allow yourself enough time to get ready, and leave for the test with plenty of time to spare so you won't have the anxiety of scrambling to arrive in time. Another reason to be early is to select a good seat. It's helpful to sit away from doors and windows, which can be distracting. Find a good seat, get out your supplies, and settle your mind before the test begins.

When the test begins, start by going over the instructions carefully, even if you already know what to expect. Make sure you avoid any careless mistakes by following the directions.

Then begin working through the questions, pacing yourself as you've practiced. If you're not sure on an answer, don't spend too much time on it, and don't let it shake your confidence. Either skip it and come back later, or eliminate as many wrong answers as possible and guess among the remaining ones. Don't dwell on these questions as you continue—put them out of your mind and focus on what lies ahead.

Be sure to read all of the answer choices, even if you're sure the first one is the right answer. Sometimes you'll find a better one if you keep reading. But don't second-guess yourself if you do immediately know the answer. Your gut instinct is usually right. Don't let test anxiety rob you of the information you know.

If you have time at the end of the test (and if the test format allows), go back and review your answers. Be cautious about changing any, since your first instinct tends to be correct, but make sure you didn't misread any of the questions or accidentally mark the wrong answer choice. Look over any you skipped and make an educated guess.

At the end, leave the test feeling confident. You've done your best, so don't waste time worrying about your performance or wishing you could change anything. Instead, celebrate the successful completion of this test. And finally, use this test to learn how to deal with anxiety even better next time.

Review Video: Test Anxiety
Visit mometrix.com/academy and enter code: 100340

Important Qualification

Not all anxiety is created equal. If your test anxiety is causing major issues in your life beyond the classroom or testing center, or if you are experiencing troubling physical symptoms related to your anxiety, it may be a sign of a serious physiological or psychological condition. If this sounds like your situation, we strongly encourage you to seek professional help.

Online Resources

Due to our efforts to try to keep this book to a manageable length, we've created a link that will give you access to all of your online resources:

mometrix.com/resources719/osatagred

It's Your Moment, Let's Celebrate It!

Share your story @mometrixtestpreparation